Rebellion, Invasion and Occupation

The British Army in Ireland, 1793–1815

Wayne Stack

Helion & Company

Dedicated to Susanne, Seamus, and Niamh

Helion & Company Limited
Unit 8 Amherst Business Centre
Budbrooke Road
Warwick
CV34 5WE
England
Tel. 01926 499619
Email: info@helion.co.uk
Website: www.helion.co.uk
Twitter: @helionbooks
Visit our blog at http://blog.helion.co.uk/

Published by Helion & Company 2021
Designed and typeset by Mach 3 Solutions Ltd (www.mach3solutions.co.uk)
Cover designed by Paul Hewitt, Battlefield Design (www.battlefield-design.co.uk)

Text © Wayne Stack 2021
Cover: A private of the Downshire Regiment of Militia, 1793 by Christa Hook (www.christahook.co.uk) © Helion & Company 2021
Illustrations © as individually credited.
Maps by George Anderson © Helion & Company

Every reasonable effort has been made to trace copyright holders and to obtain their permission for the use of copyright material. The author and publisher apologise for any errors or omissions in this work, and would be grateful if notified of any corrections that should be incorporated in future reprints or editions of this book.

ISBN 978-1-914059-83-4

British Library Cataloguing-in-Publication Data.
A catalogue record for this book is available from the British Library.

All rights reserved. No part of this publication may be reproduced, stored in a retrieval system, or transmitted, in any form, or by any means, electronic, mechanical, photocopying, recording or otherwise, without the express written consent of Helion & Company Limited.

For details of other military history titles published by Helion & Company Limited, contact the above address, or visit our website: http://www.helion.co.uk

We always welcome receiving book proposals from prospective authors.

Contents

Preface		iv
Chronology		v
1	The British Military in Ireland in the Eighteenth Century: Towards Crisis	11
2	The Militia	19
3	The Yeomanry	38
4	British Military Presence and the Management of the Irish Garrison up to 1798	59
5	The 1798 Rebellion	88
6	Defeat of the French Invasion	134
7	The British Military Occupation of Ireland	153
8	Conclusion	172

Appendices
I	Return of Permanent Barracks in Ireland, August 1811	179
II	Return of Temporary Barracks in Ireland, August 1811	181
III	Irish Militia Regiments by Seniority and Colour Facings, 1793	183
IV	English and Scottish Fencible Regiments that served in Ireland in 1798	184
V	Camden's Proposed Changes to Irish Garrison – 21 March 1796	186
VI	Selected Orders of Battle – Ireland, 1798	189

Bibliography	192

Preface

After 18 years in the New Zealand Police, and then with a young family, I considered it time that I re-evaluated my career options. So, in 2003 I enrolled at the University of Canterbury to study for a degree in history. During my undergraduate study I was fortunate enough to enrol in *Eighteenth-Century Rebellions in Britain*, a course taught by Professor John Cookson. This course introduced me to the 1798 Irish Rebellion, a revolt which I had previously known little about, but which now intrigued me, especially due to my Irish ancestry. The decision to conduct a study of the military history of Ireland during the period of 1793–1815 for my MA thesis proved a natural choice in that it combined my longstanding interests in military and Irish history. This book is based on my thesis.

In this book I have attempted to provide a balanced view of the military history of Ireland during these turbulent times, by examining the various elements of the Irish military establishment within the British Army, the roles they played and the events with which they were involved. What became obvious early in my research was that the Irish played a significant part in the defence of Britain, as well as their own country. Until recently, the traditional British bias against the Irish has been responsible for the limited recognition of this, especially regarding the Irish militia. Generally lacking the training, discipline and professional supervision of regular regiments, the militia provided the majority of troops who effectively contained and extinguished the 1798 United Irish rebellion prior to the bulk of the reinforcing British regiments arriving from Britain.

My sincere thanks go to Emeritus Professor John Cookson, whom I am heavily indebted to regarding this work. It was he who initially suggested the thesis topic to me and agreed to supervise my MA. Not only did he provide me expert advice and guidance in ensuring that my thesis developed from the raw draft initially presented to him, but he also provided me with his collection of primary source notes and microfilm which proved invaluable. I am also indebted to Graeme Dunstall, who as my senior supervisor provided sound guidance and critique that ensured the improved structure of the thesis. I also wish to thank Rob Griffith, my editor from Helion and Company, whose guidance has ensured an improved narrative for the reader.

Undoubtedly, my greatest thanks must go to my wife, Susanne, my son, Seamus, and daughter, Niamh, whose support, and sacrifice ensured that I have been able to take my passion for history to another level. So, it is to my family that I dedicate this book.

Chronology

1689
12 March: King James II lands in Ireland, leading to the Irish Williamite War between Jacobites (supporters of Catholic King James) and Williamites (supporters of Protestant Prince William of Orange).

1690
1 July: Battle of the Boyne, Co. Louth – Jacobite army defeated, with James fleeing to France.

1691
12 July: Battle of Aughrim, Co. Galway – Jacobite army defeated and withdraws to Limerick and Galway, both are besieged.
3 October: Treaty of Limerick – Jacobites surrender, ending the war. Treaty articles include protection for civil rights of Catholic Jacobite gentry to retain property, practice their religion and hold civil office if they swear allegiance to King William III.

1695
Series of harsh penal laws enacted by the Protestant Irish Parliament – Catholics unable to own land, practice their religion or hold government positions. Much of the Irish population became impoverished, leading to increasing resentment towards the Protestant ascendancy.

1791
A secret revolutionary group known as the Society of the United Irishmen is formed from mainly Presbyterian gentry (along with some middle-class Catholics) dedicated to the overthrow of the existing Irish regime and to the establishment of a French-style republic based on Liberty, Equality, and the Rights of Man.

1793
April: Irish Militia Act introduced and led to the creation of 38 regiments of militia. Catholics to be included within the militia units and used to defend the kingdom.

REBELLION, INVASION AND OCCUPATION

1796

November: Large areas of Counties Down and Armagh are proclaimed under the Insurrection Act.

21 December: A large French fleet carrying an expeditionary force of approx. 15,000–20,000 men, led by *Général de division* Louis Lazare Hoche, anchors in Bantry Bay, Co. Cork. Storms scatter the fleet and prevent any landing of the invasion force, which then returns to France.

1797

March: Lieutenant General Gerard Lake placed in command of a mixed force of militia, yeomanry and fencibles to subjugate rebels in Ulster. A wholesale policy of military terror leads to house burnings, floggings, mass arrest and murder aimed at the recovery of weapons and extinguishing the smouldering rebellion.

1798

12 March: Arrest of 16 United Irish leaders, including the Leinster Executive, at Oliver Bond's residence in Dublin cripples the movement.

14 March: Lieutenant General Sir Ralph Abercromby, commander-in-chief of the British military forces in Ireland, formally ordered to arrange the disarming of Counties Kildare, Queen's, and King's. His passive approach was unpopular among the Ascendancy.

26 March: Abercromby forced to resign, with effect from mid-April.

30 March: Lord Camden, lord lieutenant, declares the Kingdom of Ireland to be in a state of rebellion and proclaims martial law.

25 April: Abercromby replaced by Lake as commander-in-chief, who promotes draconian measures in pacifying the population.

19 May: United Irish leader Lord Edward Fitzgerald is mortally wounded while resisting arrest in Dublin. He dies in prison three weeks later.

20 May: Climax of disarming in Kildare and Wicklow. Impending insurrection reported to the government.

23 May: Pitch-capping of Anthony Perry and other violent measures in Wexford. Floggings at Carnew, Gorey, Camolin and Ballycanew.

23–24 May: The rebellion begins with rebel forces gathering in the Midlands and southern counties. Co-ordinated attacks on Dunslaughlin and Dunboyne (Meath), Clondalkin (Co. Dublin), Clane, Prosperous and Naas (Kildare). Most attacks unsuccessful but Crown forces lose 50 men at Prosperous and 22 at Naas. United Irish losses over 200 but they succeed in burning the mail coaches at Naas and Santry, which signals the start of the insurrection to supporters.

24 May: Rebel attack on Old Kilcullen results in 30 soldiers killed, along with 150 rebels. Lieutenant General Sir Ralph Dundas withdraws to Dublin, leaving much of Kildare to be occupied by the United Irishmen.

24–25 May: 58 suspected United Irish prisoners are executed in Co. Wexford. Rebel attacks on Carlow, Hacketstown and the Wicklow garrisons at Ballymore, Dunlavin, Stratford and Baltinglass are beaten off.

25 May: Abortive attacks on Lucan (Co. Dublin), Kilcock (Meath) and Leixlip (Kildare). United Irish forces regroup at Dunboyne camp.

CHRONOLOGY

25–26 May: Crown forces execute 28 prisoners at Dunlavin (Wicklow) and 28 more at Carnew (Wexford), which spreads terror among the population.

26 May: Around 4,000 rebels are attacked and defeated at Hill of Tara (Meath) by a small force of 300 Fencibles and Yeomanry. The defeat prevents the rebellion spreading throughout Meath and the northern approaches to Dublin. Rebels overrun Rathangan (Kildare) and massacre the garrison. Rumours of United Irish victories in Kildare reach Wexford. A popular rising begins in Wexford, led by Father John Murphy of Boulavogue and Father Michael Murphy of Ballycanew. Rebels kill Lieutenant Thomas Bookey and members of the Camolin yeomanry.

27 May: A sizable force of rebels surrender to Dundas at Knockallen Hill. Around 1,000 Wexford rebels, led by Father John Murphy, defeat a force of 110 North Cork Militia and 20 local yeomanry under Lieutenant Colonel Richard Foote at Oulart Hill. Battle of Tara (Meath) where Crown forces destroy the United Irish army, killing about 350 rebels for the loss of 13 killed and 28 wounded.

28 May: Wexford rebels, led by Father John Murphy, attack and defeat Crown troops at Enniscorthy. Over 100 men of the garrison killed. Rebels capture Ferns and burn the town. Recapture of Rathangan by Crown forces.

29 May: More rebels surrender at Gibbet Rath (Kildare), which results in the massacre of more than 300 rebel prisoners by the Dublin Militia, regular dragoons and local yeomanry commanded by Major General Sir James Duff. A column of Crown forces is ambushed and destroyed at Three Rocks, near Wexford town.

30 May: The town of Wexford is abandoned to the rebels, who then establish a committee of public safety. Rebel army defeat Crown forces at Three Rocks near Wexford town.

31 May: Bagenal Harvey is appointed commander of rebel army in Wexford. Massacre of 350 rebels when surrendering at Gibbet Rath (Kildare).

1 June: Unsuccessful rebel attack on Newtownbarry (Wexford), preventing rebel moving into Co. Carlow.

4 June: A column of around 750 Crown troops under the command of Colonel, the Honourable Horatio Walpole is ambushed and destroyed at Tubberneering (Wexford). Rebels capture Gorey (Wexford).

5 June: Rebels led by Bagenal Harvey unsuccessfully attack New Ross (Wexford), losing over 2,000 men. In retaliation a rebel mob massacres more than 100 loyalist prisoners, including women and children, at Scullabogue House. Father Philip Roche replaces Bagenal Harvey as rebel commander.

6 June: Rebellion finally breaks out in Co. Antrim and Co. Down, Ulster.

7 June: Approx. 20,000 rebels are severely defeated at Arklow (Wicklow) by a Crown force of 1,600 regulars, fencibles and yeomanry commanded by Major General Francis Needham and Colonel John Skerrett. Battle of Antrim where rebels led by Henry Joy McCracken attack Antrim and Larne (Antrim). Attacks repulsed and rebels lose 300 men. Randalstown and Ballymena briefly occupied by rebels but later recaptured.

9 June: Henry Joy McCracken leads an unsuccessful rebel attack in Antrim town, ending in a crushing defeat of the rebels. In contrast, Co. Down rebels win a victory over Crown forces at Saintfield and capture Newtownards. Rebel camp formed at Ballynahinch under leadership of Presbyterian Henry Munro. Battle of Arklow where rebel army led by Father John Murphy loses 300–400 men and failed to advance into Co. Wicklow and on to Dublin.

11 June: United Irish camp at Donegore Hill (Antrim) is abandoned. McCracken escaped but is later captured and hanged.

12–13 June: About 4,000 Co. Down rebels, led by Munro, are decisively defeated by a Crown force of 2,000 troops led by Major General George Nugent at Ballynahinch. Munro is captured and hanged. This effectively ends the rebellion in the north of the kingdom.

16 June: First British regular reinforcements (100th Foot) to arrive in Dublin are landed.

19 June: Rebels in the Midland counties defeated at Ovidstown Hill.

20 June: Wexford rebels defeated at Foulkes Mills. Rebels led by Thomas Dixon massacre Loyalist prisoners on Wexford Bridge.

21 June: Battle of Vinegar Hill, near Enniscorthy (Wexford), where a United Irish army of 20,000 led by Father Philip Roche is decisively beaten by Crown forces under the command of Lieutenant General Lake. Atrocities committed by the Crown troops include the burning of the rebel hospital at Enniscorthy. Wexford town is recaptured, but several thousand rebels escape. Execution of rebel leaders, including Father Roche, Bagenel Harvey and Mathew Keogh, followed by widespread atrocities committed by Crown troops.

21–27 June: Abortive attempts by Wexford rebels, led by Father John Murphy, to link up with remnants of the Kildare rebels, resulting in the battle of Castlecomer (23 June) and Hacketstown (25 June).

22 June: Lord Cornwallis replaces Lord Camden as Lord Lieutenant of Ireland.

10 July: Wexford rebels finally reach Kildare but fail to reignite rebellion.

11 July: Rebel attack on Clonard (Kildare) repulsed.

20 July: Surrender of Kildare rebels under conditional amnesty, but numerous leaders executed.

6 August: *Général de brigade* Joseph Humbert sails from Rochefort with a small French expeditionary force to support the rising.

23 August: Humbert and his force of approximately 1,100 men land at Killala (Mayo).

27 August: Battle of Castlebar – French force, supported by rebels, defeats, and routs a larger Crown force of 1,700 men led by Lieutenant General Lake.

4 September: United Irish leader, James Napper Tandy, sails with a small French force from Dunkirk.

4–6 September: Rebel rising in Counties Longford and Westmeath in hope of linking up with French forces but crushed by Crown forces at Granard (Longford).

5 September: French defeat a small Crown force at Collooney (Sligo).

6 September: Rebels defeated by Crown fencible and yeomanry units at Wilson's Hospital (Westmeath), with 600 rebels killed.
8 September: Crown forces led by Cornwallis and Lake intercept Humbert and his combined French and rebel force at Ballinamuck (Longford). Humbert is forced to surrender, and hundreds of rebels summarily killed.
12 September: Repulse of fresh rebel attack on Castlebar after it had been recaptured by Crown troops.
16 September: Napper Tandy lands at Rutland Island (Donegal).
17 September: A squadron of nine French ships carrying around 3,000 troops, along with United Irish leader Wolfe Tone, sail from Brest.
23 September: A Crown force of 1,200 troops, led by Major General Eyre Power Trench, defeat a force of several thousand rebels, led by French officers, at Killala (Mayo). Atrocities committed on rebels. This is the last engagement of the campaign.
12 October: French squadron from Brest is intercepted off Tory Island on the Donegal coast by a Royal Navy squadron led by Commodore Sir John Warren. Wolfe Tone is captured. He later dies in Dublin Prison from self-inflicted wounds.

1800–1815

Irish 'Protestant' yeomanry replaces militia as primary defence force due to strong anti-Catholic feeling – this move has great political significance. Primary role of Irish militia now as a 'nursery' for the regular British army.

1801

1 January: Act of Irish Union with Britain. Irish parliament dissolved – a direct result of the 1798 Rebellion.

1803

United Irish coup led by Robert Emmet in Dublin fails.

1805

Bounties offered to Irish militiamen to join regular regiments – 3,000 join per year. 'Protestant' yeomanry force reaches 60,000 and now controlled at national level.

1811

Militia Interchange Act authorised removal from Ireland of up to one third (10,000) of Irish Militia on an annual basis to serve in Great Britain. Replaced in Ireland by English and Scottish militia regiments.

1815

Irish recruitment into the British Army exceeds 90,000 from 1800 – boosted by 28,499 Irish militiamen from 1806 to 1813.
June: Napoleon's defeat in the 100 Days Campaign leads to the end Napoleonic Wars and any further threat of foreign invasion of Ireland and Great Britain.

REBELLION, INVASION AND OCCUPATION

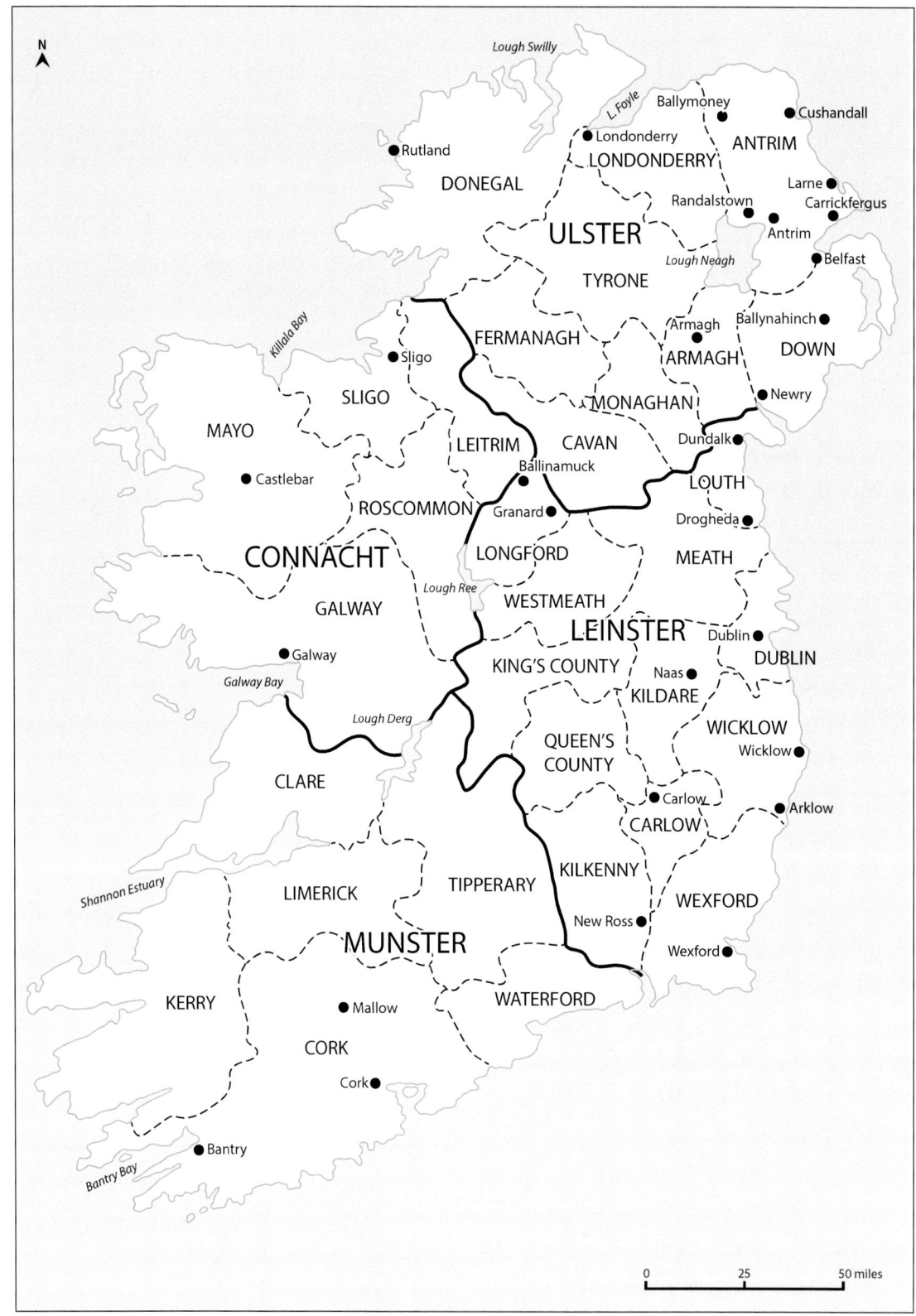

Ireland in the eighteenth century.

1

The British Military in Ireland in the Eighteenth Century: Towards Crisis

The history of Ireland is colourful and complex, and has been plagued with religious, political, and military influences that have created divisions within its population for nearly 1,000 years. Ireland's experience throughout the French Revolutionary and Napoleonic Wars highlighted and intensified such divisions, and has influenced Irish society into the twenty-first century.

The period of 1793 to 1815 was a critical era in British and Irish history. The consequences of the events and government policies of that time helped to determine the social and political divisions within Ireland for the following two centuries. A close examination of the military history of the kingdom during these crucial years provides a better understanding of how the Irish became, and remained, a socially and politically divided people, while being subjected to the political dominance of Britain. These years saw the rise in militant republicanism that was influenced by the ideology of the French Revolution and was popular amongst some factions of the middling classes. In response there was resurgence of militant Protestant loyalism that had initially evolved in the early 1780s. Revolutionary politics of the mainly Protestant middle-class, coupled with traditional agrarian grievances of the rural Catholic peasantry, led to the rise in internal violence and destruction of property.[1] Renewed war with its traditional foe, France, along with the need to counter increasing insurgent activities, forced Britain to augment its military forces in Ireland on an unprecedented scale. Ireland became an important facet of the tactical and strategic thinking of both the French and British governments at this time, with Britain needing to defend the kingdom against any possible invasion to secure its own defence, while France intended to capitalise on Irish unrest in an effort to distract British military resources from campaigns in the Caribbean and on the Continent.[2] This resulted in

---

1   Mike Cronin, *A History of Ireland* (Basingstoke: Macmillan, 2001), p.105.
2   Donald R. Come, 'French Threat to British Shores, 1793-1798', *Military Affairs*, vol.16, no.4 (Winter, 1952), pp.174–188.

the British military occupation of a kingdom whose population had been polarised by civil rebellion, invasion and renewed religious bigotry.

Ireland became a military and political enigma for Britain during the Revolutionary and Napoleonic Wars. The essential defence of the kingdom created a few dilemmas that compounded the manpower issues facing the British government in time of war. Compared to France, Britain's relatively small population ensured it had limited manpower resources for either defensive or offensive operations. Heavily committed on the Continent and in the West Indies, operational requirements forced the British army to transfer regular infantry regiments from the Irish establishment. In response, in 1793 British Prime Minister, William Pitt (the Younger), instigated the formation of the Irish militia to make use of the largely untapped Catholic male population that his government had recently permitted to bear arms in defence of their country. However, this caused conflict with the majority of the ruling Protestant Ascendancy in Ireland who feared the rise of the Catholic majority, claiming that they could not be trusted due to their traditional Jacobite sympathies and allegiances to the Pope and Catholic monarchy of France.[3] The army also had to deal with the conflicting demands of counter-insurgency operations while having to deploy a sufficient force to meet any invasion. The subsequent events of 1798 illuminated the problems faced by the authorities in Dublin Castle, the seat of government in Ireland, who had to quell rebellion and defend against invasion, while attempting to temper factions of zealous Protestants whose continued violence towards the Catholic population promoted further internal unrest. This did not prove easy as the contradictory ideologies and tactics of the military high command promoted confusion and ill-discipline within the army, fostering further violence; Ascendancy-minded generals, Lieutenant General Henry Luttrill, 2nd Earl Carhampton, and Lieutenant General Gerard Lake, encouraged counter-terror tactics, while Lieutenant Generals Sir Ralph Abercromby and Charles, the Marquis Cornwallis, favoured a more liberal and humane approach.[4]

The Protestant Ascendancy caused the greatest predicament for Britain in Ireland in the 1790s. The nationalistic fervour of the armed volunteers of the 1770s and 80s during a time of war with the American colonies and France had seen Britain relinquish legislative power to the Irish parliament in 1783. However, by the early 1790s the rise of the republican movement and its potential for Catholic emancipation led the Ascendancy to seek the military support of Britain to maintain their control of the kingdom. This led to a change of direction for the Protestant minority who now saw closer ties to Britain as the only means to protect their interests. The Protestants focused on religion as a tie to Britain, openly displayed through the rise of the Orange orders that were incorporated into the yeomanry. It was such fervour that led Britain to reclaim political control of Ireland through the Act

---

3   J.E. Cookson, 'Arming Catholics: The Irish Militia, 1793-1815,' Unpublished paper presented at A.M.B.H.A. Conference, February 1995, p.5.
4   Charles Ross (ed.), *Correspondence of Charles, First Marquis Cornwallis* (London: John Murray, 1859), vol.2, p.355.

of Union in 1801. The chaos caused by constant civil unrest and the excessive violence against Catholics, encouraged by the Ascendancy, convinced liberals such as Pitt and Cornwallis that the only alternative was for Ireland to be incorporated into the United Kingdom.[5] The few military reverses of 1798 were unfairly blamed on the militia to hide the inadequacies of the high command and its policies, further promoting the mistrust of Catholics. This was endorsed by the Ascendancy who called for the augmentation of the predominantly Protestant yeomanry, which it claimed was the only national force that could effectively defend its and Britain's interests in Ireland.[6] This resulted in the militia being marginalised to be mainly seen as a source for regular recruits, with the Irish garrison being further reinforced by British fencibles and militia.

The French revolutionary principles of 'Liberty, equality and fraternity' were popular within certain sectors of the Irish population in the 1790s and such philosophies helped to determine the crucial events of 1798. These principles were embraced by the Presbyterians of Ulster, whose religious beliefs were in line with the democratic doctrine, and who hoped to gain the political power that was denied them as religious dissenters. Factions within the Irish peasantry also incorporated some of these principles with their separate agrarian issues, especially in County Armagh and the Ulster borderlands where violence became prevalent by 1796. Such principles also gained support to varying degrees from the four million disenfranchised Roman Catholics who, until 1793, could not buy or sell land, practise law, teach, enter university, vote or enter parliament, bear arms, or purchase commissions in the armed forces.[7] Political agitation was fuelled by publications such as Tom Paine's *The Rights of Man* and Wolfe Tone's *An Argument on behalf of the Catholics in Ireland,* leading to the formation of new political societies.[8] The 'Society of United Irishmen' campaigned for radical reform and the limitation of English influence in Ireland, while supporting the re-instatement of Catholics into Irish politics. Their ultimate aim was for total independence from Britain and the formation of a republic, although initially such policies were not publicised.[9] Political tension grew within the kingdom, with the British prime minister, William Pitt, arguing that concessions needed to be made to Irish Catholics to counter revolutionary ideas, regardless of the position of the Irish parliament in Dublin.[10] This led to the removal of some of the Penal Laws in 1793 that had legally deprived Catholics of their civil rights for most of the eighteenth century. Other

---

5   Cronin, *A History of Ireland*, pp.114–116.
6   Allan Blackstock, *An Ascendancy Army: The Irish Yeomanry, 1796–1834* (Dublin: Four Courts Press, 1998), pp.289–290.
7   Thomas Bartlett, 'Defence, counter-insurgency and rebellion: Ireland, 1793–1803', in Thomas Bartlett & Keith Jeffery (eds), *A Military History of Ireland* (Cambridge: Cambridge University Press, 1996), p.247.
8   David Dickinson, Daire Keogh & Kevin Whelan (eds), *The United Irishmen: Republicanism, Radicalism and Rebellion* (Dublin: The Lilliput Press, 1993), pp.256–258.
9   Dickinson, et.al, *The United Irishmen*, pp.256–258.
10 Ivan F. Nelson, *The Irish Militia, 1797-1802: Ireland's Forgotten Army* (Dublin: Four Courts Press, 2007), pp.30–33.

moves which proved unpopular with the Protestant Irish oligarchy included the disbandment of the old Volunteer movement and its replacement with a militia controlled by the government. Catholics were entitled to enlist in the militia, ensuring they were now armed, which led to protests from Protestant sectors and increased sectarian tension. Starting in County Armagh, clashes between Catholic 'Defenders' and Protestant 'Peep o' Day Boys' led to the formation of Loyal Orange societies that quickly became powerful elements within Irish society and were initially looked upon with some concern by the British authorities at Dublin Castle. However, by 1796 the government was more preoccupied with the suppression of the clandestine activities of the United Irish and the Defenders that were actively promoting rebellion.

The army in Ireland had the dual tasks of maintaining the peace and defending the kingdom from invasion. Up until the 1790s this was successfully achieved by the small number of British regular regiments stationed there. However, war with France from 1793 created added pressure on the Irish military forces. The shortage of troops required to fight in overseas campaigns led to a rapid reduction in the number of regular infantrymen on the Irish establishment. The creation of the 38 militia regiments that year ensured the augmentation of the infantry component of the garrison at a time when internal security was seriously threatened, although the loyalty and competency of the predominantly Catholic and poorly trained militia was questioned by many.[11] When the United Irishman, Wolfe Tone fled from Ireland in 1795 he succeeded in persuading some of the French Directory that Ireland was a weak spot in Britain's defence system and that a French invasion would spark a mass popular uprising that would end British rule. By 1796 the Irish army was fully stretched with few regular troops to provide a sufficient force to repel an invasion, while most of the militia regiments were dispersed into small detachments throughout the kingdom to counter insurgency.[12] The fact that a large fleet carrying a sizable French army led by *Général de division* Louis Lazare Hoche had managed to evade the Royal Navy blockade and anchored in Bantry Bay in December 1796 proved that the security of Ireland was seriously under threat and emphasized the inadequacies of the government's defence strategy. Fortunately for the British, a storm scattered the French fleet, and the proposed invasion was abandoned.

The threat of invasion accelerated the polarisation of Irish society. The outlawed United Irishmen established an underground military organisation and allied themselves with the Defenders to gain mass support from the Catholic peasantry. In response to demands from Protestant gentry for the means to defend themselves from insurgent activities, and as a safeguard against invasion and insurrection, a force of yeomanry was established that year that actively enlisted the vehemently Protestant Orangemen. Tension mounted with the introduction of the Insurrection Act of 1796 which enabled the lord lieutenant to proclaim certain areas to be 'in a state of disturbance'.[13]

---

11   Nelson, *The Irish Militia*, pp.15–16.
12   The National Archives (TNA): HO 100/60: Home Office Papers, Earl of Camden to the Duke of Portland, 19 March 1796.
13   Bartlett, 'Defence, counter-insurgency and rebellion: Ireland, 1793–1803', pp.262–265.

This act allowed for searches, curfews, press-ganging of suspected insurgents, calling out of the yeomanry and the quartering of soldiers in the homes of citizens without compensation. Such moves proved highly unpopular and led to excesses and acts of cruelty by government troops that went unpunished and fuelled resentment. As more areas were proclaimed to be in a state of disturbance and searches led to arrests and the seizure of weapons, pressure grew on the United Irish to act before their organisation was too weak to be effective.[14] Thus, in May 1798 the long-awaited rebellion erupted without the support of a French invasion that was essential to give it any chance of success.

The 1798 uprising was a tragic episode in Irish history that had political and social ramifications for future generations of Irishmen. Massacres and atrocities were perpetrated by both government and rebel forces, each feeding on long-held hatred that was sponsored by religious bigotry. A bloodbath ensued in the few counties where the rebels succeeded in gaining active popular support, especially in Meath, Kildare, Wicklow, and Wexford, with the hated yeomanry and hundreds of innocent Protestant civilians being targeted by Protestant and Catholic insurgents.[15] The rebels fought bravely, and though poorly armed and ill-organised, initially inflicted some reverses on detachments of government troops that mainly consisted of militia and yeomanry. However, once the government forces were concentrated into sizable bodies the rebel armies were contained and quickly defeated. Due to the lack of experienced leadership and significant active popular support within the United Irish movement in Dublin and its surrounding counties, the rebel forces in Meath and Kildare lacked direction and soon after the outbreak of the uprising lost the initiative and were either captured, surrendered, or were killed by government forces. It was only in County Wexford, where the combination of factors ensured the rebellion gained significant popular support. Recent counter-insurgent operations, combined with the limited number of troops stationed in the county and economic hardship had inspired some Protestant gentry, as well as the Catholic peasantry, to rise against the government.[16] The county was quickly captured by the rebels and a short-lived republic was established that seriously threatened the internal security of the kingdom.

However, all attempts to expand the republic into neighbouring counties were defeated. The United Irish suffered heavy reverses at Arklow and New Ross, losing the military initiative. Lacking essential military experience within the senior leadership, the rebel forces remained disorganised and eventually concentrated at Vinegar Hill, near Enniscorthy, where they were easily defeated by several converging government columns. The rebel army was dispersed, with hundreds being slaughtered in the rout, including

---

14 Nancy J. Curtain, *The United Irishmen: Popular Politics in Ulster and Dublin, 1791–1798* (Oxford: Clarendon Press, 1994), pp.65–66.
15 Thomas Pakenham, *The Year of Liberty: The bloody story of the great Irish Rebellion of 1798* (London: Weidenfield & Nicholson, 1972), pp.132–140.
16 Daniel Gahan, 'The Rebellion of 1798 in South Leinster', in Thomas Bartlett, et.al. (eds), *1798: A Bicentenary Perspective* (Dublin: Four Courts Press, 2003), pp.109–111.

women and children.[17] And although a small number escaped into the Wicklow Mountains to continue guerrilla-style operations up until 1803, the uprising had been effectively dealt with. The failed rebellions in Ulster in June 1798 proved even less successful for the United Irish movement and were decisively extinguished within two weeks. Government counter-insurgent operations in the province had successfully weakened the revolutionary organisation that ensured that the risings in counties Antrim and Down were uncoordinated and lacked experienced leadership.[18] As with the uprising in Dublin, government spies had successfully penetrated the rebel movement ensuring that military forces could be mobilized to counter insurgent activity.

The subsequent French invasion in August the same year came too late to aid the rebel cause. After landing on the coast of county Mayo, the small force of 1,100 men led by *Général de brigade* Jean Joseph Humbert, captured the town of Castlebar and established a republic.[19] The defeat and ignominious rout of the government troops, known as the 'Castlebar Races,' became a stain on the reputation of the British Army, and for which the blame was placed unfairly on the Irish militia. However, the outnumbered and isolated French column was eventually surrounded and forced to surrender at Ballinamuck, County Longford, on 8 September after Humbert had attempted to march on Dublin to release imprisoned rebel leaders. The invasion failed to inspire the mass popular support that the exiled United Irishmen, such as Wolfe Tone and Napper Tandy, had promised. And although there were minor risings in counties Longford and Westmeath, where rebels had hoped to link up with the French force, the insurgents were easily defeated by government troops. At Granard, County Westmeath, an ill-conceived and disorganised attack on the garrison was dispersed, while at Wilson's Hospital in County Longford, an estimated 200 rebels were slaughtered in the hospital grounds after they had negotiated a surrender.[20] Some United Irishmen from these defeated groups did manage to join the French only to be killed at Ballinamuck. The massacre of 500 rebels who were forced to flee after the French had surrendered was followed by the summary execution of the majority of the 90 insurgents who were captured.[21] Further atrocities were committed by government troops in mopping-up operations in the recapture of Killala in County Mayo.[22] And although the rebellion was over, reprisals continued that ensured further unnecessary deaths that fostered permanent division between the Protestant Ascendancy and the Catholic majority.

Despite the repression of the rebellion, military resources in Ireland had been severely tested. The continued demand for regular troops to be taken from the Irish establishment ensured that Dublin Castle accepted the offer of English militia regiments to serve in Ireland, alongside the numerous English and Scottish fencibles units that remained in the

---

17   James Hewitt (ed.), *Eye–Witnesses to Ireland in Revolt* (Reading: Osprey, 1974), p.92.
18   Bartlett, 'Defence, counter-insurgency and rebellion: Ireland, 1793–1803', p.281.
19   Richard Hayes, *The Last Invasion of Ireland* (Dublin: Gill & MacMillan, 1979), pp.140–146.
20   Pakenham, *The Year of Liberty*, pp.370–372.
21   Pakenham, *The Year of Liberty*, pp.370–372.
22   Harmen Murtagh, 'General Humbert's Futile Campaign', in Thomas Bartlett, et.al (eds), *1798: A Bicentenary Perspective* (Dublin: Four Courts Press, 2003), p.186.

kingdom until their disbandment in 1802. Exaggerated and politically motivated reports concerning the undisciplined behaviour of the 'Catholic' Irish militia regiments during the events of 1798 promoted a reputation of untrustworthiness that was to affect the components of the Irish garrison in the post-rebellion years.[23] The uprisings were portrayed by the Ascendancy as a Catholic rebellion set on the removal of the Protestant oligarchy.[24] Therefore, the predominantly Catholic militia could no longer be fully trusted in the defence of the kingdom, ensuring that greater reliance was now placed on the yeomanry to provide internal security. Loyalism was now rampant within the Protestant population, including the Presbyterians of Ulster, leading to a massive augmentation of the yeomanry that eventually saw membership exceeding 80,000.[25] This was more than four times that of the militia which had been restricted by law not to exceed more than 25,000 men.[26] The militia became an embarrassment to the government and, apart from a few 'Protestant' regiments together with the ad-hoc elite light company battalions who were considered worthy enough to be incorporated into the army reserve, the majority of the militia regiments were relegated to secondary roles of garrison duty in Ireland and Britain. In effect, the Irish establishment became a Protestant army of occupation with the marginalisation of the militia, the expansion of the yeomanry and the increased number of British auxiliary troops in Ireland.

Nevertheless, Ireland continued to provide a flood of recruits to the militia and regular regiments, despite the events of 1798. At a time when enlistment in the army was entirely voluntary, there was a steady flow of Irish Catholics recruited into the British Army throughout the Revolutionary and Napoleonic Wars. However, by comparing the rapid expansion of the yeomanry to the estimated Protestant male population at the time, it is clear that Protestant Irishmen generally preferred to defend their interests in Ireland rather than serve overseas.[27] It appears that such trends may have been encouraged by the government to ensure internal security by legally removing thousands of potentially volatile military-age Catholics from the kingdom while increasing the number of armed loyal Protestants. Home Office archives indicate that regiments sent to recruit in Ireland post-1798 were stationed in counties with high Catholic populations, with few being posted in Ulster where the concentration of the Protestant population and yeomanry corps was greatest.[28] However, it could also be argued that these regiments were simply posted to locations that provided the greatest number of recruits in the shortest time, and no doubt this must have been a consideration of Horse Guards with the constant demand for troops during the period. Ultimately, Irishmen, whether Protestant or Catholic, enlisted for self-interest. Protestants joined the yeomanry to protect family and property,

---

23 Nelson, *The Irish Militia*, pp.228–229.
24 A.T.Q. Stewart, *The Summer Soldiers: The 1798 Rebellion in Antrim and Down* (Belfast: The Blackstaff Press, 1995), p.40.
25 Blackstock, *An Ascendancy Army*, p.12.
26 Nelson, *The Irish Militia*, pp.45–46.
27 Nelson, *The Irish Militia*, pp.114–115.
28 TNA: HO 100/90: Circular from Adjutant General's office, 23 January 1800.

while the Catholic peasantry generally enlisted to provide an income for their families in a time of economic hardship. Whatever the motivation, the Irish proved to be reliable soldiers and an essential element of the British army both in home defence and overseas operations.

The historiography surrounding the Irish establishment during the period has been influenced by political intrigue and religious intolerance. This is most evident in the lasting reputations of the militia and yeomanry where the 'Catholic' militia became synonymous with ill-discipline, disaffection, and disloyalty, while the 'Protestant' yeomanry established a reputation for loyalty and reliability. Such attitudes were promoted by contemporary Ascendant politicians and historians, such as Sir Richard Musgrave, who played on the fears of Catholic domination in Ireland to secure their own interests through British military support. Exaggeration of massacres became the orthodoxy of a reinvigorated conservative Protestantism in Britain and Ireland with the publication of Musgrave's memoirs in 1801 which further fuelled the underlying fear of slaughter by Catholics that had remained in Protestant psyche from the stories of the massacre of Protestants in 1641 during the English Civil War and the Williamite War of the early 1690s.[29] By focusing on atrocities committed by the Catholic rebels against Protestants during the uprisings and emphasizing the perceived poor performance of the militia, these zealous loyalists intended to prove that the Irish Catholic population could not be trusted and were not deserving of emancipation. Thus, by depriving the Catholic majority of any political power, the Protestant minority could maintain control of the kingdom. Irish Catholics had traditionally supported the Jacobite cause and their supply of recruits to the Irish Brigade of the French army throughout the eighteenth century was seen as proof of disloyalty to the Hanoverian regime. Such strategies proved fruitful in preventing emancipation for a time and secured the military dominance of Britain over Ireland through to the early twentieth century. However, it was not until the late twentieth century that in-depth study has revealed a less partial account of the era.

---

29 James Kelly, 'We were all to have been massacred: Irish Protestants and the experience of the rebellion', in Thomas Bartlett & Keith Jeffrey (eds), *1798: A Bicentenary Perspective* (Dublin: The Four Courts Press, 2003), pp.312–315.

2

The Militia

The arming of the Irish population through the formation of the militia and yeomanry was a necessary consequence of war with Revolutionary France. The demand for regular army regiments outside the British Isles led to a massive reduction of the Irish establishment and posed a serious threat to Britain's defence system. When war was first declared in 1793 the Irish establishment, then consisting of 11,094 regular troops, was well under strength from the 15,000 men set by the British government in 1769.[1] However, this number was further reduced to less than 4,000, with battalions being required for campaigns in Flanders and the West Indies.[2] Securing Ireland from external invasion and internal rebellion was necessary for maintaining Britain's defence system and a substantial military force was needed to ensure this. An immediate solution was found in the posting of English and Scottish fencibles (temporary militia units raised in times of war or rebellion to serve on home soil only) to Ireland from 1794, as only a few regiments of the newly established Irish militia were operational at the beginning of that year and the Irish-recruited regular regiments were being immediately shipped out of the kingdom once they had reached full strength.[3] At this time it was considered that the raising of the militia, and the later yeomanry, from within the local population would provide the necessary manpower for a substantial garrison that was not available from Britain. However, the creation of these forces, the way they were employed and the reputations that they acquired during this turbulent period were to have a dramatic effect on the future political and social development of Ireland.

The Militia Act of 1793 provided Ireland with a citizen army for its defence. A similar act had been introduced to Ireland in 1778 during the American War of Independence but had never been enforced. What had subverted the formation of an Irish militia during this time was the creation of patriotic volunteers into independent armed associations from 1776

---

1 Nelson, *The Irish Militia*, p.13.
2 TNA: HO 100/40: Home Office Papers, Earl of Westmorland to Sir Henry Dundas, 25 September 1793.
3 TNA: HO 100/40: Home Office Papers, Earl of Westmorland to Sir Henry Dundas, 25 September 1793.

until 1793. These formations were independent of any formal government control, with the politically ambitious and democratically elected leadership of landed gentry and middle-class professionals, supported by the rank and file, eventually gaining substantial political influence that assisted Ireland in gaining full legislative independence in 1782.[4] This ensured that the volunteer movement became a subject of suspicion, and was perceived as a threat to British influence in Ireland. The Earl of Rutland claimed that it was 'impossible to bring them under subordination' and that there was a need to restore 'the sword to the executive'.[5] The creation of the militia was seen by the administration at Dublin Castle as an opportunity to remove this threat, as well as the threat of increased rural disturbances created through the rise of Catholic Defenderism, by providing a government-controlled armed force for internal security. In December 1792, the Earl of Westmorland, then the Lord Lieutenant of Ireland, wrote to the British Prime Minister, William Pitt, stating that the Irish cabinet had decided that it was now essential to form a militia to put down the volunteering spirit.[6] Once the Militia Act was introduced and the militia regiments embodied, the numerous volunteer corps were forced to disband through a proclamation by the lord lieutenant.

The Irish militia was a subject of controversy from its inauguration. The Militia Act authorised the formation of 38 single battalion regiments to be established from each county as well as from a small number of cities, such as Dublin, Limerick, and Cork.[7] In 1793 many members of the Irish Ascendancy, including the Earl of Westmorland, insisted that only Protestants be recruited into the militia. They argued that Catholic loyalty could not be trusted and that only a Protestant militia could restore the confidence of the Irish and British governments.[8] However, Pitt and Major General David Dundas, who had previously been Adjutant General in Ireland, disagreed. They argued that the creation of the militia provided an opportunity to establish a regulated instrument of government that would defend against anarchy and misrule in Ireland. They stated that by promoting the formation of a militia that included Catholics, they were advancing the interests of Protestant Ireland and the Empire as a whole, in that by 'conciliating the Catholics as much as possible' it would make them an effectual body of support.[9] Others supported their stance, with Lord Darnley stating in the Irish House of Lords in January 1793, that the militia must not be exclusive to Protestants as this would only promote 'bad blood'.[10] Thus, when the Militia Act was passed into law by the Irish parliament in April 1793, enlistment into the regiments was open to both Protestants and Catholics. Only Lord Kingsborough, the commanding officer of the North Cork Militia, openly encouraged Protestant enlistment

---

4 Marianne Elliott, 'Ireland', in Otto Dann & J.R. Dinwiddy (eds), *Nationalism in the Age of the French Revolution* (London: Hambleton Press, 1988), pp.71–86.
5 Sir Henry McAnally, *The Irish Militia, 1793–1816: A Social and Military History* (London: Clonmore & Reynolds, 1949), p.6.
6 McAnally, *The Irish Militia*, p.10.
7 McAnally, *The Irish Militia*, p.10.
8 Bartlett, 'Defence, counter-insurgency and rebellion: Ireland, 1793–1803', p.253.
9 Bartlett, 'Defence, counter-insurgency and rebellion: Ireland, 1793–1803', p.253.
10 McAnally, *The Irish Militia*, p.58.

into his regiment by promising land allotments to non-Catholic recruits at the end of their service.[11]

The balloting system used to raise the militia proved contentious and unpopular as it saw the introduction of compulsory conscription in an era when service in the army had been traditionally voluntary. To meet the emergency response of raising an establishment of 16,000 men for the new militia, each parish within the counties was to provide a list of names of all eligible males between 18 and 45, with professions or occupations to be included.[12] Names were then drawn from a ballot by a local magistrate to ensure each parish provided the required number of recruits allocated to serve in the county regiment. However, in some areas this system was extremely unpopular and resulted in rioting. Throughout March, April, May and June of 1793, more than 230 people were killed in protests against the embodiment of the militia that occurred across the county.[13] This was five times the number of casualties sustained in the previous 30 years of agrarian disturbances, but considerably less than the fatalities recorded concerning protests against raising militia in England.[14] Rioting was particularly prevalent in counties that had a strong United Irish presence, such as those of eastern Ulster and border counties such as Armagh and Monaghan. Riots in other counties, such as Roscommon, were not only aimed at the ballot system but were also stimulated by traditional agrarian complaints regarding church tithes and rents.[15] Although initially successful in quickly raising the required numbers for some county militia regiments, the ballot system was eventually abandoned due to a combination of its unpopularity, that it was considered slow, expensive, and inefficient, and that it had been made redundant by the number of volunteers.[16]

Some historical claims surrounding difficulties in raising the militia regiments have been exaggerated. The population of some counties peacefully accepted the ballot system, with 17 out of the 32 counties having no reported riots or incidents.[17] Numerous counties were able to dispense with balloting altogether due to the number of men who voluntarily enlisted. Examples include the County Kerry and City of Limerick militias that were able to raise their full complements in one day, solely from volunteers.[18] Others such as the Queen's County regiment took only 10 days. It could be argued that the large number of volunteers was due to numerous benefits and the comparatively good wages paid to the rank and file once it had been determined that militia would remain on permanent duty, effectively making the militiamen full-time soldiers. One incentive for recruits was the limited enlistment period of

---

11   McAnally, *The Irish Militia*, p.58.
12   McAnally, *The Irish Militia*, p.29.
13   Thomas Bartlett, 'An End to Moral Economy: The Irish Militia Disturbances of 1793', *Past and Present*, No.99 (May 1983), pp.41–64.
14   Bartlett, 'An End to Moral Economy: The Irish Militia Disturbances of 1793', pp.41–64.
15   Nelson, *The Irish Militia*, p.60.
16   Nelson, *The Irish Militia*, p.68.
17   Nelson, *The Irish Militia*, p.63.
18   McAnally, *The Irish Militia*, p.40.

four years, with the right of re-enlistment once the period had expired.[19] The majority of the militiamen were either labourers or tradesmen. The skilled recruits from cities and provincial towns tended to be Protestant, while those unskilled labourers from rural areas tended to be Catholic, with many seeing the militia as providing a regular income in times of economic depression.[20] A high proportion of the unskilled and semi-skilled married recruits would have been attracted by regular full-time pay, extra allowances for wives and children under 10 years old, promotion, and in the early 1790s, no risk of service outside Ireland.[21] One notable benefit was provision for children of militiamen to attend school at a time of high illiteracy and no formal state-funded education system. Evidence for this is provided in the Carlow Militia enrolment book; the only known complete surviving contemporary record of militia enlistment in the 1790s. However, any general conclusions must be treated with caution due to a lack of similar records to compare it to when considering there were 38 battalions of Irish militia.

Regimental establishments varied in size when they were first raised in 1793. Lord Hillsborough, the chief designer of the bill put to the Irish House of Commons, suggested an initial total strength of 16,000 militiamen, based on 500 men per county.[22] The total number of troops initially raised, excluding officers and non-commissioned officers, was 14,948.[23] The ability to raise troops was determined by regional economic, political, and religious influences, as well as the reaction of the local population to the ballot system and proposed conditions of service. Lord Hillsborough's Royal Downshire Regiment had the largest complement with a strength of 770 rank and file divided into 12 companies.[24] Tipperary, Wexford, Galway, Donegal, Londonderry and Tyrone all had strengths of 560 men distributed into 10 companies, while most other county militia varied between 300 to 500 men in five to eight companies.[25] The smallest unit was that of the Drogheda Militia which had only 183 militiamen formed into three companies.[26] The total number of troops within the Irish militia fluctuated from year to year due to medical discharges, desertions, deaths and availability of recruits. In February 1795, Earl Fitzwilliam, the Lord Lieutenant of Ireland at the time, reported that the militia amounted to 13,366 rank and file.[27] The same year authorisation was given for militia companies to be augmented from 50 to 70 men, as it was considered easier to find recruits for the militia than regular regiments.[28] From that time there was a steady increase fostered by a wealth of volunteers and substitutes, ensuring that by January 1798 the militia

---

19   McAnally, *The Irish Militia*, p.40
20   Nelson, *The Irish Militia*, p.129.
21   Nelson, *The Irish Militia*, p.129.
22   Andrew Martin, 'Reform and Change Within the Irish Army and Military System, 1763–1818', Unpublished M.A. thesis (Christchurch: University of Canterbury, 1990), p.104.
23   McAnally, *The Irish Militia*, p.24.
24   Nelson, *The Irish Militia*, p.46.
25   Nelson, *The Irish Militia*, p.46.
26   Nelson, *The Irish Militia*, p.46.
27   TNA: HO 100/53: Home Office Papers. Earl Fitzwilliam to the Duke of Portland, February 1795.
28   McAnally, *The Irish Militia*, p.73.

consisted of 22,728 men.[29] The size of the militia was significant in that when the rebellion broke out in May of the same year, the militia constituted 64 percent of the total military forces available in Ireland.[30]

The command structure of the Irish militia was predominantly Protestant. Initially, in February 1793 a militia force of 16,000 was proposed, with a qualification of income of £2,000 per annum for commanding officers ensuring only landed magnates became colonels.[31] This ensured that most regiments would be led by Protestants, with very few Catholic nobles having sufficient funds to qualify. This in turn led to most junior officers also being of the Protestant faith, gaining their commissions through patronage. This system of acquiring positions by taking advantage of family and local connections was the accepted practice within British and Irish military and political spheres during this period, providing structures of loyalty that fostered stability.[32] Evidence of this is provided by Lieutenant John Dobbs of the Armagh Militia, who later gained a regular commission in the 52nd Regiment of Foot:

> In the same year [1805], I being fifteen years old, Lord Gosford gave me a Lieutenancy in the Armagh Militia, in which my brother Francis was Captain. I joined them at Ennis in the county Clare, whence we marched to Tuam in Galway, where I had some hard night duty, 'still-hunting.' We were then sent to Eyrecourt, leaving detachments at Banagher and Shannon Bridge, at which places I was successively stationed. While here, our men were trained to the great guns in the batteries. During my stay at Shannon Bridge, my brother and I visited Ballinasloe during the great fair held there, and were witnesses to a great faction fight. There was a large body on each side, and they fought through the streets with sticks and stones to the terror of all persons peaceably inclined. All the shops were closed, shutters put up, and business suspended. Such was the state of most of the large towns in Ireland at this period, and it continued so till sometime after Peel's Act for the establishment of the present Police. Soon afterwards we were moved to Naas, near Dublin, where I received my appointment to the 52nd, (Sir John Moore being an old schoolfellow of my father's) in which regiment my brother Joseph was a captain.[33]

However, although this practice restricted the number of Catholic officers in the Irish militia, the same system also led to some Catholic gentry, who were tenants of the landed magnates, being offered commissions either by the very few Catholic colonels or by liberal-minded Protestant commanding officers. An example of this was Lord Fingal, who as head of the Catholic branch of the influential Plunkett family, rose to the rank of lieutenant colonel of

---

29   Nelson, *The Irish Militia*, p.248.
30   Nelson, *The Irish Militia*, p.248.
31   McAnally, *The Irish Militia*, p.18.
32   McAnally, *The Irish Militia*, pp.58–60.
33   J. Dobbs, *Recollections of an Old 52nd Man* (Waterford: Harvey, 1859), p.v.

the Meath Militia in 1797 after he had been offered a captaincy in the same regiment in 1793.[34]

In contrast to the officer corps, the rank and file of the militia was predominantly Catholic. In the 1790s Catholics accounted for approximately 75 per cent of the population of Ireland and clearly without their enlistment into the regiments, only the units raised in Protestant Ulster would have been able to achieve their effective strength. The enlistment of Catholics was actively encouraged by the government, being made possible by the Catholic Relief Acts of 1792–1793. These removed restrictions on Catholics holding firearms, from entering the army, and holding commissions. This was a total reversal of previous government policy, although Irish Catholics had been unofficially recruited into the British army since the Seven Years War in the 1750s.[35] The heavy demand on manpower on the small British army during the American War of Independence from 1775 to 1783 had led to constant recruiting in Ireland, where the legislation preventing the enlistment of Catholics was pragmatically ignored. During the eighteenth century it was customary for recruits to enlist for service for life, only being released from the army due to medical discharge through illness, age, or wounds.[36] This meant that by the time the Relief Acts were introduced in the early 1790s, thousands of Irish Catholics had already proved their loyalty through service in the British army.

The demographics of the Irish population influenced the identity of each militia regiment. Most records pertaining to the individual regiments were destroyed during the Irish Civil War of 1921–1922. However, other relevant contemporary documentation such as official government correspondence, journals, newspapers, and personal memoirs, provide a clear picture of how the regiments were formed and of the reaction to the raising of the militia. In 1793 Ireland was divided into 32 administrative counties, varying in population size and religious persuasion. Catholics made up the majority of people in most counties, with only the bulk of the population of the counties in Ulster being Protestant.[37] But there was further division amongst the Protestant population, with most of the population of several counties in Ulster being Presbyterian. This was reflected in the composition of the rank and file of the militia regiments.

With no record of the religion of individual militiamen in enrolment books, pay records or muster rolls, it remains conjecture that the county regiments reflected the religious make-up of their county of origin.[38] However, contemporary evidence collated by Edward Wakefield in 1812, was an attempt to estimate the proportion of Catholics to Protestants in the Irish militia. His findings were compiled from interviews with various regimental commanders and from records concerning the composition of the 30 militia light companies that were brought together as composite

---

34 Nelson, *The Irish Militia*, p.65.
35 Stuart Reid, *King George's Army 1740–1793: Infantry* (London: Osprey, 1995), pp.19–20.
36 Reid, *King George's Army*, pp.19–20.
37 Bartlett, 'Defence, counter-insurgency and rebellion: Ireland, 1793–1803', p.255.
38 Nelson, *The Irish Militia*, p.124.

battalions in 1802 at a brigade summer training camp at Athlone.[39] It remains the only contemporary evidence available, where he concluded that contrary to the previously accepted thought surrounding the religious composition of the militia rank and file, proportionally more Protestants enlisted than Catholics.[40] Wakefield came to this conclusion by comparing the estimated proportion of the Catholic and Protestant population of 17 counties to the proportion of Catholics and Protestants in the rank and file of the respective county militias. In almost every case the ratio of enlisted Protestants far exceeds the proportion of the Protestant population for the counties (Table 2.1).[41] However, the accuracy of such statistics will always remain in question as the only available official evidence of the Protestant/Catholic county population ratio was provided from the Hearth Tax survey of the 1730s which does not take into consideration the rapid population increase of Catholic peasantry during the late eighteenth century.

Table 2.1: Proportion of Catholics to Protestant in the Irish militia.

Regiment	Militia Proportion	County Proportion
Carlow	5:2	9:1
Cork County	7:2	11:1
Fermanagh	2:13	2:1
Galway	5:1	39:1
Kerry	5:1	79:1
Kilkenny	7:1	22:1
King's County	6:1	7:1
Leitrim	2:1	29:1
Limerick County	14:1	79:1
Louth	5:4	14:1
Monaghan	3:4	4:1
Roscommon	7:1	79:1
Tipperary	19:1	11:1
Sligo	2:1	30:1
Westmeath	2:1	29:1
Wexford	2:1	9:1

Source: Nelson, *The Irish Militia, 1793–1802*, p.124

The most extreme example is County Fermanagh which had a civilian population ratio of two Catholics for every one Protestant. However, this was not reflected in the county militia which had a ratio of two Catholics to 13 Protestants.[42] It could be argued that the small proportion of Catholics could be explained by Fermanagh being a border county where traditional agrarian disturbances and strong links to Defenderism dissuaded the Catholic peasantry from joining what may have been seen as the military arm of the

---

39 Edward Wakefield, *An Account of Ireland, Statistical and Political* (London: Longman, Hurst, Rees, Orme & Brown, 1812), vol.2, pp.630–631.
40 Nelson, *The Irish Militia*, p.124.
41 Nelson, *The Irish Militia*, p.124.
42 Nelson, *The Irish Militia*, p.124.

Protestant oligarchy. However, an examination of predominantly Catholic counties throughout Ireland, and excluding those in Ulster, also supports this. County Kerry had a population ratio of 79 Catholics to one Protestant, but the county militia ratio was only five to one. County Louth had a Catholic population majority of 14 to one, but a militia ratio of only five Catholics for every four Protestants. Only County Tipperary went against this trend having a militia ratio of 19 to one compared to a civilian population ratio of 11 to one.[43]

It is impossible to get an exact proportion of Catholic militiamen compared to Protestants or their distribution amongst the regiments. The light company returns submitted from the battalions formed for summer camp training, and used by Wakefield, are the only known official records to provide the relevant information (Table 2.2). This suggests that only two thirds of the total militia rank and file were Catholic.[44] Possibly 15 out of the 38 regiments included one third or more enlisted Protestants, but official information concerning the religious make-up of the battalions was not published due to the government concern for the deepening sectarian bitterness.[45] The Irish administration at Dublin Castle was hopeful that the militia would be seen as a national defence force, free from religious labelling. However, from the time of its establishment, the Irish militia was dismissed by the Protestant Ascendancy as being hostile to the Protestant population, mainly due to the perceived proportion of Catholic militiamen.[46] Historians generally agree with the estimation that Catholics provided two-thirds to three-quarters of the total militia rank and file during its existence.[47] This indicates that Protestants made up a substantial percentage of enlisted militiamen, negating the myth that the Irish militia was exclusively a Catholic institution. However, the militia remained predominantly Catholic in the rank and file, which was unprecedented in eighteenth century Ireland.

Initially, the Militia Act empowered the governors of each county to call out the militia once a year for 28 days of training in times of peace.[48] However, the increase in violence throughout the kingdom, accompanied by the constant threat of invasion through war with republican France and the upsurge in the volunteer movement, posed a serious risk to the internal and external security of the nation. This resulted in heated debate within the Irish parliament as to the proposed length of embodiment after the cabinet had already authorised expenditure for 12 months wages for each regiment.[49] This then led to the lord lieutenant in the summer of 1793 directing that the Irish militia be placed on permanent service for the duration of the war with France. Although this contradicted the terms in which the recruits were enlisted, resulting in some desertions, there appears to have been no serious

---

43 Nelson, *The Irish Militia*, p.124.
44 J.E. Cookson, 'Arming Catholics: The Irish Militia, 1793–1815', (Unpublished article, presented at AMBHA Conference, February 1995), p.4.
45 Cookson, 'Arming Catholics: The Irish Militia, 1793–1815', p.4.
46 Cookson, 'Arming Catholics: The Irish Militia, 1793–1815', p.5.
47 Nelson, *The Irish Militia*, p.21.
48 Nelson, *The Irish Militia*, p.46.
49 McAnally, *The Irish Militia*, p.53.

Table 2.2: Irish Militia, 1802: Catholic and Protestant rank and file, Light Infantry Brigade

Regiment	Catholic	Protestant	Percentage Catholic
Cork City	95	1	
Galway	97	2	
Carlow	78	4	
Longford	90	6	
Waterford	89	6	
Clare	91	7	
Limerick County	89	7	
Limerick City	84	7	
Meath	90	9	
Kildare	91	9	
Westmeath	85	10	
Kerry	83	13	
Tipperary	85	15	
Dublin City	84	16	
Roscommon	82	16	
North Cork	81	18	
Louth	72	25	
Queen's County	73	26	
South Cork	73	26	
Tyrone	58	29	
Londonderry	55	45	
Sligo	48	42	
Leitrim	50	50	
North Down	44	51	
Wicklow	44	54	
Armagh	26	69	
Fermanagh	24	76	
Monaghan	18	82	
South Down	13	87	
Cavan	5	95	
Total	1,997	903	68.8

(Source: Wakefield, *An Account of Ireland, Statistical and Political,* vol. 2, pp. 630–631)

protest from the rank and file. What concerns the men did have mainly regarded the initial lack of provisions made for their families. However, such anxiety soon dissipated once allowances, pensions, and schools were provided by government funding for dependents of all militiamen on permanent service and serving outside their home county.[50] In effect, permanent service was welcomed by many of the rank and file as it provided clothing, food, accommodation, and regular pay in a time of economic uncertainty.

The reputation and performance of the militia officer corps proved controversial. Most criticism came from experienced senior regular army officers such as Lieutenant General Sir Ralph Abercromby and Lieutenant General Charles, Marquis Cornwallis, who were highly critical of the lack of

---

50   McAnally, *The Irish Militia*, pp.266–267.

leadership within the militia during 1797 and 1798. As commander-in-chief of the army in Ireland from late 1797 until April 1798, Abercromby used his criticism of the militia to highlight the flaws of the strategic policy that had been implemented. He argued that its dispersal into small detachments throughout the countryside to guard against insurgency hindered training and supervision by officers, thus reducing discipline and morale.[51] Subsequent to a general inspection of the army conducted throughout Ireland in December 1797, he described the militia as 'licentious' and was critical of the lack of professionalism and responsibility displayed within the officer corps.[52] He found that many militia officers were absent from their commands, preferring to maintain their social lives by residing in cities and provincial centres. In a private letter to the Duke of Portland in June 1798 when the government forces had successfully contained the uprising, Cornwallis expressed his disgust at the cruelty shown by officers of the Irish militia and yeomanry: 'It shall be one of my first objects to soften the ferocity of our troops, which I am afraid, in the Irish corps at least, is not confined to the private soldiers.'[53] A month later, when post-rebellion clean-up was in full swing, he reinforced his feelings in a letter to Major General Sir Charles Ross when he stated, 'The Irish Militia with few officers, and those chiefly of the worst kind, follow closely on the heels of the yeomanry in murder and every kind of atrocity.'[54]

Another senior officer, Major General Sir John Moore, who held a command in Cork, that the difference in religion between the officers and the other ranks was heightened by the attitudes and behaviour of the officers: 'The officers of the Militia are in general Protestants, the men Roman Catholic. The hatred between these different persuasions is inveterate to a degree, and the officers have so little sense or prudence as not to conceal their prejudices.'[55]

Regular officers constantly criticized their colleagues in the militia. An example is Colonel Robert Craufurd, who was later to gain fame as a major general leading the Light Division in the Peninsular War, claiming that the Irish militia officers were 'nothing more than brutes and uneducated farmers' sons.'[56] However, he was aware that there was a significant difference in attitude to duty between the regular and militia officers:

> The officers, too, in the Line, are obliged, to behave like gentlemen, and men of honour, even if they are not naturally so, for a man who enters as an officer, into a regiment of the Line, makes the army his profession, he gets out of all other habits and conditions in life, and feels that if he was to lose the hold he has in the army, he would be plunged into the depths of misery and ruin… In the militia, the case is widely different … militia officers do not feel the necessity of endeavouring to

---

51   McAnally, *The Irish Militia*, p.116.
52   McAnally, *The Irish Militia*, p.116.
53   Ross, *Correspondence of Charles, First Marquis Cornwallis*, pp.354–355.
54   Ross, *Correspondence of Charles, First Marquis Cornwallis*, pp.368–369.
55   Major General Sir J. F. Maurice (ed.), *The Diary of Sir John Moore* (London: Arnold, 1904), pp.274–275.
56   Bartlett, 'Defence, counter-insurgency and rebellion: Ireland, 1793–1803', p.258.

imitate the conduct of men of honour, because they know that at most you can only take from them that situation which at any rate they will lose in a year or two.[57]

Some criticism came from within the militia itself with Colonel Charles Vallancey, commander of the Tyrone Militia, complaining that his junior officers were self-indulgent and had no sense of duty to the regiment or their men.[58] An example of this was the Hon. Robert Ward who was a captain in the Royal Downshire Regiment and who failed to accompany his regiment when it marched to defend against the threatened French invasion at Bantry Bay in late 1796. He was chastised in a letter from Lord Carhampton, who made his expectations clear:

> It is my duty to make sure that every officer in this kingdom does his duty…You are a captain in the Royal Downshire Regiment, you receive pay as such, you have neglected doing duty with the regiment for some time past. This neglect of yours has not been noticed as it ought to have been, but it was not to be supposed that a gentleman of your rank should have heard that the regiment in which he was a captain, and received pay for it, was marching towards an enemy, threatening every hour to invade his country and that you should hesitate a moment to fly to join it… Every moment you remain at Castle Ward after the receipt of my order is … an aggravation of your neglect of duty and disobedience of my orders and without any personal disrespect to you I will vindicate the order I have given.[59]

Even after their involvement in extinguishing the rebellion and defeating the French, Lord Castlereagh, secretary to Cornwallis and a previous militia officer himself, wrote in September 1798 that the militia was commanded by 'bad officers' who perpetually solicited leave of absence and that they had 'a total ignorance and inexperience of every military duty beyond that of a common parade'.[60] Even within the militia itself there were complaints from senior officers regarding subordinate officers of their regiments. An example is a letter written by Major George Matthews, Lord Annesley, of the Royal Downshire Militia to the Marquis of Downshire in 1798:

> The more I see of the Irish militia the more I am convinced that they are totally unfit to take the field against regular troops, we have not officers, for my own part I am at our own officers every day about their duty, but all in vain. Nature never intended them for war, except for a few they are not worth their salt. I can't get anything done, as it ought to be, all your last batch are worse than useless.[61]

---

57 TNA: HO/100/79/116: Home Office Papers, Colonel Robert Craufurd to Wickham, 19 November 1798.
58 Bartlett, 'Defence, counter-insurgency and rebellion: Ireland, 1793–1803', p.258.
59 National Library of Ireland (NLI): KP/ 1081/24: Kilmainham Papers, Lord Carhampton to the Hon. Robert Ward, 2 January 1797.
60 Ross, *Correspondence of Charles, First Marquis Cornwallis*, p.406.
61 Public Records Office of Northern Ireland (PRONI): D/607/F/410: Downshire Papers, Major George Matthews to the Marquess of Downshire, 15 September 1798.

It was statements such as these, made by respected military authorities, which reinforced the perpetual stigma that was attached to the militia and its officer corps.

However, the alleged general reputation of the leadership within the militia must been seen in its context. There is more than sufficient evidence to prove that the officer corps of the militia was not of the professional standard of the regular army. It could not be expected to achieve that level. The militia, by definition, was a military force of trained civilians to be used in times of emergency. The only officers required to have previous military service were the regimental adjutants, ensuring that many unsuitable officers were offered commissions purely on their financial qualifications or family connections.[62] Most of the peers and gentry, who made up much of the officer corps, also had civil duties as county governors, magistrates, and land magnates. Examples were Lord Abercorn of the Tyrone Militia, Lord Portarlington of the Queen's County Militia, and the Duke of Leinster in the Kildare Militia, who gained their appointments as colonels due to their local influence and loyalty to the government.[63] These were administrative appointments in the militia and the day-to-day running of the regiments was carried out by the lieutenant colonels. However, there was an expectation that the colonels would provide leadership when required. Having dual responsibilities led to many being absent from their units for long periods of time, especially when required to attend county assizes.[64] Admittedly, many officers would have used such occasions as excuses to escape the boredom of military life in unfavourable rural and provincial locations. This is evident in the correspondence received by the lord lieutenant from disgruntled regimental commanders seeking permission to replace officers who had continually refused to return to their units.[65]

The absence of officers from regiments had a detrimental effect on training for both officers and the rank and file, and there is an obvious link between the criticism of the quality of the officers and the ill-discipline of the men.[66] In the eighteenth century officers in the British Army learned their profession through studying the numerous manuals written for junior officers, guidance from experienced colleagues, by being provided drill lessons from senior non-commissioned officers and through experience in times of war.[67] The ability of many officers to gain leave to foster their civilian interests ensured that they and their men did not achieve the level of professionalism expected by the Irish administration. However, much of the blame for this situation lay with the colonels of the regiments. All leave was given at the discretion of the colonel, with each battalion officially required to have one field officer (major, lieutenant colonel or colonel) and two thirds

---

62 McAnally, *The Irish Militia*, p.21.
63 McAnally, *The Irish Militia*, pp.88–91.
64 McAnally, *The Irish Militia*, pp.88–91.
65 TNA: HO 100/68: Home Office Papers, Lord Carhampton to the Earl of Camden, 19 October 1797.
66 Nelson, *The Irish Militia*, p.25.
67 J.A. Houlding, *Fit For Service: The Training of the British Army, 1717–1795* (Oxford: Clarendon Press, 1981), pp.45–57.

'The Auckward Squad' by Isaac Cruikshank, 1793. This caricature of militia training shows the various uniforms used by the militia in the 1790s. (Anne S.K. Brown Military Collection)

of all other officers present with the regiment at all times.⁶⁸ In reality, leave tended to be given indiscriminately. The absence of many officers then led to much of the individual, company and battalion drill and tactical training being conducted by the non-commissioned officers, such as sergeant majors and sergeants.⁶⁹ This was especially so when the battalions were broken up into small sections and detachments to be stationed in small hamlets.

Detached service also proved damaging to the effectiveness of the militia, and it is surprising that the semi-trained regiments performed as well as they did during the uprising and French invasion in 1798. It not only hindered essential large formation training which was required to be effective in linear-style actions against regular troops, but also proved difficult in establishing and maintaining regimental discipline and morale.⁷⁰ Postings to dispersed locations ensured a lack of officer supervision when battalions were broken up into company and squad size detachments that were commanded by either inexperienced junior officers or NCOs.⁷¹ Small squads were posted in villages and hamlets to protect individuals and property, negating any form of battalion or company training that was essential to effectively perform the drills and formations of the British army during the period.⁷² An example

---

68 Nelson, *The Irish Militia*, p.108.
69 Nelson, *The Irish Militia*, p.24.
70 Nelson, *The Irish Militia*, p.24.
71 Nelson, *The Irish Militia*, p.137.
72 Stuart Reid, *British Redcoat 1740-1793* (London: Osprey, 1996), pp.24–26.

was the Royal Downshire Militia which in 1796 had its headquarters at Drogheda, while one of its companies was stationed at Navan and another at Bilgriggan. However, smaller detachments of the regiment were stationed at Swords, Rateath, Lusk, Malahide, Dunshaglin, Westpanstown, Collon, Torkphecklan, Slane and Parsonstown; six being commanded by a junior officer with the other four by sergeants.[73] Morale and discipline suffered due to exposure to corruption, drunkenness and constant use in unpopular policing duties in assisting magistrates against the local population, among whom the militiamen had to reside.[74] Regiments were restricted from being stationed within the same localities from which they recruited because it was felt that possible family connections and local sympathies would affect unit discipline. It was such postings away from their home counties, together with the shock of military life that initially led to a significant number of desertions within regiments. Within the first six months of service the County Wexford regiment lost 27 out of a complement of 207, the Downshire regiment lost 14 from 649, County Meath lost 45 from 298, and the City of Dublin regiment lost 33 out of 291.[75] Such desertions became less frequent once conditions for the troops improved, such as provisions for wives and children to the live within barracks and the establishment of battalion schools.

Much of the indiscipline shown by the militia was officially encouraged. In March 1793, Major General Richard Whyte urged his troops to rampage through Belfast, attacking homes and businesses of known radicals.[76] The 1795 pacification of Connacht by Lord Carhampton, the commander-in-chief of the army in Ireland at the time, also aided the breakdown in discipline with those militia units involved. This civilian rebellion came about through rising unrest and the inadequacy of the magistrates to deal with the disaffected population. On 17 May 1795 a proclamation was issued authorising the military to act in dispersing unlawful assemblies without the need to wait for the direction of a magistrate, although they could not act on their own accord if a magistrate was present.[77] The proclamation order was signed by seven privy councillors who were all colonels of militia regiments.[78] Continuous searches of civilian property, floggings, numerous house burnings and the illegal sending of suspected Defenders and United Irishmen to serve in the Royal Navy without trial were characteristics of this campaign as well as similar operations in Ulster later that year.[79] Thomas Pelham, the lord lieutenant's chief secretary at the time defended such practice and praised the conduct of the militia: 'It cannot be denied that some things were done that are to be regretted, but at the same time I believe

---

73 McAnally, *The Irish Militia*, p.88.
74 Nelson, *The Irish Militia*, p.137.
75 Nelson, *The Irish Militia*, p.73.
76 Thomas Bartlett, 'Indiscipline and disaffection in the armed forces of Ireland in the 1790s', in Patrick J. Corish (ed.), *Radicals, Rebels and Establishments* (Belfast: Appletree Press, 1985), p.118.
77 Nelson, *The Irish Militia*, p.137.
78 Nelson, *The Irish Militia*, p.137.
79 Bartlett, 'Indiscipline and disaffection in the armed forces of Ireland in the 1790s', p.118.

no army ever behaved better under similar circumstances and I venture to say no army was ever placed in exactly the same situation.'[80]

The illegal operations carried out under veiled approval from the government were linked to the indiscipline of the militia regiments involved.[81] The dispersal of battalions and the blurring of vital distinctions between civil and military authority could only add confusion and lack of restraint to troops who were not properly trained in such use. Even the severest critic of the Irish army, Lieutenant General Sir Ralph Abercromby, admitted that some of its indiscipline stemmed from the situation in Ireland: 'the dispersed state of the troops is really ruinous to the service. The best regiments in Europe could not stand such usage.'[82]

To remedy the effects of detached service, summer training camps were established in 1795 where several battalions could come together. These camps, situated at Ardfinnan, near Clonmel in County Tipperary, Blaris, near Belfast, and Loughlinstown, near Dublin, provided opportunities for company, battalion and brigade level training in firing and marching that were essential in forging the militia into an effective military force. Although initially established as temporary encampments for the summer months, they eventually became permanent camps with huts being erected for the troops. In the first year of their operation the Kildare, Clare, Donegal, Limerick City and Wexford militias were ordered to remain at Loughlinstown over the winter, while the Carlow, Wicklow and Kerry regiments remained at Blaris.[83] The traditional dispersal of the regiments had led to a decline in regulation dress, parade drill and arms exercise, due in part to the boredom and negligence of many officers.[84] It was proposed that a rotational system of postings to the above camps would increase the standards within the militia regiments. However, it appears that these camps were not used to their full potential. The lack of contemporary documentation relating to training at the camps makes it difficult to ascertain an accurate record of which regiments attended these camps as well as what training they received. However, official returns and reports from newspapers such as the *Dublin Journal*, indicate that only 27 out of the 38 militia regiments trained together between 1795 and 1797.[85] No regiment attended the camps in all three years, as was initially intended, and only the Clare, Donegal, Wexford, Armagh, Westmeath, Limerick City and Cavan militias had attended twice. There were also a decreasing number of units available to attend summer training, with 21 in 1795, 10 in 1796 and only three in 1797.[86] These figures demonstrate how the dispersal of the regiments throughout the country was ruinous to the proficiency of the corps.

---

80 TNA: HO 100/70: Home Office Papers, Thomas Pelham to the Home Secretary, July 1797.
81 Bartlett, 'Indiscipline and disaffection in the armed forces of Ireland in the 1790s', p.119.
82 James Abercromby, *Lieutenant General Sir Ralph Abercromby: a memoir by his son* (Edinburgh: Edmonston & Douglas, 1861), p.86.
83 Nelson, *The Irish Milia*, p.82.
84 Houlding, *Fit For Service*, pp.45–57.
85 Nelson, *The Irish Militia*, pp.82–83.
86 Nelson, *The Irish Militia*, pp.82–83.

REBELLION, INVASION AND OCCUPATION

'The Salute' by James Gillray. The uniforms depicted are typical of militia uniforms from 1793 to 1800. (Anne S.K. Brown Military Collection)

In general, the initial stationing of the militia regiments between 1794 and 1798 appeared to be free from any official system of religious bias. Once the regiments had been fully embodied, they were marched from their counties of origin, only to return when being disbanded in 1802 and again in 1816. A system of annual rotation was introduced which saw most battalions serving at various locations throughout Ireland. This was proposed to counteract any unwanted sympathies and relationships that the militiamen may have developed for and with the local population that were deemed detrimental to the policing duties required of the militias.[87] In practice the regiments were posted to places far from their county of origin as it was thought that discipline would improve and training would be more efficient with the officers and men away from their home influences.[88] This is evident when examining the militia return for March 1796 which showed the Kerry Militia stationed at Newry in County Down, the Derry Militia at Limerick, the Fermanagh Militia at Waterford and the North Cork Militia at Sligo.[89] The only exception to this was the Royal Downshire Militia, recruited from the large Presbyterian population of County Down in Ulster, which appeared to have been permanently stationed at Drogheda. One explanation

---

87   McAnally, *The Irish Militia*, p.62.
88   McAnally, *The Irish Militia*, p.62.
89   TNA: HO 100/60: Home Office Papers, Camden to the Duke of Portland, 21 March 1796.

for this could be the strength of the United Irish in this part of Ulster whose large Presbyterian population were considered dissenters from the Anglican Church and mistrusted by the Irish Ascendancy. By stationing this unit at Drogheda, situated halfway between the army reserves at Blaris, near Belfast, and Dublin, the government would have been able to react quickly with superior forces should the regiment mutiny. The quartering of the regiments changed so frequently to prevent attachments occurring that the militia developed into a nomadic force.[90]

An exact account relating to the annual stationing of the militias is impossible to collate due to most records having been destroyed. However, the few surviving regimental annual returns provide some indication of how the units were distributed. In March 1796, Camden wrote to the Duke of Portland with his proposed changes to the Irish garrison for the summer of that year, seeking authority from the Home Secretary to establish permanent camps to help formulate a defensive strategy against foreign invasion. By 1796 British intervention in Europe against France had failed ensuring that the British Isles were now a likely target of French attack. Camden's letter shows that the Irish militia was to be dispersed as individual battalions throughout the 32 counties, with 10 regiments to be concentrated at the training camps. These camps were established not only to provide opportunities for battalion and brigade formation training, but also provided concentrations of ready reserves against rebellion or any invasion attempts.[91] The regiments selected for the various camps were a balance between battalions with Catholic and Protestant rank and file majorities. The force to be stationed at Blaris in Ulster consisted of two 'Catholic' units, the City of Limerick and Queen's County militias, which were accompanied by three 'Protestant' regiments, the Cavan Militia together with the Fife and York Fencibles. At Loughlinstown the 'Catholic' Clare Militia was to serve with the Kildare and Donegal militias, which both had a sizable minority of Protestant militiamen. Whilst the force at Ardfinnan consisting mainly of 'Protestant' units, the Antrim and Armagh militias, was balanced by the presence of the 'Catholic' Wexford Militia and the Louth Militia that had a large minority of Catholic troops.[92] However, the lack of available regular army units and the desperate need to police the rural heartland of Ireland, as well as the strategic ports of Dublin, Cork and Belfast, ensured that the government was initially forced to rely upon the loyalty of the 'Catholic' militia regiments in assisting in the national security.

The militia lacked the required effective training to raise it to the level of the regular army. In contrast to the regular regiments, when first raised the militia battalions generally lacked a cadre of experienced officers and non-commissioned officers to provide drills and experience. Heavy reliance was placed on the few who had previous military experience to forge the officers and rank and file into a disciplined and effective unit.[93] Some regiments resorted to recruiting former English NCOs to provide the

---

90 McAnally, *The Irish Militia*, p.62.
91 TNA: HO 100/60: Home Office Papers, Camden to Portland, 21 March 1796.
92 TNA: HO 100/60: Home Office Papers, Camden to Portland, 21 March 1796.
93 McAnally, *The Irish Militia*, pp.55–56.

necessary experience.⁹⁴ The few diligent officers who remained with their regiments were required to study the new drill manual written by Dundas in 1793 to become proficient with the current military standards. It took time for the rank and file to adjust to the rigours of military life, with discipline instilled only after months of constant marching and musket drill. Failure of the government to initially supply accoutrements and weapons led to some units, such as the Kerry Militia, parading and training without muskets for a number of months.⁹⁵ However, by early 1794 all but the Cavan and Kildare Militias had reached their required strengths and were deemed proficient enough for service at a minimum level required for internal security.⁹⁶ In a dispatch to London in January 1794, the lord lieutenant, the Earl of Westmorland reported that 'the militia are about 10,000 strong and are becoming fit for garrison duty and purposes of police but could not well be relied on against a disciplined enemy without the intermixture and aid of a body of regulars.'⁹⁷ It was clear that as a force the militia was not capable of defending Ireland against an invasion by regular troops.

Yet, in contrast to its poor reputation, the Irish Militia was effective in providing internal security. The large number of battalions ensured that the rural and isolated regions of Ireland could now be policed against the rising incidents of violence. This had not previously been possible due to the few remaining available regular troops being required to guard strategic points such as Dublin and Cork. Lieutenant General William Dalrymple, commanding in Belfast, reported in September 1795 that in service against Defenders 'In all the circumstances that have yet occurred the behaviour of the regiments of militia has been excellent … the conduct … has been firm and obedient and that of good soldiers.'⁹⁸ Lord Camden had previously made his favourable opinion of the militia known when he reported in May of the same year that 'on all occasions that militia have behaved with the greatest spirit and showed the most loyal attachment to his majesty's government.'⁹⁹

The most notable incident where the militia proved effective prior to the 1798 rebellion was in the quelling of the mutinies of regular battalions in Cork and Dublin in 1795. At Cork the Louth, King's County, Meath, and Roscommon Militias displayed discipline and loyalty when they assisted the 32nd Foot and the 7th Dragoon Guards in subduing the mutineers of the 105th and 113th Foot who were protesting being posted to the Caribbean. In Dublin the Westmeath, Londonderry and Longford Militias combined with the Essex and Breadalbane Fencibles in suppressing the 104th and 111th Foot who had mutinied for the same reason.¹⁰⁰ In reporting on these incidents and other operations against rural insurgents, Camden stated that 'The militia

---

94 McAnally, *The Irish Militia*, pp.55–56.
95 McAnally, *The Irish Militia*, pp.55–56.
96 McAnally, *The Irish Militia*, pp.55–56.
97 TNA: HO 100/47: Home Office Papers, Earl of Westmorland to the Duke of Portland, 14 January 1794.
98 McAnally, *The Irish Militia*, p.84.
99 McAnally, *The Irish Militia*, p.84.
100 Nelson, *The Irish Militia*, p.156.

are the finest troops it is possible to see and have universally behaved well.'[101] While this comment may be an exaggeration stimulated by exuberance and relief in eliminating potential threats to Camden's administration, the militia had proven itself to have developed into a reliable and effective auxiliary force. This in part could be attributed to the increased supervision and leadership provided by the augmentation of the militia in 1795, which led to an increase in the NCO to men ratio to one to five.[102] This was much higher than the NCO to private ratio of the regular regiments. Contrary to the post-rebellion reputation of the Irish militia, most regiments had proven themselves to be loyal and disciplined, qualities that would be reinforced in 1798.

The conventional view of the Irish militia as an ill-disciplined and poorly trained Catholic corps that had been infiltrated by the United Irishmen, was subject to subversion, and thus could not be trusted in the defence of Ireland was reinforced by exaggerated, and sometimes false, reports concerning negative behaviour of individual militia regiments during the rebellion and French invasion of 1798. Political expediency, religious bias, mistrust, and fear of the Catholic peasant majority by the Protestant minority can account for these unfavourable attitudes towards the militia. However, contrary to such adverse views, in general, the militia played a significant role in the defence of Britain, either in dealing with rebels during the rebellion or by providing thousands of semi-trained recruits to regular British regiments. This highlights the importance of the corps in the broader defence of Britain during the period.

---

101   TNA: HO 100/58: Home Office Papers, Camden to the Duke of Portland, 24 July 1795.
102   TNA: HO 100/50: Home Office Papers, 'Return for Strength of Army and Militia in Ireland', 1 March 1795.

3

The Yeomanry

The formation of the Irish yeomanry in 1796 marked the second phase in the official arming of the Irish population. This force came about through the increasing political and sectarian disturbances that had occurred in Ulster and the bordering counties of Ulster, Leinster, and Connacht during that year. Escalating violence in rural areas led to the demand for effective protection for individuals and property from the propertied classes that included the gentry, farmers, landowners, and merchants.[1] Heightened support for the formation of localised armed forces eventually led to official recognition of the many defence associations that had already mushroomed in the troubled areas. The establishment of the yeomanry was also perceived at this time as being of significant strategic value in that it would free the militia from many civil duties so that it could be more effectively used in counter-invasion operations.[2] Although the yeomanry was predominantly Protestant, and in later years became the military arm of the Protestant Irish Ascendancy, many Catholics enlisted in the corps, with some gaining commissions.[3] However, the events of 1798 led to a greater polarisation of the Irish population, with the increased distrust of Catholics leading to most being purged from the yeomanry. It was the hardening of attitudes and ill-discipline of many troops within the para-military organisation that tarnished the reputation of the corps.

The yeomanry was founded on a tradition of duty in self-defence. The majority of yeomanry corps were established in Ulster where the Protestant population had relied on voluntary military service since the founding of the Elizabethan plantations in the sixteenth century to provide the necessary protection from Catholic aggression.[4] The collusion of the militant United Irishmen and the Catholic Defenders in the mid-1790s led to increased fears throughout Protestant society and a call for greater measures to ensure the safety of lives and property. Anxiety was increased through comments recorded from Protestant leaders such as Lord Clare who feared

---

1 R.G. Morton, 'The Rise of the Yeomanry', *The Irish Sword*, vol.8 (1967), pp.58–64.
2 TNA: HO 100/61: Earl of Camden to the Duke of Portland, 22 September 1796.
3 Blackstock, *An Ascendancy Army*, p.60.
4 Bartlett, 'Defence, counter-insurgency and rebellion: Ireland, 1793–1803', p.267.

a repeat of the massacres committed by Catholics in 1641.⁵ Localised armed associations began to be formed based around already established Protestant groups known as Boyne societies, such as the 'Apprentice Boys' and various other 'Orange' factions.⁶ These initially functioned as social organisations. However, by 1795 the ability of Protestants to lawfully carry arms saw many of these factions coming together to provide armed security to their communities, which the army was unable to provide.

The need to provide public safety inspired the establishment of the corps. As tension increased rural gentry and merchants increasingly became targets of the disaffected. Defenders (a Catholic agrarian secret society formed in Armagh to provide local defence against Protestant Peep 'o Day Boys) and United Irishmen carried out raids on the houses of the landed classes to seize firearms necessary for rebellion. Such raids led to numerous deaths and destruction of property. Due to the isolated locations of many of the houses, the response from the military stationed in provincial towns was inadequate, resulting in calls for the creation of official localised bodies of volunteers to counter such activities.⁷ The gentry began to lobby for government support in such measures, which were initially rejected. Although such calls received considerable positive response in the Irish Houses of Commons and Lords, the British and Irish administrations quashed such initiatives, fearing the power any such organisation may hold over the government.

The experience of dealing with the Irish Volunteers initially hindered the introduction of the yeomanry. The Irish Volunteers were established in 1778 and existed until the organisation was outlawed by the Irish government in 1793. Although the movement was established during the American War of Independence primarily to provide an auxiliary force for the defence of Ireland from potential French and Spanish invasion, it eventually became a strong political force. At its peak in 1782, it could boast 89,000 members and was influential in promoting the re-establishment of the Irish parliament that year, as well as gaining more favourable trade concessions from Britain.⁸ The Volunteers became the strongest expression of Protestant defence tradition and could not be controlled by the government. As the movement was based purely on volunteers, received no funding from the government and had not been formed through any legislative power, the authorities had no control over delegating commissions for officers or the distribution of arms. Ironically, it was the legislation that allowed Protestants to bear arms that allowed the Volunteers to develop into a strong, armed movement and powerful political force that was considered a destabilizing faction by the British government. Many feared that the creation of the yeomanry would lead to a similar situation.

Although the establishment of the yeomanry eventually proved to be a decisive move in aiding political stability in Ireland, the authorities in Dublin

---

5   Blackstock, *An Ascendancy Army*, p.42.
6   Morton, 'The Rise of the Yeomanry', pp.58–64.
7   Morton, 'The Rise of the Yeomanry', pp.58–64.
8   Allan Blackstock, 'The Irish Yeomanry and the 1798 Rebellion', in Thomas Bartlett et. al. (eds), *1798: A Bicentenary Perspective* (Dublin: Four Courts Press, 2003), p.332.

REBELLION, INVASION AND OCCUPATION

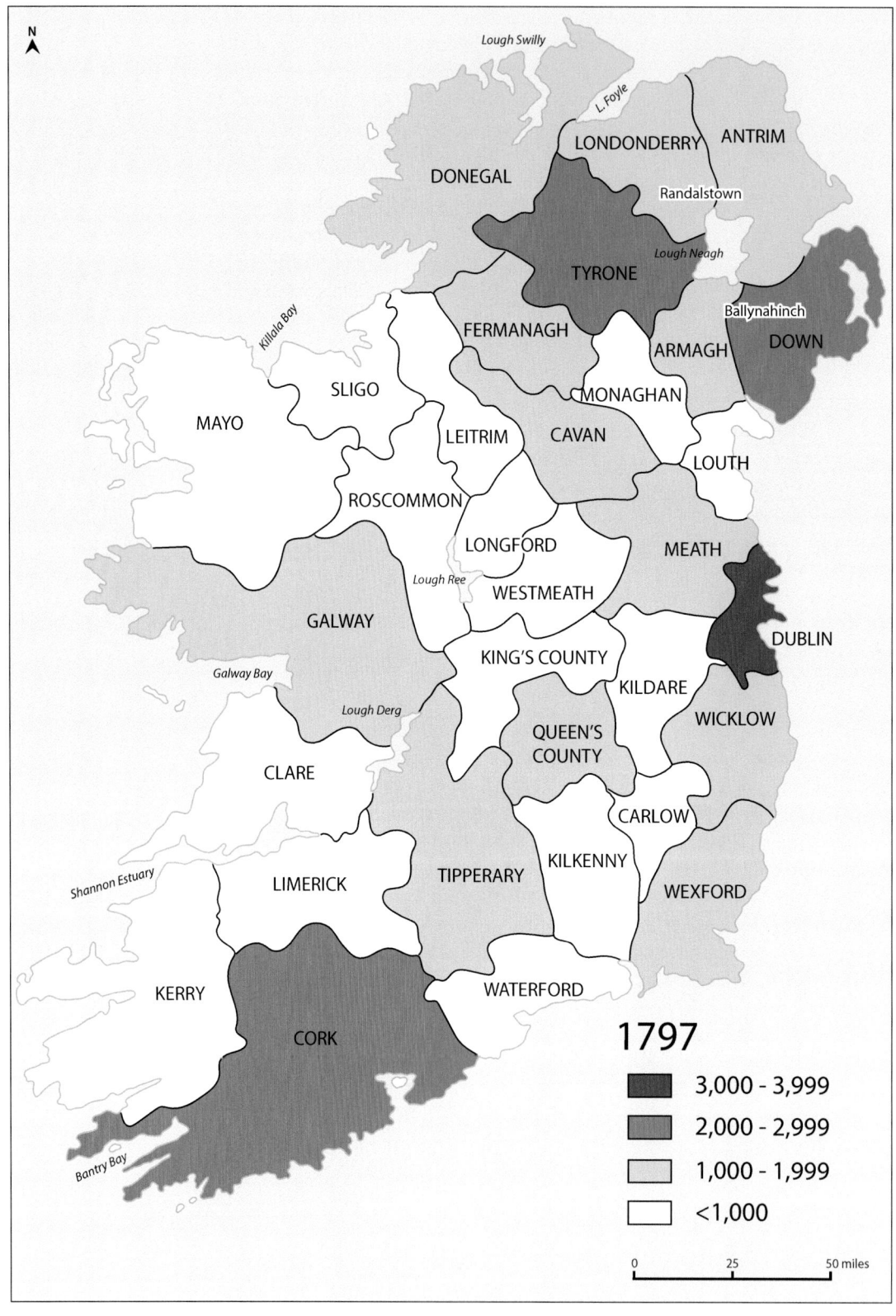

Irish Yeomanry: County density, 1797 (Source: Blackstock, *An Ascendancy Army*, p.119)

THE YEOMANRY

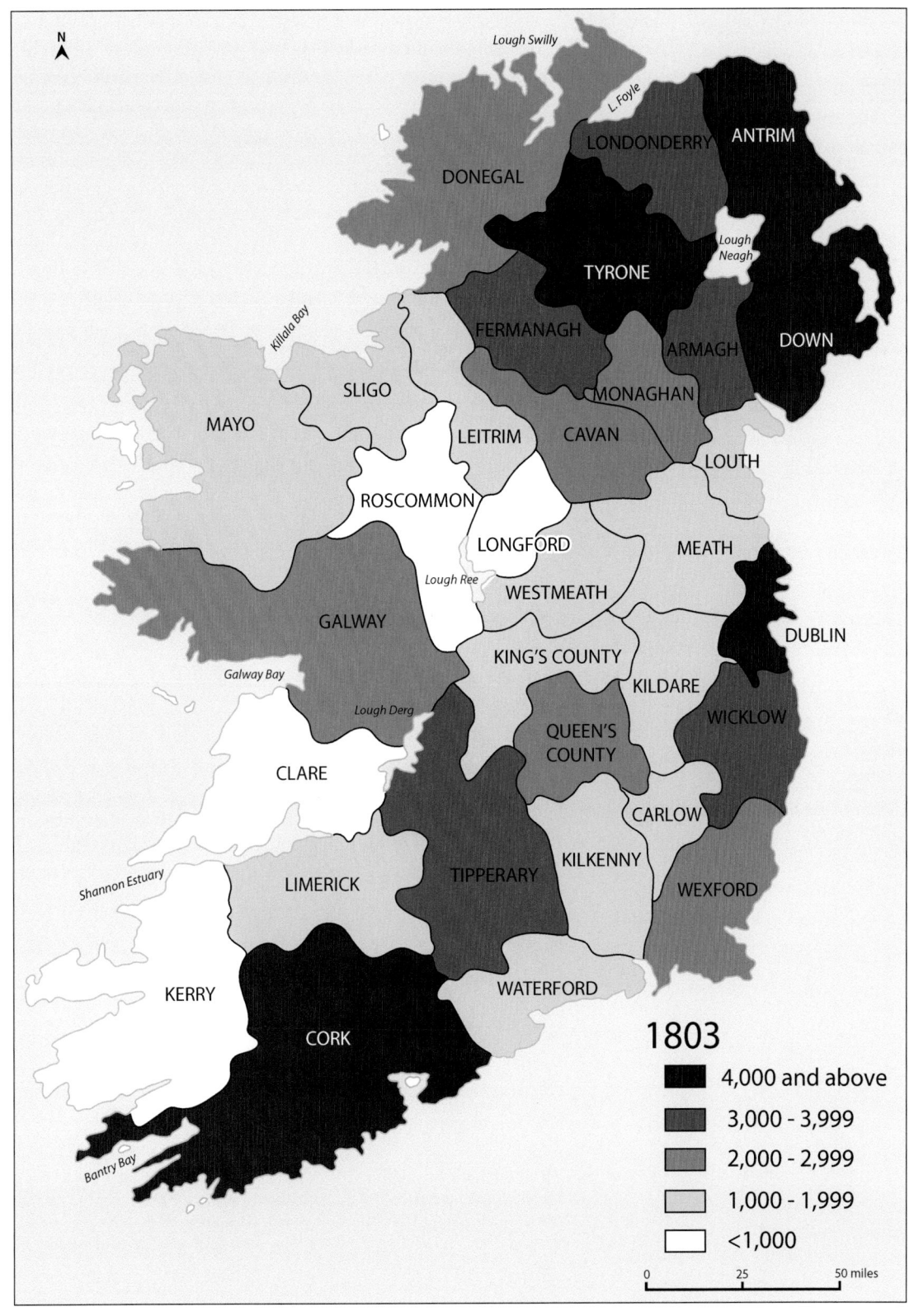

Irish Yeomanry: County density, 1803 (Source: Blackstock, *An Ascendancy Army*, p.120)

Castle initially viewed any sort of volunteering as a destabilizing influence. They saw the rise of the independent armed associations as a potential threat and feared armed power in the localities in case it formed into radical political opposition.[9] To counteract this, it was argued that such groups could be controlled by drafting them into a government-established yeomanry. Through this process, the Irish government could offer commissions to those it considered loyal to the regime and control them through pay and patronage. Lord Fitzwilliam, the liberal lord lieutenant in Ireland in 1795, argued for the formation of a yeomanry that would include Catholics: 'We must endeavour to form a strength upon the principle of the English Yeomanry which will have the double effect of a defence against an invasion and an additional power in support of the magistracy.'[10] He proposed that the yeomanry would include the better sorts of people whose social status fell between the landlords and the peasantry, which would include Catholic gentry, except in Ulster.[11] However, this proposal proved contentious in that it was seen by the Ascendancy as being revolutionary, by placing power in the hands of Catholics, and was one of the concerns that eventually led to Fitzwilliam's recall.[12]

The Irish Yeomanry came into being in September 1796, based on a plan proposed by Thomas Knox of Dungannon, an MP for Tyrone. In February of that year several armed Protestant and district defence associations were formed amongst the tenants of County Tyrone, pledging assistance to local magistrates in enforcing the law. The idea spread with numerous associations being formed in the other border counties of Ulster. By June 1796, the Dungannon Association had formulated a plan that was submitted to Dublin Castle by Knox. The plan called for a gentry-sponsored law and order association which would include reliable inhabitants signing loyal resolutions and submitting offers of service under government control.[13] Although initially sceptical, the new lord lieutenant, the Earl of Camden, soon warmed to the idea. In a letter to the Duke of Portland he pointed out the positive aspects of the proposal, arguing that the yeomanry might be the foundation of a useful plan to strengthen the government in Ireland.[14] However, he believed that any forthcoming legislation should exclude the clause from the Dungannon plan that proposed the force could be used 'to oppose the French should they attempt to invade.'[15] Camden feared that United Irishmen could easily infiltrate the yeomanry and prove a disruptive element in the case of any invasion.

Political pressure played a major part in the creation of the yeomanry. Increasing internal violence, civil unrest and the impending threat of invasion forced Camden to act. He was under pressure from advisors, such

---

9   Blackstock, 'The Irish Yeomanry and the 1798 Rebellion', p.332.
10   TNA: HO 100/56: Fitzwilliam to the Duke of Portland, 10 January 1795.
11   TNA: HO 100/56: Fitzwilliam to the Duke of Portland, 10 January 1795.
12   Ernest Smith, *Whig Principles and party politics: Earl Fitzwilliam and the Whig party, 1748–1833* (Manchester: Manchester University Press, 1975), p.177.
13   TNA: HO 100/61: Earl of Camden to the Duke of Portland, 22 September 1796.
14   Blackstock, *An Ascendancy Army*, p.56.
15   Blackstock, *An Ascendancy Army*, p.56.

THE YEOMANRY

Dublin Castle c.1816. (Anne S.K. Brown Military Collection)

as Lords Clare and Carhampton, prominent leaders within the Protestant Ascendancy, to form yeomanry corps along the lines of the English model, based solely on cavalry. However, this would prove impractical, especially in Ulster where many poorer Protestants would be unable to provide their own horse. There was a need for infantry corps to be incorporated into the plan as there were not enough gentry in some areas, such as Donegal, to raise cavalry. This would then lead to lower-class membership within the infantry and raised the thorny question as to religious composition. As commander-in-chief, Carhampton had voiced his frustration at being unable to concentrate a sufficient force to challenge an invasion due to the army being distributed throughout the provinces to provide security for the gentry. He argued that such a dilemma could be solved by allowing the formation of gentry-led yeomanry corps to provide localised security against insurgents, thus allowing the release of most of his troops to concentrate on external threats.[16] Portland had authorised Camden to raise 'provincial levies' but hesitated in using the term 'yeomanry' due to the unfavourable reception given to Fitzwilliam's rejected plan.[17] He advised that any move to make the force exclusively Protestant risked alienating Catholics and fostered further unrest. Camden was fully aware of the political implications

---

16   Peter Karsten, 'Irish soldiers in the British Army, 1792-1922: Suborned or subordinate?', *Journal of Social History*, vol.17 (1983–1984), pp.31–63.
17   Blackstock, *An Ascendancy Army*, pp.65–66.

and sensitivity required over the matter and took measures to appease all parties. By allowing only reliable Catholics and Dissenters (Presbyterians) of property to enlist he addressed a major concern of Protestants by preventing the inclusion of lower-class Catholics from the infantry without alienating the Catholic gentry. This ensured sufficient support for the measure to be introduced through parliament.

The Irish yeomanry was established after much deliberation, and prior to any authorising enactment being passed. On 17 September 1796 the official plan for raising yeomanry corps was announced and published throughout national newspapers. It included a critical amendment that set the organisation apart from the English model: 'Troops of cavalry will be preferred ... but as it has been represented in certain parts of the kingdom where it might be difficult to raise cavalry alone that many respectable persons would readily serve on foot, the proportion of mounted and dismounted men in each troop must depend on local circumstances.'[18] This led to an immediate flood of offers from local associations and individuals, especially from Ulster and the northern counties of Leinster and Connacht, to raise local corps even before the Yeomanry Bill was introduced in October.[19] Over-subscription proved an issue, with the government unsuccessfully attempting to cap the membership of each corps at 50 when recruits of up to 70 had volunteered.[20] County governors and land magnates called meetings of local magistrates and gentry who were tasked to administer the raising of units and the selection of suitable recruits. What resulted was a diversity of opinion as to the admissibility of Catholics due to local circumstances and lack of direction from the government.

Insufficient government directives saw a varied approach to the formation of individual corps. The yeomanry gained official recognition with the passing of the Yeomanry Bill in the Irish parliament on 25 October 1796, becoming an act of parliament after it gained royal assent two days later.[21] This allowed the organisation to emerge as a uniform national structure which simultaneously contained territorially discrete, regionally diverse, and complex elements. The lack of official directives regarding membership contributed to religious and political exclusiveness in some counties, which represented the local balance of power within parishes.[22] Existing social hierarchies that traditionally dominated parishes and towns tended to gain control of local units, sometimes at the expense and exclusion of political and religious rivals.[23] Protestant leaders within the Irish parliament quietly encouraged this as it was felt that this represented the natural order within Irish society and would provide stability, especially in the volatile rural areas, such as the border counties of Ulster.[24] This *laissez-faire* approach to

---

18 *Freeman's Journal*, 17 September 1796, quoted in Blackstock, *An Ascendancy Army*, p.70.
19 Blackstock, *An Ascendancy Army*, p.71.
20 Blackstock, *An Ascendancy Army*, p.71.
21 Blackstock, *An Ascendancy Army*, p.73.
22 Morton, 'The Rise of the Yeomanry,' p.63.
23 Morton, 'The Rise of the Yeomanry,' p.63.
24 British Library (BL): Add. MS 33102: Camden to Pelham, 28 August 1796, quoted in Morton, 'The Rise of the Yeomanry', p.64.

recruiting by the government ensured that the yeomanry was to eventually become a solely Protestant institution that was to provide the security required to maintain the Ascendancy.

Many members of the dissolved volunteer associations enlisted in the yeomanry. This was somewhat ironic as it was the political power that the movement had previously acquired that Camden and his associates feared, resulting in his initial hesitance in accepting the raising of the yeomanry.[25] An examination of surviving documentation reveals that many names of officers from the volunteers also appear in the returns of yeomanry corps. In the 1970s a study of surviving volunteer lists, yeomanry documentation and journals was conducted and found considerable correlation between volunteer and yeomanry membership. It revealed that in counties Monaghan, Donegal and Roscommon around 50 percent of surnames recurred in yeomanry lists.[26] In Meath, from 88 yeomanry surnames, 20 of the same were recorded in volunteer lists, while in Limerick and Roscommon, the location continuity rate was around 50 percent, with 43 percent in Monaghan.[27] Although this evidence is limited in that there are very few volunteer lists available for comparison due to the secret nature of the organisation and the few surviving yeomanry returns only record the names of officers, it does give an indication of strong linkages between the membership of the two organisations.

However, this should not be surprising as it was the minor gentry, merchants and farmers from the middling classes that had gained influence in the provinces and feared the loss of their prosperity through peasant rebellion or invasion by French republican forces. By 1792–1793 the volunteers were increasingly dominated by more radical elements within the middle-classes of Irish society compared to the more inclusive organisation of the period 1778–1783, and included many United Irishmen, especially in Ulster. The quashing of the volunteers in 1793 may have ensured the disarming of an increasingly radical armed group but it had also left a void in the ability of this class to maintain any localised self-defence force and the raising of the yeomanry provided an opportunity to resume the tradition.

The radical Protestant 'Orange' movement also provided a significant membership within the yeomanry. Extreme 'Orange' loyalism had grown from the ranks of lower-class Anglicans in County Armagh in response to the increasing level of violence sponsored by Catholic Defenders during the mid-1790s. The movement proved popular and quickly spread to neighbouring counties. However, the inclusion of Orangemen within the yeomanry was treated with much suspicion by the authorities in Dublin Castle, who viewed the democratic and anti-Catholic stance of the loyalists as a potential threat to internal stability. Camden voiced his concerns in a letter to the Duke of Portland: 'How impolitic and unwise … to refuse the offers of Protestants to enter the yeomanry … yet how dangerous is even any encouragement to the Orange spirit, whilst our army is composed of Catholics, as the militia

---

25   Bartlett, 'Defence, counter-insurgency and rebellion: Ireland, 1793–1803', p.266.
26   Blackstock, *An Ascendancy Army*, p.76.
27   Blackstock, *An Ascendancy Army*, p.76.

generally is.'[28] His concern had some foundation, with a detachment of the Kerry Militia, a predominantly Catholic regiment, being ambushed near Stewartstown, County Tyrone, Ulster in September 1797 by a combined force of local yeomanry, the Tay Fencibles, and the regular cavalry of the 24th Light Dragoons.[29] This resulted in a number of casualties and strained relationships within the Irish garrison. Nevertheless, the Orangemen were openly encouraged into the yeomanry at local levels and played a significant role in the policing of their communities.

The Orange elements of the yeomanry were mainly limited to the counties within, or those that bordered, Ulster. In 1796 Orangeism was geographically limited to mid-Ulster, with official membership being estimated at only several thousand men. However, the movement quickly spread and by early 1797 approximately 30,000 Orangemen had enlisted in yeomanry corps.[30] This was significant in that by December 1797 there were only 35,000 men enlisted in the yeomanry, 14,290 of which came from corps within Ulster (Table 3.1).[31] And although exact figures cannot be obtained, it is estimated that eventually one-in-three serviceable Protestant males aged between 18 and 45 were to join the yeomanry, where in Ulster almost every Protestant of military age was to become a yeoman.[32] This also indicates how quickly the movement had spread, with another 15,000 Orangemen registered as members of other corps throughout the country.[33] However, the reliability of these figures must be treated with caution as reliance has been placed mainly on official returns forwarded to the Home Office.

Table 3.1: Yeomanry: Provincial Comparison

	1797	1798	1799	1803	1810	1817
Ulster	39 %	36 %	40 %	42 %	45 %	64 %
Leinster	33 %	33 %	32 %	31 %	29 %	21 %
Munster	18 %	22 %	19 %	19 %	17 %	7 %
Connacht	11 %	10 %	9 %	8 %	9 %	8 %

Source: Blackstock, *An Ascendancy Army*, p. 122.

'Orangeism' spread rapidly throughout the yeomanry corps in the north of Ireland. Anti-autocracy and anti-Catholic traditions played a part in this, combined with the perceived physical and political threats Protestants felt with the recent concessions given to Catholics. The failed French invasion attempt at Bantry Bay in late December 1796 further increased the anxiety of the civilian population, leading to an upsurge in patriotic fervour and a willingness to assist in the defence of the kingdom through joining armed loyalist associations.[34] Brigadier General John Knox, the commander-in-chief of the military forces in County Tyrone and a Protestant land magnate

---

28 TNA: HO 100/77: Camden to the Duke of Portland, 11 June 1798.
29 Bartlett, 'Defence, counter-insurgency and rebellion: Ireland, 1793–1803', p.270.
30 Blackstock, *An Ascendancy Army*, p.92.
31 Blackstock, *An Ascendancy Army*, p.117.
32 J.E. Cookson, *The British Armed Nation, 1793–1815* (Oxford: Clarendon Press, 1997), p.167.
33 Blackstock, *An Ascendancy Army*, p.117.
34 Morton, 'The Rise of the Yeomanry', p.64.

in that county, actively supported the arming of Orange associations by proposing the formation of Orange fencibles. When this move was rejected by the government, he then promoted the inclusion of these organisations into the yeomanry as a defence measure against the perceived threat posed to Protestants by the posting of Catholic militia in Ulster.[35] In a letter to Edward Cooke, Camden's under-secretary, in August 1796 he argued for the inclusion of Orangemen within the yeomanry: 'As to the Orange Men we have rather a difficult card to play, they must not be entirely discountenanced, on the contrary, we must, in a certain degree, uphold them, for, with all their licentiousness, on them must we rely for the preservation of our lives and properties, should critical times occur.'[36] Knox was a greater advocate for the inclusion of Orangemen in the yeomanry than his letter to Cooke suggests. In early 1797 many parts of Ulster were proclaimed under the Insurrection Act that gave magistrates unprecedented power to search and seize arms. At this time, not only did he indicate to the yeomanry in Armagh not to seize weapons of Orangemen, but he also fostered their inclusion into yeomanry corps by seeking specific permission from Thomas Pelham, Camden's chief secretary, to add these radical loyalists as supplementary men to the corps led by James Verner.[37] He further sought to create a new corps entirely of Orangemen, who would display their loyalty by wearing orange ribbons.[38] The inevitability of such measures became apparent to others such as Lord Auckland who spoke of a pragmatic approach to the worsening situation in Ireland: 'These Orange Boys … are growing numerous and are most inveterate against the United Irishmen. They are a dangerous ally; however, to a certain extent, it is necessary to use them.'[39]

The creation of the yeomanry was an essential strategic measure. By 1796 the threat of invasion together with increased civil unrest throughout Ireland had placed immense pressure on the army and the government. The demands of Britain's foreign military operations had led to a massive reduction in the number of regular troops on the Irish Establishment, ensuring that the inexperienced and dispersed militia became the largest element within the army. It became apparent that this force was inadequate to provide both the necessary internal security against insurrection as well as providing an effective counter-invasion force. Camden was reluctant to establish a para-military force of armed civilian volunteers, mainly due to the political power previously achieved by the volunteer movement in the early 1780s.[40] However, the worsening domestic and foreign situation in 1796 forced his hand: 'I do not like to resort to yeomanry cavalry or infantry or

---

35   Morton, 'The Rise of the Yeomanry', p.93.
36   National Archives, Ireland (NAI): Rebellion Papers 620/24/106: Knox to Cooke, 13 August 1796, quoted in Blackstock, *An Ascendancy Army*, p.61.
37   BL: Pelham Papers, Add. MS 33103: ff 379-380, Knox to Pelham, 2 January 1797, quoted in Blackstock, 'The Irish Yeomanry and the 1798 Rebellion', p.335.
38   BL: Pelham Papers, Add. MS 33103: ff 379-380, Knox to Pelham, 2 January 1797, quoted in Blackstock, 'The Irish Yeomanry and the 1798 Rebellion', p.335.
39   BL: Add. MS 37308: f. 132, Wellesley Papers, Auckland to Lord Mornington, 22 April 1798, quoted in Blackstock, 'The Irish Yeomanry and the 1798 Rebellion', p.340.
40   Morton, 'The Rise of the Yeomanry', p.60.

armed associations if I can help it, but I can see no other recourse at the present time – the army must be withdrawn from many of its present quarters and must be drawn together to act in larger units than it has lately done.'[41] His repeated requests for reinforcements of regular regiments from Britain had largely proved fruitless, ensuring that rural Ireland could not effectively be policed. The formation of a government-controlled yeomanry was thus seen as the only alternative to provide the security being demanded by the propertied population.

The landed magnates provided the political leadership in the yeomanry. It was powerful and wealthy Protestant Irish peers, such as the Duke of Leinster, the Marquis of Abercorn and Lord Downshire, that the lesser classes looked to for patronage in forming the corps.[42] Such men not only had political influence in ensuring government support for the formation of the yeomanry at a national level, but they also provided leadership at the local level, where many held positions as county governors. Although the yeomanry was centrally controlled from Dublin Castle, the county governors and landed magnates maintained a greater influence over the corps within their localities.[43] It was these men who mostly determined who received officer commissions within individual units and it was through their patronage that these were confirmed by the lord lieutenant.[44] The system of patronage was well established and accepted within eighteenth century British and Irish society due to its perceived ability to maintain stability within the social hierarchy.[45] Thus, it was in the interests of the aristocrats to support any self-defence measures proposed by the middle classes that would defend against the serious threat posed to them by militant republicans and the rebellious Catholic peasantry. However, although many Irish peers (some of whom were already colonels of militia regiments, such as Lord Downshire) also provided financial backing and accepted colonelcies for numerous yeomanry corps, especially those from their estates, most only provided nominal leadership roles, preferring to leave active command to county squires.[46]

It was the gentry who provided the practical leadership within the yeomanry. This social class potentially had the most to lose through rebellion of the peasantry and it was the drive for self-interest and self-preservation that saw thousands offer their service and allegiance to the Crown. It had been these people, together with farmers, merchants, and other middling classes, who had been seeking greater protection from the state after being the main victims of insurgent activities.[47] The gentry had successfully argued their traditional local leadership should be reflected in the yeomanry where they could maintain the law and prevent the rise of vigilante groups. The government looked to establish individual corps based on the traditional

---

41 BL: Add. MSS 33102: Camden to Pelham, 28 August 1796, quoted in Morton, 'The Rise of the Yeomanry', p.63.
42 Blackstock, *An Ascendancy Army*, p.103.
43 Blackstock, *An Ascendancy Army*, p.103.
44 Blackstock, *An Ascendancy Army*, p.103.
45 Nelson, *The Irish Militia, 1793–1802*, pp.54–55.
46 Blackstock, *An Ascendancy Army*, p.128.
47 TNA: HO 100/61: Camden to Portland, 22 September 1796.

parish system where each county was divided into smaller administrative districts. This was seen as providing stability within communities by transferring the accepted civilian hierarchy into leadership roles within the yeomanry. Thus, the influence that these landholders held within their districts made them natural leaders and ensured the required support within the parish to rapidly establish local troops or companies.[48] Patronage ensured that mostly substantial farmers or minor gentry were offered commissions. Although the right of election of officers remained within each corps, ballots were discouraged by the hierarchy for being too democratic, with elections sometimes provoking social tension.[49] Family and professional connections also proved instrumental in gaining commissions in yeomanry corps, as well as the militia, as John Dobbs recalled:

> At this time [1798] the defence of Ireland depended on her Militia and corps of Yeomanry, which were formed wherever a sufficient body of loyal subjects could be collected. In Dublin there were the Lawyers', Attorneys', Merchants' and College Corps, and several others, amongst which, one called Beresford's bore a prominent part. The loyal male members of every family were attached to one of them, and on the ringing of the alarm bells, and the drums beating to arms, each repaired to the alarm-post of his corps, leaving the women and children in a state of anxiety. My father, four brothers, one uncle and five first-cousins, were at this time in arms for the defence of Ireland.
>
> My brother William commanded a company of the Armagh Militia at Ballynamuck, and my brother Francis was engaged with the Lisburn Yeomanry at Ballynahinch.[50]

Each corps was initially established within specifications directed by the government. Infantry units were to be around 100 men strong, with cavalry corps being around 50, but no less than 40.[51] Each cavalry volunteer was required to provide his own horse, with many gentry providing mounts for those tenants, servants, retainers, and volunteers who lacked sufficient funds to do so themselves. The yeomanry was to comprise mainly of cavalry and infantry, although there were also some small components of artillery. Examples of this include the Dublin Lawyers Corps, which although an infantry unit, had a small artillery section, as well as the Loyal Loughlinstown Yeomanry, whose gunners manned the defences at Loughlinstown army camp, 12 miles south-east of Dublin.[52] However, the size of corps could fluctuate depending on the current political situation. This occurred in April 1798 when several supplementary yeomanry units were created and attached to corps as unpaid and un-uniformed auxiliaries to serve in emergencies or

---

48   Blackstock, *An Ascendancy Army*, p.72.
49   Blackstock, *An Ascendancy Army*, p.72.
50   Dobbs, *Recollections of an Old 52nd Man*, p.iv.
51   Blackstock, *An Ascendancy Army*, p.98.
52   Blackstock, *An Ascendancy Army*, p.72.

to fill vacancies.[53] The majority of these volunteers came from within 'Orange' organisations.

Each corps was commanded by a captain, who was to be assisted by lieutenants, and cornets. Often in rural areas the captain's residence became the administrative headquarters of the unit. This proved a practical measure in that the strongly built substantial homes of the gentry provided rallying points in troubled times that could be used as defensive strongholds. Such tactics were also implemented in urban centres where stone-built government buildings provided the focus for the yeomanry defence system. The defence measures for Dublin provide the prime examples of this where the Lawyers Corps headquarters were at the Four Courts and the Revenue Corps headquarters were at the Custom House.[54] Metropolitan centres such as Dublin and Cork had sufficient population to raise several yeomanry corps based on, and named after, their professions. These included the aforementioned Lawyers and Revenue Corps, along with units formed from students from Trinity College. In rural areas the units were usually named after the parish from which the volunteers came.

The establishment of each corps was determined through a combination of government directives and local influence. The lord lieutenant issued officers commissions in the name of the King to those who were nominated by the local county governor or aristocrats who were raising corps from within their own estates. Dublin Castle stipulated that each corps was to have a minimum of two officers, a captain and a lieutenant, with other commissions being offered as required.[55] The state provided wages for a permanent sergeant to be attached to each unit. These men were usually retired regular soldiers who were employed to instil formal drill and discipline into the untrained volunteers. The government also provided for the full-time employment of a drummer or trumpeter for each corps. However, once the cadre of the corps were established, a more democratic approach was allowed within each unit. Committees were formed from unit members to regulate discipline, finances, and membership. Prospective members required voting support from two-thirds of the committee to be eligible to join the corps.[56] It was this practice that ensured that many Catholics and political rivals of officers were refused entry. It was only when placed on permanent duty that the yeomanry lost their democratic rights, coming under strict military discipline and the command of district generals and the commander-in-chief.

Discipline within the corps was self-regulating. Enrolment in the yeomanry was seen as socially acceptable and fashionable amongst the middle classes in Britain and Ireland during the period. Peer pressure ensured that volunteers conformed to the accepted political attitudes and social behaviours within their local communities. Corps committees determined disciplinary practices within individual units, although these were based on behaviour codes formulated by captains for their troops. Those who breached such

---

53 Blackstock, *An Ascendancy Army*, p.72.
54 Blackstock, *An Ascendancy Army*, p.72.
55 Blackstock, *An Ascendancy Army*, pp.102–103.
56 Blackstock, *An Ascendancy Army*, pp.102–103.

codes risked banishment from the corps and social embarrassment. It was only in times of war, when under direct command of the military that serious breaches of conduct resulted in capital punishment. During the rebellion of 1798 a small number of yeomen were executed for desertion, with some having sided with the rebels.[57] However, men who deserted from their corps after this time were spared by agreeing to military service overseas. The lax discipline within the armed forces of Ireland during the 1790s can be largely traced to the enormous expansion in numbers, especially in the yeomanry where most officers lacked any formal military experience, and that training was generally limited to several days per week.[58]

The state maintained some control over the yeomanry by providing every corps with pay, uniforms, and arms. To promote efficiency and martial appearance, the government had agreed to pay wages for each yeoman to train with his corps two days per week. Undoubtedly, these wages would have been claimed, but there is little surviving evidence to indicate how often the individual units spent training. It is most likely that the amount of training carried out by units would have been determined by the level of enthusiasm of commanding officers.

To deviate from the old volunteer units, the government attempted to regulate the uniforms issued to the corps. Infantry units were to wear uniforms like those of regular infantry regiments: white breeches, red coats with blue collar and cuffs, but without facings, as well as the ubiquitous black felt cocked hats.[59] However, most yeomanry uniforms were designed at the discretion of the senior officer, who usually paid for them. The colour of facings varied from red, blue, yellow, and white, while many units wore a fur-crested 'round' hat, rather than the unpopular military cocked hat.[60] The yeoman cavalry were dressed similarly to the light dragoons of the regular army and their yeomanry counterparts in the United Kingdom: white riding breeches, knee length boots, short blue or red jackets and 'Tarleton' helmets. However, in practice, there was a variety of uniforms worn, with the government having to compromise to promote *esprit de corps* within the yeomanry.[61] Providing sufficient weapons posed a problem for the government with the distribution system unable to cope with the demand. Infantrymen were to be issued with cartridge boxes, bayonets and 'Brown Bess' muskets, while cavalrymen were to receive pistols and light dragoon sabres. However, in January 1797 only 14,000 out of 24,000 yeomen had been issued arms, with most of these weapons being in poor condition.[62] Many volunteers purchased their own weapons through necessity, keeping them at their homes instead of being secured at the unit headquarters. Although this was a practical measure to provide personal safety, it also made many yeomen

---

57 Blackstock, *An Ascendancy Army*, p.106.
58 Bartlett, 'Indiscipline and disaffection in Ireland in the 1790s', p.116.
59 Blackstock, *An Ascendancy Army*, p.107.
60 Reid, *Armies of the Irish Rebellion 1798*, p.18.
61 Blackstock, *An Ascendancy Army*, p.107.
62 Blackstock, *An Ascendancy Army*, p.111.

REBELLION, INVASION AND OCCUPATION

'Yeomanry Cavalry!!' by George Moutard Woodward, 1796. (Anne S.K. Brown Military Collection)

targets for rebel activities, with houses being raided to secure firearms for the planned rebellion.

Contrary to the views promoted by some nationalist historians concerning the yeomanry, there was no official anti-Catholic or anti-Presbyterian policy regarding recruiting, Camden had told Lord Waterford that it was unwise to refuse Catholics into the yeomanry as it may cause further unrest amongst the population and then wrote to Lord Downshire stating that trustworthy Catholics and dissenters should be included in his corps.[63] However, the enlistment of Catholics and religious dissenters proved to be a contentious issue, especially in Ulster. Catholic enlistment was actively discouraged by the opposition within the Irish parliament, as well as the influential 'Catholic Committee,' an organisation established in the early 1790s to promote Catholic interests, which consisted of leading Catholic gentry, businessmen and clergy who saw the yeomanry as a tool of oppression against the Catholic peasantry.[64] However, in a later letter to the Duke of Portland, Camden made it clear that he was supportive of Catholics enlisting as individuals into existing corps rather than joining *en masse* and forming their own units.[65] The rarity of complete muster rolls makes it hard to determine a definitive denominational breakdown of the yeomanry corps, although there are a number of known examples where Catholics played a significant role.

---

63 PRONI: D 607/D/142: Downshire Papers, Camden to Lord Downshire October 1796.
64 Connelly, *The Oxford companion of Irish History*, pp.78–79.
65 TNA: HO 100/69: Camden to Portland, 3 January 1797.

Allan Blackstock argues that an examination of the surviving 'Derry Muster Rolls' suggests that there is a correlation between Catholic membership and the concentration of native Irish surnames. These records show that the Banagher Yeomen Cavalry had 14 Catholics, all with native surnames, out of a membership of 53.[66] The dismounted section of the same corps had 81 with native names out of a total of 82 members. The Faughan Glen Yeomen Infantry proved to be a mixed unit with Catholics outnumbering Protestants 34 to 18 in 1798 and 33 to eight in 1800.[67] What makes these figures so significant is that even after the events of 1798, Catholics continued to be retained in reasonable numbers in some corps. This indicates that Catholics were readily accepted into the yeomanry in areas, such as Counties Derry and Donegal, where Catholics owned land and there were few Protestants.

Trustworthiness appears to have been the main government criteria for membership within the yeomanry, rather than religion. The gentry and other persons of property who had the most to lose from rebellion assumed the trust of the state on the grounds that they would be determined to defend the status quo, regardless of religious denomination. The chief aim of Whig policies in Ireland was to reconcile the Catholic gentry and moneyed class to the British state and to cement a 'union of property' against Jacobin subversion.[68] Allowing prominent Catholics to raise yeomanry corps to prove their loyalty was an obvious tactic to achieve these goals. This was evident with Catholic peers, such as Lord Gormanston, receiving official authority to raise and command a cavalry corps in County Meath that consisted of 40 Catholics.[69] Lord Donoughmore's Cork Legion consisted of many wealthy Catholics, where native surnames were prevalent, while Lord Kenmare raised a predominantly Catholic cavalry corps in Killarney.[70]

There also appears to be a strong correlation between Catholic membership and wealth and property, which was the general criteria for acceptance into yeomanry cavalry corps throughout Ireland, excepting certain counties in Ulster. Each yeoman had to provide his own horse and uniform, the cost of which proved prohibitive to both Catholic and Protestant peasants, ensuring that yeoman cavalry corps consisted of members of the gentry and the middle-classes, along with some of their retainers.[71] It is estimated that there were 2–3,000 Catholics in the yeomanry in 1797, with most of them in cavalry units in the south of the country.[72] This was at a time when the yeomanry had a total strength of 35,000, of which 14,000 were in Ulster.[73] Statistics recorded by the Protestant, Sir Richard Musgrave, in a pamphlet published in 1799, indicate strong Catholic membership in the various cavalry corps of Leinster, especially in Wexford, where the majority of infantry corps consisted of Catholics. Examples include the Shelmaliere

---

66 PRONI: T1021/3: Derry Muster Rolls, quoted in Blackstock, *An Ascendancy Army*, p.130.
67 PRONI: T1021/3: Derry Muster Rolls, quoted in Blackstock, *An Ascendancy Army*, p.130.
68 Smith, *Whig Principles and Party Politics*, p.177.
69 Blackstock, *An Ascendancy Army*, p.132.
70 Blackstock, *An Ascendancy Army*, p.134.
71 Bartlett, 'Defence, counter-insurgency and rebellion: Ireland, 1793-1803', p.265.
72 Blackstock, *An Ascendancy Army*, p.134.
73 Blackstock, *An Ascendancy Army*, p.134.

Cavalry that contained 24 Catholics, the Castletown Cavalry that had 46 and the Coolgreary Cavalry that boasted 16. Musgrave also claims that one third of the Clane Cavalry in Kildare consisted of 'papists', while the Rathcoole infantry contained three Catholic officers and 42 privates.[74] The reliability of Musgrave's figures remains in question due to his overt bias towards the Ascendancy where he has attempted to use these figures to argue a Catholic conspiracy with the United Irishmen in the rebellion. However, what they indicate is that there was a limited level of trust placed in wealthy Catholics, and the extent of their involvement within the yeomanry prior to the rebellion of 1798.

The yeomanry was considered a key element in the defensive strategy for Ireland, especially after the attempted French invasion at Bantry Bay in December 1796. At this time, it was feared that any such invasion would be supported by a simultaneous internal rebellion led by the United Irishmen. The military strategy formulated after the failed landing called for the concentration of the bulk of the regular forces and the militia regiments to form a sizable army to either confront the enemy in open battle or to man defensive lines based on geographical boundaries, such as the rivers Shannon and Blackwater.[75] The yeomanry had three important roles to play in this strategy. Firstly, the main duty of the corps was to maintain law and order in their localities and to quickly deal with any insurgent activities that may occur. The yeomanry was expected to perform town garrison duties, including providing guards at gaols, in the case of invasion.[76] The second role was to aid the military forces by keeping the lines of communication open so that the army could receive dispatches, munitions and other supplies required to maintain it in the field. The third role involved the yeomen cavalry acting as irregular forces in enemy-held territory. It was envisaged the mounted corps would slow the movement of the French by employing *petite guerre* tactics of harassing lines of communication, destroying bridges, attacking supply convoys, and supplying the army with essential information regarding enemy troop movements.[77] This strategic use of the yeomanry was sound in theory as the volunteers would have lacked the training and discipline required to confront the enemy in open battle.

The yeomanry most effective in policing roles

Prior to the rebellion and invasion of 1798, the yeomanry became an essential tool of the government in dealing with civil unrest. Throughout 1797–1798 there had been an increasing breakdown in law and order in parts of Ireland, especially in the northern counties, where the yeomanry was heavily relied

---

74 Sir Richard Musgrave, *Observations on a pamphlet lately published by an officer entitled 'Imperial relation of the military operations which took place in Ireland* (Dublin: T. Stuart, 1799), quoted in Blackstock, *An Ascendancy Army*, p.131.
75 D.A. Chart, 'The Irish Levies During the Great French War', *English Historical Review*, vol.32 (1917), pp.497–516.
76 NLI: MS 809: General Dalrymple to Thomas Pelham, 1 February 1797.
77 NLI: MS 809: General Dalrymple to Thomas Pelham, 1 February 1797.

upon to provide local intelligence and manpower for the escalating counter-terror operations promoted by the government. In practice, it was the quality of leadership and discipline within individual corps that determined how effectively the yeomanry carried out its specified roles. Magistrates came to depend upon the corps to help enforce the Insurrection Act. The yeomanry was immediately available and could provide local knowledge which the regulars, fencibles and militia lacked. It was the localised nature of the yeomanry that was the main feature of its military strength; as the first potential victims of insurrection, the yeomen had a vested interest in immediately and vigorously reacting to any threat. In March 1797 Lieutenant General Lake was given discretion to act independently of local magistrates if he felt conditions were justified. This led to some districts coming under de-facto martial law, with the subsequent security operations that followed being known as the 'dragooning' of Ulster.[78] The lack of troops available to carry out such measures ensured that Lake and his subordinate, Knox, were reliant on the yeomanry to perform the required duties of searching and seizing arms and suspects. Yeomanry corps were also used in similar operations in Dublin and some disturbed southern counties in early 1798. This included County Wexford in March and April of that year where the yeomanry was heavily relied upon to maintain the peace due to the insufficient number of troops stationed there, with Pakenham claiming their over-vigorous actions promoted the civilian uprising.[79] However, in general, where the yeomanry proved most effective was functioning as a deterrent, where its very existence meant a constant local presence of armed strength.

The weak infrastructure of law and government in Ireland at this time ensured some local autonomy for the yeomanry corps. In the provinces the government was reliant on local magistrates to ensure law and order, although the magistrates had to rely on the army and yeomanry to enforce the law. This situation contributed to disorder spreading throughout the country where in some localities the authority of the law was supplanted by the personal interests of the commanding officers of the yeomanry. In many areas local magistrates had become impotent in administering civil law due to intimidation and fear of being murdered by rebels, leading to the temporary introduction of martial law. This then ensured that local army commanders, who could be impatient of, and contemptuous of, civil authority, could conduct their counter-insurgent operations without the 'niceties' of the legal system. Brigadier General Knox, a strong promoter of yeomanry intervention in Ulster argued that the law was insufficient to quell rebellion: 'Laws though ever so strict will not do … severe military execution alone will recover the arms from the hands of the rebels.'[80] Camden and his advisors advocated counter-terror tactics and encouraged excessive behaviour by the army and yeomanry by proclaiming the suspension of civil rights in disaffected areas, thus removing restrictions that some saw

---

78 Blackstock, 'The Irish Yeomanry and the 1798 Rebellion', pp.336–337.
79 Pakenham, *The Year of Liberty*, pp.162–165.
80 PRONI: T 2542/1B3/6/10: Knox to Abercorn, 21 March 1797, quoted in Bartlett, 'Defence, counter-insurgency and rebellion: Ireland, 1793-1803', p.270.

as preventing the maintenance of order and forestalling insurgency.[81] This provided unscrupulous yeomanry officers with the opportunity to exceed their authority and seek revenge on local political rivals. Such activities included destruction of property, imprisonment without trial, and murders for which few was held accountable.[82] The 'independence' of the yeomanry was shown to its full effect in 1798 where the increasingly violent activities of insurgents were countered by retaliatory actions of local yeomanry who acted without seeking orders from higher authorities.[83] It was this inability to effectively control the largely untrained and ill-disciplined yeomanry corps that not only fostered disorder leading up to the rebellion, but also ensured the government remained sensitive to the challenge the corps posed to the state's monopoly of armed force in Ireland.

The Unsavoury Reputation of the Yeomanry

The yeomanry force crucially functioned as an agent of counter-revolution in the period 1796–1798, where 'terror' was increasingly used by both sides and reached a climax with the atrocities committed during the rebellion. Patriotic fervour and over-zealous actions within the corps led to numerous official complaints to the government.[84] This was especially so concerning the operations in Ulster, where the indiscriminate violence used by the yeomen, such as hanging suspects by their feet and lashing them with ropes and belts, was possibly encouraged, and at the very least, ignored by superior officers.[85] The use of terror in counter-terror operations was seen at the time as the best deterrent to rebellion, and coupled with the indiscipline of the yeomanry, ultimately led to numerous floggings, houses burning and deaths.[86] The most notorious incident occurred in July 1797 at Newry where defenceless civilians, including children, were murdered by local yeomanry and members of a Welsh fencibles regiment known as the 'Ancient Britons'.[87] And although an official excuse was given that such action was taken in response to the murder of a local magistrate, on this occasion even loyalists protested at the 'wanton and gratuitous ferocity of the attack'.[88] However, in general, most complaints related to the destruction of property, that, if not sanctioned by the government, were certainly encouraged by Knox who had openly spoken of the need for 'spiriting up' opposition to the United Irishmen by opposing violence with violence.[89] This was further fostered by members of the Irish

---

81 Bartlett, 'Indiscipline and disaffection in Ireland in the 1790s', p.120.
82 G.A. Hayes-McCoy, 'The Government Forces Which Opposed the Irish Insurgents of 1798', *The Irish Sword*, vol.4 (1959), p.17.
83 Hayes-McCoy, 'The Government Forces Which Opposed the Irish Insurgents of 1798', p.17.
84 Stewart, *The Summer Soldiers*, p.52.
85 Stewart, *The Summer Soldiers*, p.52.
86 Blackstock, 'The Irish Yeomanry and the 1798 Rebellion', pp.336–337.
87 Allan L. Carswell, 'The Scottish Fencible Regiments in Ireland', *The Irish Sword*, vol.21 (1998), pp.155–159.
88 Blackstock, 'The Irish Yeomanry and the 1798 Rebellion', pp.336–337.
89 PRONI: T 2541/183/610: Abercorn Papers, Knox to Lord Abercorn, 21 March 1797, quoted in Bartlett, 'Indiscipline and disaffection in Ireland in the 1790s', p.120.

parliament resurrecting the Williamite traditions of 1690 through emotive speeches that cast the conflict in apocalyptic terms, portraying it as a struggle for survival.[90]

Although based on the self-defence traditions of the volunteers, the yeomanry never represented the old Protestant nationalism promoted by that organization. The volunteers had been formed in some part as a protest to the economic restrictions placed on the Irish by Britain that had led to anger and calls for self-determination.[91] However, in the 1790s, instead of voicing their need for greater political independence that had been the catch-cry of the late 1770s and early 1780s, the Protestant Ascendancy was reliant on Britain as an ally to ensure the maintenance of power and control in Ireland. British military and naval support were essential in dealing with the increasing threats of internal rebellion and invasion that could potentially see the oligarchy of the Ascendancy replaced with a republic. The inclusion of the Orange orders into the corps also influenced the character of the yeomanry. Orangeism was based on loyalty to the Crown, with strong religious connections through the Anglican Church.[92] With most of the Protestant members of the corps being either Orangemen, Anglicans, or both, it is quite clear why, although being an Irish institution, the yeomanry as an organisation would be more supportive of retaining its British links. The fear of the rise of Catholic peasantry who were a substantial percentage of the population was also a huge incentive for the yeomanry to support internal intervention by Britain. The increase in sectarian violence fostered fears amongst the Protestant minority of religious extermination, who argued for Britain to supply a significant increase in loyal troops for the garrison to ensure their safety.

The yeomanry became an integral element within the military establishment of Ireland from the time of its inception in 1796 and throughout the years of war with France. Dublin Castle was forced to actively support the formal creation of the corps to ensure control over the numerous armed reactionary groups that were being established in the troubled counties to provide local security for the gentry and middle classes. Through rapid augmentation the yeomanry became an essential force in the defence strategy of the Ireland where the corps were to be used as an internal police force, especially in counter-insurgent operations, thus in theory freeing the militia and regular troops to concentrate on counter-invasion defence (Table 3.2). Issues of ill-discipline, murder, nepotism, and corruption, coupled with the religious fervour of the Orangemen who were incorporated into the corps in large numbers, led to the tarnishing of the reputation of the yeomanry, although such issues were generally overlooked by authorities at the time. Ultimately, the yeomanry developed into a powerful para-military organization that not only proved essential in the defence of the country,

---

90 Myers & McKnight, *Sir Richard Musgrave's Memoirs of the Irish Rebellion of 1798*, pp.161–162.
91 Martin, 'Reform and Change within the Irish Army and Military System', pp.57–59.
92 Peter R. Newman (ed.), *Companion to Irish History: From the submission of Tyrone to Partition, 1603–1921* (London & New York: Facts on File, 1991), p.8.

but more importantly for some, it also ensured the armed protection of the interests of the Protestant Ascendancy.

The Irish yeomanry remains a contentious subject within Ireland. Historical memories of oppression and atrocities by the corps against the United Irish rebels and the Catholic peasantry which were fostered by Irish nationalists in the nineteenth century have been continued through to the twenty-first century.[93] However, in Ulster, where the yeomanry were most prevalent, the organisation is seen positively as an expression of loyalism to the British Crown, although its initial purpose was to serve the interests of both Protestant and Catholic gentry and the middle-classes.[94] The perception that the yeomanry provided the armed strength of the Protestant Ascendancy that was determined to maintain power through the domination of the Catholic majority has, until recently, ensured the unpopularity of the organisation amongst Irish nationalist historians. What is evident is that the yeomanry was not only the physical embodiment of the Ascendancy, but that it proved to be an essential political tool in achieving increased military support from Britain, ensuring the maintenance of Ascendancy power in Ireland until the early twentieth century. Contrary to the views of some nationalist historians, the yeomanry corps were not a tool of British oppression but became one of Protestant Irish oppression over the Catholic peasantry. The British government never fully trusted the Ascendancy and ultimately, it was the armed strength of the yeomanry and the potential threat it posed to stability in the kingdom that ensured Britain increased its military presence in Ireland.

Table 3.2 – Yeomanry Corps Establishment, 1796-1815

Date	Establishment	Effectives	Date	Establishment	Effectives
Dec. 1796	21,000		Nov. 1804	70,000	64,000
Dec. 1797	35,000		Dec. 1805		70,000
May 1798	50,000		Apr. 1806	82,000	64,000
1799	66,000		May 1807	69,000	61,000
1800	54,000		Apr. 1808	80,000	75,000
Nov. 1801	52,000		Mar. 1810	85,000	
June 1802	51,000		Dec. 1815		45,000
1803	83,000	70,000			

(Source: Blackstock, *An Ascendancy Army*, p. 114)

---

93   Connelly, *The Oxford Companion to Irish History*, p.633.
94   Connelly, *The Oxford Companion to Irish History*, p.633.

4

British Military Presence and the Management of the Irish Garrison up to 1798

Britain had maintained a substantial military presence in Ireland since the Williamite Wars of the early 1690s and throughout the eighteenth century. The perceived threat posed to the Protestant oligarchy by Catholics, who accounted for an estimated three quarters of the population, ensured the need for a significant number of troops being permanently stationed in Ireland.[1] Throughout the century Britain was also in near constant conflict with France which necessitated a strong garrison to defend against the repeated threats of invasion.

During this period Ireland was seen by the French and the British as a key strategic location that offered both offensive and defensive opportunities that could not be ignored. The policies concerning the distribution and management of the armed forces stationed in Ireland were determined by numerous factors such as internal politics, threat of rebellion, threat of invasion, rising sectarian tension and the constant demand for troops for military operations in the West Indies and on the Continent. The war with Revolutionary France from 1793 increased the demand for troops and significantly altered the dynamics of the British Army in Ireland. What resulted was the introduction of conflicting defensive policies: counter-invasion, which required the concentration of the army to provide a force large enough to defeat any invasion, and counterinsurgency, which required the dispersal of the armed forces to police against increasing rebel activity throughout the kingdom. These incompatible strategies created tension within Irish political circles, as well as amongst the military leadership. Although the threat of French incursion remained constant, political pressure from the Ascendancy due to increasing internal violence ensured the dispersal of the army throughout the kingdom, seriously hindering its ability to deal with any sizable invasion force.

---

1   Blackstock, *An Ascendancy Army*, p.19.

REBELLION, INVASION AND OCCUPATION

'Consequences of a successful French invasion' by James Gillray, 1798. (Anne S.K. Brown Military Collection)

When the Revolutionary French government declared war on Great Britain in February 1793 the British were militarily unprepared. In the 10 years following the 1783 Treaty of Versailles that ended the American War of Independence, the British Army had been cut back to 44,000 officers and men.² This was hardly enough to maintain the weak overseas garrisons, with only a few thousand men remaining for the defence of the British Isles or to carry out any offensive operations. The British government was now forced to rapidly mobilise its military forces through heavy recruitment drives throughout the British Isles, including Catholic Ireland. At this time Britain had entered a coalition with a number of continental states that were also at war with France, such as Spain, the Dutch Republic, Austria and numerous German states, and had committed itself to provide a small army for operations in Flanders.³ Established regiments of seasoned and experienced soldiers had to be found quickly, resulting in the reduction of British garrisons throughout the empire. Ireland had the largest garrison and its proximity to the area of operations ensured that the number of troops within the kingdom was rapidly and seriously depleted. This posed a major problem for those responsible for the security of the country.

---

2   Allan Shepperd, *The Connaught Rangers* (London: Osprey, 1972), p.3.
3   Shepperd, *The Connaught Rangers*, p.3.

The Irish government was responsible for the military forces in Ireland in the late eighteenth century, with the Irish parliament providing financial support under the direction of the lord lieutenant. Prior to 1793 the official 'Irish Establishment' consisted solely of regular regiments of the British army that had been posted to Ireland to perform permanent garrison duties, or had been temporarily sent to the kingdom for the purpose of recruiting. However, at the outbreak of war with France in 1793 Ireland was largely independent of Great Britain in military matters. The Irish government was financially responsible for all the troops stationed in the kingdom and even funded a number of regiments for overseas service.[4] The establishment was maintained with resources, such as wheat, barley and horses, from within the kingdom and even the army's gunpowder and small arms were produced by the Ordnance Department at the arsenal in Dublin.[5] However, Ireland became increasingly reliant on Britain to provide additional troops for its defence to counter the dual threats of rebellion and invasion. Sea links in the Irish Sea remained controlled by the Royal Navy ensuring reinforcements could be quickly transported when required, although such forces could take weeks to embark due to the few regiments available in Britain, as transpired in 1798.[6] The Irish establishment was directly under the control of the lord lieutenant, who acted as the representative of the king, having the title of 'Captain General and Commander-in-Chief,' although most viceroys concentrated mainly on civil matters. In 1769 the official peace-time strength of the establishment had been increased from 12,000 rank and file to 15,000 which had been decided by a vote in the Irish Parliament and was to be financed by the Irish government.[7] It was argued that the security of Ireland had to be maintained not only due to its close proximity to Britain but also due to its importance in maintaining trans-Atlantic shipping routes that Britain, and thus Ireland, relied on for increasing commercial prosperity.

Military appointments and commissions were made by the lord lieutenant, subject to the approval of the king. Ireland had its own War Office that was established as the military department of the chief secretary's office. This department was administered by an under-secretary who presided over six sub-branches that co-ordinated the logistical requirements of the military establishment: the Commissariat which was responsible for food and forage; the Muster Master-Generals office which provided monthly returns of regimentals strengths; the Barrack Board and Board of Works responsible for the quartering of troops and maintenance of barracks; the Ordnance Department which administered the Royal Irish Artillery Regiment and Engineers, while also ensuring the supply of small arms; the Army Medical Board (established in 1795); and the Army Accounts Office

---

4   Martin, 'Reform and Change within the Irish Army and Military System, 1763-1818', pp.12–14.
5   Martin, 'Reform and Change within the Irish Army and Military System, 1763-1818', pp.12–14.
6   Hayes-McCoy, 'The Government Forces Which Opposed the Irish Insurgents of 1798', *The Irish Sword*, vol.4 (1959), p.28.
7   Chart, 'The Irish Levies during the Great French War', pp.497–516.

which was established by Cornwallis in 1799.[8] The establishment also had an army 'commander of the forces' who was directly responsible to the lord lieutenant and not to the Duke of York, who was the commander-in-chief of the British Army for most of the period. The commander of the forces was supported by a general staff that included an Adjutant General, Quarter Master General, Judge Advocate General and a Master General of Ordnance, as well as numerous clerks tasked with the daily correspondence required to administer the army.[9]

In 1793 the military force in Ireland was neither formidable in numbers nor quality. The official garrison strength of 15,000 men had never been reached but the importance Britain placed on Ireland was evident in that in 1792 a third of the regiments in the small British Army were stationed in the kingdom.[10] In January 1793 the establishment had only 10,199 troops recorded on the strength, which included 1,711 cavalry and 8,488 infantry.[11] The garrison comprised ordinary cavalry and infantry regiments of the line that had been mostly raised and recruited throughout Britain, as well a number of companies of the Royal Irish Artillery and detachments of invalids – soldiers who were no longer fit for active service but who were used to man the numerous harbour forts protecting Cork, Dublin and Waterford. There were very few locally raised Irish infantry regiments before 1793, with only the 18th (Royal Irish) and 27th (Inniskilling) regiments of foot being distinctive Irish infantry units in British service.[12] This was most likely due to the official anti-Catholic recruiting policies of the British Army throughout most of the eighteenth century that ensured that Irish recruiting generally occurred in the Protestant strong-holds of Ulster and the Pale (Dublin and its surrounding counties). However, much of the rank and file of numerous cavalry regiments were raised within Ireland, with four of the dragoon regiments having served in the garrison for so long that they were collectively known as 'Irish Horse'.[13]

However, the cavalry regiments based in Ireland until 1798 were of poor quality. This was generally due to a lack of active military service and inadequate training, supervision, and leadership from officers. Regiments had been dispersed throughout the counties to provide small troop-sized garrisons for provincial towns, which negated essential regimental drill training, while it was common practice for officers to be absent from their troops while seeking a social life in the urban centres. The 12th Light Dragoons had been stationed continuously in Ireland from 1717, while the 13th and 14th Dragoons were raised in the kingdom and remained there until after the events of 1798.[14] This made the troops more susceptible to

---

8 Martin, 'Reform and Change within the Irish Army and Military System, 1763-1818', pp.4–7.
9 Martin, 'Reform and Change within the Irish Army and Military System, 1763-1818', pp.4–7.
10 Cookson, *The British Armed Nation*, p.153.
11 State Papers Office, Ireland (SPOI): MS 620/50/56: 'Return of Effectives for January 1793,' quoted in K.P. Ferguson, 'The Army in Ireland from the Restoration to the Act of Union' (PhD thesis, Trinity College, Dublin, 1980), p.149.
12 Chart, 'The Irish Levies during the Great French War', p.497.
13 Chart, 'The Irish Levies during the Great French War', p.497.
14 Houlding, *Fit For Service*, p.353.

THE IRISH GARRISON UP TO 1798

harbouring sympathies for the local population from which they were recruited from and had lived amongst for so long. The most recognised example of this was the 5th Dragoons that was disbanded in 1799 at the direction of the lord lieutenant, Lord Cornwallis, due to the sympathies held by a significant number of the Irish troops towards the plight of Irish rebels. Twenty troopers had been tried for high treason and desertion to the enemy during the rebellion, with a number shot or hanged. Many within the regiment were sworn United Irishmen who were in the habit of drinking seditious toasts and were insubordinate, affecting the discipline and reliability of the regiment.[15] Lieutenant General Sir Ralph Abercromby, appointed as commander-in-chief of the Irish military force in late 1797, inspected the army in Ireland shortly after his appointment and was highly critical of the cavalry regiments. In his famous general order to the army of 26 February 1798, he singled out the cavalry: 'It is of utmost importance that the discipline of the dragoon regiments should be minutely attended to … and that they should be employed only … on military and indispensable business.'[16] However, no measures to improve efficiency were implemented before the rebellion. In early 1798 Thomas Pelham, Camden's chief secretary, wrote to the Duke of Portland describing the condition of the cavalry regiments stationed at the camp at Curragh. He claimed that the six regiments encamped there appeared to be 'perfectly ignorant of the new [cavalry] exercises' and that from one regiment alone '365 horses were lost or died in the course of two years, notwithstanding that no glanders or epidemic disorder appeared to have prevailed in that regiment.'[17] Desertion and death from disease were also rife amongst the cavalry regiments during this period. Taking the above into consideration, it is no wonder that this branch of the service proved of little account against the insurgents.

Royal Irish Artillery, c. 1773. (Anne S.K. Brown Military Collection)

The outbreak of war in 1793 led to further reductions in the number of regular troops in the Irish garrison. Due to its relatively small army, Britain struggled to provide sufficient troops to fulfil its commitments to the operations with its continental allies in Flanders and Holland, as well as to defend its possessions in the West Indies. The Relief Acts of 1792–1793 had provided the Irish government with the ability to raise a substantial permanent militia from the relatively untapped Catholic population to replace the regular infantry line regiments of the garrison which were

---

15   Ross, *Correspondence of Charles, First Marquis Cornwallis*, p.422.
16   McAnally, *The Irish Militia*, p.323.
17   McAnally, *The Irish Militia*, p.118.

desperately needed for overseas operations. This ensured that the Irish establishment was systematically stripped of most of its regular infantry. In August 1793 five regiments of infantry and three of cavalry, as well as two companies of the Royal Irish Artillery were transferred from Ireland for foreign service.[18] By the end of 1794 most of the regular regiments that had formerly been part of the Irish establishment had been sent on active service, leaving only a small number of under-strength regular battalions that had been specifically sent to the kingdom to recruit. Once these units had recruited to full strength they were quickly posted to overseas theatres of operation. Between July 1793 and January 1798, the number of rank-and-file regular infantry in Ireland was significantly reduced from 11,094 to 1,830.[19] However, the number of regular cavalry troops available for the defence of Ireland substantially increased. For the same period as above the number of regular rank and file troopers stationed in the kingdom increased from 2,793 to 3,943.[20] It is most likely that the main reason the establishment maintained and augmented its cavalry force in Ireland was that the theatres of operations involving the British army at this time were not suitable for large scale mounted action. It was also thought at the time that mounted troops would be more suitable for internal policing operations due to the ability to respond quickly to areas of disturbance and the intimidation factor of cavalry against ill-disciplined civilians.[21] The available cavalry numbers fluctuated slightly during this period; however, it was this arm of the regular army that the government was forced to heavily rely on to provide professionalism in the garrison.

Although war with France led to an immediate reduction in the number of regular infantry in Ireland, the period 1793 to 1798 saw an unprecedented rise in the available troops on the Irish establishment. And although there is some minor discrepancy between these figures obtained from the State Papers Office (Ireland) and those in Table 4.1 taken from official Home Office returns, they give an indication of the limited number of regular troops available in Ireland (Table 4.1). However, the demands of war led to a massive recruitment drive to bring the established regiments up to full strength of 600 men for foot regiments and 400 for cavalry. Once at full strength the regiments usually embarked for overseas service leaving a void in the garrison. The majority of the 38 new Irish militia regiments were quickly raised and were used to replace the regular infantry battalions, significantly augmenting the number of foot soldiers in Ireland. However, many in the Ascendancy questioned the reliability and loyalty of the untrained, inexperienced, and mostly Catholic, militiamen. To further increase the available troops for the defence of the kingdom, as well to provide a force to safeguard against any

---

18 SPO: MS 620/50/56: quoted in K.P. Ferguson, 'The Army in Ireland from the Restoration to the Act of Union', p.149.
19 SPO: MS 620/50/56: quoted in K.P. Ferguson, 'The Army in Ireland from the Restoration to the Act of Union', p.149.
20 SPO: MS 620/50/56: quoted in K.P. Ferguson, 'The Army in Ireland from the Restoration to the Act of Union', p.149.
21 SPO: MS 620/50/56: quoted in K.P. Ferguson, 'The Army in Ireland from the Restoration to the Act of Union', p.149.

possible treasonable action by the militia, the Irish government sought the services of newly raised fencible cavalry and infantry from Britain.

Table 4.1: The armed forces of the crown in Ireland, 1 January 1793 to 1 January 1800

	Cavalry		Infantry			Yeomanry	Total
	Regulars	Fencibles	Regulars	Fencibles	Militia		Total
Jan. 1793	1,510		8,134				9,644
Jan. 1794	2,331		8,087		9,627		20,155
Jan. 1795	2,715	300	6,126	537	12,847		22,525
Jan. 1796	2,296	508	1,480	10,210	17,162		31,656
Jan. 1797	3,640	664	1,699	9,085	18,188		33,276
Jan. 1798	3,957	1,820	1,812	10,788	22,358	36,854	77,589
Jan. 1799	4,151	3,139	5,572	13,516	32,583	43,221	102,181
Jan. 1800	1,742	3,738	2,657	16,823	25,542	66,082	116,584

Sources: 'Return of the effective men in the British army stationed in Ireland,' Jan. 1793-Jan. 1806 (TNA: HO 100/176/429); 'Numerical Strength of the Yeomanry, 1797-1799 (NAI: Rebellion Papers 620/48/56)

Compared to the rapid augmentation of the army from 1793, there appears to have been only a small-scale programme of barrack building in Ireland prior to 1798. Permanent barracks were already established in strategic locations such as Belfast, Dublin, Cork, Londonderry, Galway, and Duncannon Fort near Waterford, although some were in a poor state of repair. An Army Medical Board report issued in 1801 was highly critical of the general state of barracks in Ireland: 'Permanent and temporary barracks have been from necessity greatly over crowded ... many of these latter buildings are unfavourably placed, badly constructed and worse ventilated.'[22] The issue of providing adequate accommodation for the troops did lead to the construction of a number of new barracks prior to the rebellion, such as Clonmel in 1793, Belfast and Island Bridge in 1797, and at Tralee in 1798, although the number of permanent barracks proved to be insufficient in some areas leading to the unpopular practice of billeting of troops amongst the local population.[23] In 1798 there was so little suitable accommodation for the 2,000 troops stationed between Cork and Limerick that it was suggested that two regiments should be encamped in tents on open ground.[24] What makes this so significant is that this region was identified as a likely location for a French invasion in 1796 and obviously inadequate measures had been taken to house the sizable force that was to garrison the area during the years of hostilities. However, it appears that a few small barracks that could accommodate up to 100 men were established throughout the kingdom during the 1790s, either from the construction of new buildings or from modifications made to existing structures, in areas where insurgents were

---

22 A. Aspinall & E.A. Smith (eds), *English Historical Documents, 1783–1832* (London: Oxford University Press, 1959), p.862, quoted in Martin, 'Reform and Change within the Irish Army and Military System, 1763-1818', p.9.
23 McAnally, *The Irish Militia*, pp.62–63.
24 NLI: Kilmainham Papers, Section 2, p.179, Lieutenant General Lake, 8 May, quoted in Martin, 'Reform and Change within the Irish Army and Military System, 1763–1818,' p.9.

active. Typical of such buildings was Ross Castle, near Killarney, where a single company of the Kerry Militia was stationed in 1797.[25] What is obvious is, that prior to 1798, the military authority's policy of billeting troops in Ireland had failed to provide suitable and sufficient accommodation for the increasing number of troops in the kingdom, especially regarding the fencible regiments sent from Britain.

The Fencibles

Fencible regiments proved to be an essential element in the defence of the British Isles during the Revolutionary War and played a significant role in the defensive strategy of Ireland until their disbandment in 1802, during the pause in the war which followed the Treaty of Amiens. Fencible cavalry and infantry regiments were initially raised in Britain as an emergency measure to supplement the war-time home-defence force. Civilians were enlisted for full-time service for a limited period, which was usually for the duration of hostilities, as opposed to the life-time service of the regular army that discouraged many to enlist. Units were quickly and easily raised due to the favourable conditions of length of service and the promise that recruits would not serve abroad. Between 1793 and 1802 approximately 34 regiments of fencible cavalry and 59 battalions of fencible infantry were raised, of which 12 cavalry and 34 infantry units were Scottish.[26] Cavalry regiments usually consisted of 300 troopers, while infantry battalions had a full strength of 600 men. In all, 12 regiments of fencible cavalry, including four Scots units, and 34 battalions of fencible infantry served in Ireland during the period, with 21 of the infantry units being Scottish.[27] This indicates that Scots played a significant role in the defence of Ireland during the period, where they equated to a third of the fencible cavalry force and nearly two thirds of the fencible infantry.[28]

The negative view held by many British and Irish historians regarding the composition and efficiency of the regiments of fencibles that served in Ireland during this time is contentious. There were two fencible light dragoon cavalry units and at least one fencible infantry battalion raised in Ireland in 1795, with Camden reporting to the Duke of Portland in July 1795 that he had recently inspected the newly raised Irish Fencible Regiment of Foot at Waterford.[29] However, most fencible regiments that served in Ireland had been sent to the kingdom from Britain, beginning in April 1795. Camden, though, took exception to three of the four regiments sent to Ireland in June of that year, which included two regular cavalry regiments and two fencible units, because three of them were entirely composed of Irishmen recruited

---

25   Nelson, *The Irish Militia*, p.85.
26   Allan L. Carswell, 'The Scottish Fencible Regiments in Ireland', *The Irish Sword*, vol.21 (1998), pp.155–159.
27   Carswell, 'The Scottish Fencible Regiments in Ireland', pp.155–159.
28   Carswell, 'The Scottish Fencible Regiments in Ireland', pp.155–159.
29   TNA: HO 100/55: Camden to Portland, 8 July 1795.

in England.[30] A lasting perception amongst traditional and nationalist historians is that, in general, fencibles were ill-disciplined, in poor physical health, and subject to committing atrocities against the civilian population. And although there is sufficient evidence to support these views regarding these regiments, there is also contemporary evidence to suggest that some individual units proved themselves to be of a proficient standard for the duties they were expected to perform.

A recurring criticism was that many of the soldiers suffered from illnesses, were of a weak physical build, and were not fit for service. In October 1795 General Robert Cunninghame, then commander-in-chief of the army in Ireland, received a report from Major General Sir James Duff concerning his recent inspection of the Perthshire Fencible Regiment. His observations were typical of the complaints regarding fencible units, stating the regiment was 'composed of old men and young boys, few of either fit for His Majesty's service.'[31] He further stated that there was a high fatality rate within the regiment due to the want of proper clothing and that he 'had not been able to prevail on the officers to have them clothed or to provide them with necessities, both of which they are … in want of.' He concluded the report by stating the new recruits mostly proved to be unfit as well. The most extreme example is that of the Leicester Fencible Infantry Regiment that disembarked at Dublin in May 1795 but immediately had 80 percent of its men returned to England as unfit for service.[32] The same month the Prince of Wales Fencibles arrived at the same port and were also sent back to Britain, as 396 out the 500-man battalion were considered unfit for duty due to being 'too old, too fat, too small, too infirm and too young.'[33]

The poor physical condition of these troops can be attributed to numerous factors. One explanation can be sought by examining where most of the recruits came from. The high death rate from natural causes of fencibles in Ireland, which was five-times higher than the militia, led to an inquiry by the Army Medical Board into the disparity in mortality between the two forces. It concluded that the Irish militia generally comprised of 'stout men in the prime of life', drawn from the peasantry and used to hard work and the Irish climate, whereas the British fencibles were 'either too young or unhealthy old men from unhealthy parts of Britain.'[34] Most of these men, especially those from England, had been artisans, mechanics and labourers recruited from over-crowded and unhealthy sprawling urban centres, and generally were less robust and strong compared to the majority of Catholic recruits of the Irish Militia who were mainly rural agricultural labourers.[35] The fencibles were also prone to disease and poor living conditions. Barracks were notoriously overcrowded and cold and damp during the winter months, which fostered numerous ailments. Duncannon Fort, near Waterford, was a typical example

---

30   Sir John Fortescue, *A History of the British Army* (London: MacMillan, 1915), vol.4, part 1, p.519.
31   TNA: HO 100/55: General Robert Cunninghame to Edward Cooke, 10 October 1795.
32   Carswell, 'The Scottish Fencible Regiments in Ireland', p.157.
33   Bartlett, 'Defence, counter-insurgency and rebellion: Ireland 1793–1803', p.259.
34   Bartlett, 'Defence, counter-insurgency and rebellion: Ireland 1793–1803', p.259.
35   Nelson, *The Irish Militia*, p.130.

where the soldiers had to share three to a bed, which led to the rapid spread of fever and deaths.[36]

Ill-discipline was another major criticism aimed at the fencibles. This occurred due to several factors, which included lack of military experience, poor training, boredom, and poor leadership. The service of the Perthshire Fencible Infantry was an example of this where it appeared to suffer from poor recruiting and an open feud between its commanding officer and some of his subordinate officers. This resulted in lax discipline, with the regiment behaving badly against the civilian population, especially after the defeat of the rebels in 1798.[37] The actions of the battalion were considered so bad that in late 1798 Cornwallis ordered the disbandment of the regiment as an example to the rest of the army.[38] Similarly to the Irish militia, the absence of officers from the fencible regiments reflected a lack of concern for their men and affected the efficiency and discipline of the troops when used in counter-insurgent operations, as well as garrison duty. This appears to have been a constant concern for the hierarchy of the army, with the military returns of October 1797 submitted by Lord Carhampton, then commander-in-chief of the army, showing that there were eight fencible officers reported absent-without-leave at that time.[39] In comparison, the return states there were only three regular officers missing, but consideration must be given to the small number of regulars stationed in Ireland at this time. The same return reported that there were also eight militia officers absent from their battalions without authority. This tends to indicate that the attitudes and professionalism of the officer corps within the fencibles and militia was generally inferior in standard to that of regular officers, which reflected the standard of discipline displayed by their troops.

Some atrocities were committed against the civilian population by individual fencible units that were instrumental in the lasting unfavourable reputation of the corps in Ireland. The most notorious unit was the Ancient British Light Dragoons, a Welsh fencible cavalry regiment commonly known as the 'Ancient Britons'. This regiment was stationed in Ulster and was involved in the combined counter-insurgent operations of 1797–1798. The officers and troops within the regiment proved ruthless towards the inhabitants of areas that were suspected of supporting the United Irishmen. In November 1797 Robert Livingstone, the agent of the Protestant loyalist, Lord Charlemont, complained to his employer, that the Ancient Britons, accompanied by yeomanry, had wrecked property, and indiscriminately beaten inhabitants of Charlemont's estate in Armagh, while seizing all arms, including those of Protestants who had lawfully registered them.[40] The counter-terror tactics used by the regiment were so severe that prominent loyalist gentry were repulsed by them. John Giffard, an Orangeman who

---

36 Bartlett, 'Defence, counter-insurgency and rebellion: Ireland 1793–1803', p.258.
37 Carswell, 'The Scottish Fencible Regiments in Ireland', p.157.
38 Carswell, 'The Scottish Fencible Regiments in Ireland', p.157.
39 TNA: HO 100/68: Lord Carhampton to Camden, 19 October 1797.
40 Historical Manuscripts Commission, Charlemont, vol.ii, pp.310–311, Livingstone to Lord Charlemont, 8 November 1797, quoted in Blackstock, *An Ascendancy Army*, p.241.

commanded a detachment of Dublin militia during the Newry arms searches in County Down, was disgusted by the behaviour of the Ancient Britons and accompanying yeomen, who burnt houses, took prisoners, and fired randomly at anyone they saw, killing up to 20 civilians who all subsequently proved to be innocent.[41] The regiment was never officially held accountable for these murders.

However, contrary to popular tradition, there are a few incidents where fencible units proved to be reliable and effective, especially during the rebellion in 1798. At the Battle of Arklow, County Wicklow, on 9 June, the Loyal Durham Fencibles were positioned on the crucial right flank of the government forces defending the town and their actions were instrumental in repulsing and defeating the rebels.[42] This proved decisive in that the large number of casualties suffered by the insurgents, forced them to withdraw and concentrate at Vinegar Hill where they were subsequently routed and destroyed, effectively ending the rebellion in Wexford. During the uprising in Ulster, where a substantial number of fencible units were stationed, the Loyal Tay Fencibles, a Scottish infantry battalion, proved most effective. The regiment had its headquarters at Carrickfergus, County Antrim, but the battalion had been dispersed into small units to provide garrisons for outlying towns and villages. When the rebellion erupted in Antrim on 7 June, a small detachment of 20 Tay Fencibles commanded by Lieutenant Andrew Small, together with a few loyal armed civilians, successfully defended the town against a substantial rebel attack.[43] At Bellair another small detachment of Tay Fencibles, together with the Glenarm Yeomanry, took the initiative by seizing known United Irish leaders in a pre-emptive strike and subsequently defended the local castle.[44]

In general, the Scottish regiments proved to be the most effective and reliable fencible troops in Ireland. The British government had capitalised on the traditional Highland relationships of loyalty to the crown which had developed since the defeat of the Scottish Jacobites in 1746 and had exploited the economic opportunities available to the landowners through the diminishing clan system by fostering patronage.[45] Major Scottish landowners and minor gentry were offered political favour or military rank in return for raising battalions or recruiting troops from their estates. An example of this is the 2nd Regiment of Argyle Fencibles, raised by Colonel Archibald McNeil of Colonsay from his estates in the Western Isles.[46] These policies ensured that whole regiments of fit and active young men could be quickly formed, with five of the seven Scottish regiments raised in 1793 being Highland units.[47] However, some of these corps were not as solely 'Highland' in composition

---

41 Historical Manuscripts Commission, Charlemont, vol.ii, pp.310–311, Livingstone to Lord Charlemont, 8 November 1797, quoted in Blackstock, *An Ascendancy Army*, p.241.
42 Hayes–McCoy, 'The Government Forces Which Opposed the Irish Insurgents of 1798', pp.16–28.
43 Stewart, *The Summer Soldiers*, p.88.
44 Stewart, *The Summer Soldiers*, p.98.
45 Stuart Reid, *Wellington's Highlanders* (Oxford: Osprey, 1992), pp.22–24.
46 Reid, *Wellington's Highlanders*, pp.22–24.
47 Reid, *Wellington's Highlanders*, pp.22–24.

as their titles suggest, with regiments increasingly being forced to recruit in Lowland areas where the population was always greater and, in the 1790s, expanding.[48] The traditional relationships between the Highland officers and their men, together with their cultural respect for military service, ensured that these troops had the potential to be excellent soldiers once trained. The Reay Fencibles, raised from the north-west of Scotland, were particularly well thought of due to their fair treatment of the local population and appear to have remained untainted by acts of atrocity or indiscipline.[49] The Highland soldiers were generally physically hardy, which made them well suited to the types of counter-insurgent operations that followed the rebellion, such as pursuing rebels into remote and mountainous terrain. An example was the service of the Dumbartonshire Fencibles, included in an elite mobile force which received praise from Brigadier General John Moore after he had led the campaign against insurgents in the Wicklow Mountains in late 1798: 'the fatigue and inconvenience of the troops has been very great. In the mountains of Wicklow we are obliged to divest ourselves of all baggage, and for a week, notwithstanding hard rain and cold, lay on the ground without tents or covering.'[50]

Cultural and religious beliefs affected how the Scottish Fencibles reacted to their duties in Ireland. Some regiments initially refused to serve in the kingdom and mutinied when they were about to embark for Ireland, although such protest was quickly quelled with the arrest of ringleaders. The majority of Lowland regiments were recruited from Protestants, ensuring many of the officers and soldiers could identify with the Protestant population, especially the Presbyterians of Ulster. This was evident through the establishment of Orange lodges within numerous battalions, which would have fostered strong partisan feelings towards rebels or suspected rebels. It is likely that such attitudes would have led to incidents of ruthless behaviour and possible atrocities against civilians, like those committed by local yeomanry and Irish militia in Ulster in 1797 and during the rebellion of 1798, by units that were susceptible to ill-discipline. The Reay Fencibles, a predominantly Protestant regiment, enthusiastically sent sergeants to act as drill masters to the newly formed Protestant yeomanry corps in Belfast in 1796. However, the relationship between this regiment and the predominantly Catholic Monaghan Militia, which was also stationed in Belfast at the time, almost led to open conflict. This was reportedly due to the militia regiment being suspected of having been subverted by the United Irishmen. However, even Scottish units were not immune from such activity, with two soldiers from the Fife Fencibles being executed at Carrickfergus in 1797 for taking the United Irish oath. In contrast, some Scots felt sympathy towards the situation of the Catholic population. The Glengarry Fencibles, a Highland regiment that was composed largely of Catholics and even had its own priest, was well

---

48   Carswell, 'The Scottish Fencibles in Ireland', p.157.
49   Carswell, 'The Scottish Fencibles in Ireland', p.158.
50   Beatrice Brownrigg, *The Life and Letters of Sir John Moore* (Oxford: Basil Blackwell, 1923), pp.82–84.

regarded for its humane treatment of the population of Wexford during and after the uprising.[51]

The reputation of the Highland fencible regiments has unjustifiably been linked to the poor press that fencibles, have received from nationalist historians, mainly due to their role in the pacification of Ulster. The Scottish fencibles were a more complex and varied force compared to the generally substandard regiments from other parts of Britain. And although the Lowland regiments generally proved to be of a less physical quality than Highland counterparts, the Scottish fencibles remained a loyal and effective military force during the times of crisis in Ireland. In contrast to England and Ireland, Scotland had no official militia prior to 1797 and it is probable that this accounted for the Scottish fencibles, in general, attracting a better class of recruit than their English counterparts. The Scots soldiers were credited with displaying remarkably good behaviour towards the civilian population. Obviously, this was not the always the case, with some isolated unsavoury incidents involving individuals from particular regiments having been recorded. However, the Scottish fencibles appear to have constituted a relatively disciplined force at a time when regular troops in Ireland were desperately in short supply. A significant indication of the quality and regard held by military authorities for some Scottish fencible regiments was the number that were recruited into regular regiments when the fencibles were disbanded in 1802, with some units enlisting *en masse* while they were still stationed in Ireland.[52]

Ireland as a Source of Recruits for the British Army

Between 1793 and 1815 Ireland proved to be a crucial source of recruits for the regular forces of the British army. During this period it is estimated that approximately 150,000 Irishmen enlisted, with the majority serving in regular regiments posted overseas.[53] The heavy recruiting conducted in the kingdom during the 1790s led to an estimated one-third of the British Army being comprised of Irishmen, with an even higher rate being achieved during the later Napoleonic wars.[54] In the period 1793–1794 as many as 30 new regular regiments were raised in Ireland, along with 44 independent companies that were recruited in Ireland and subsequently sent to Britain to be formed into battalions.[55] Although most of the troops raised in Ireland at this time were infantrymen recruited from rural peasants and poor urban artisans, four new regular cavalry regiments were raised from the more affluent farming classes. These regiments were subsequently numbered as the 30th to the 34th Light Dragoons, but disbanded within a short time.[56]

---

51   Carswell, 'The Scottish Fencibles in Ireland', p.158.
52   Carswell, 'The Scottish Fencibles in Ireland', p.159.
53   Chart, 'The Irish Levies during the Great French War', p.516.
54   Cookson, *The British Armed Nation 1793–1815*, p.154.
55   Cookson, *The British Armed Nation 1793–1815*, pp.498–499.
56   Cookson, *The British Armed Nation 1793–1815*, p.503.

Once the battalions in Ireland had been recruited to full strength they were immediately posted out of the kingdom, most never to return. The two main reasons for this can be attributed to the desperate need to boost the number of troops available to defend Britain and its overseas possessions, as well as to build a substantial army for operations against the French on the continent. However, this policy was also actively supported by the Irish Ascendancy who were against the stationing of new regular units in Ireland, as they were mainly comprised of Catholic recruits who posed a potential armed threat to the Protestant oligarchy. The experience of the 88th Foot, commonly known as the 'Connaught Rangers,' was typical of regular regiments established in Ireland. Raised mainly from within the counties of Connacht in 1793 by the Honourable John de Burgh, once it had reached its full complement it was immediately shipped to England and the following year sent to Flanders as part of the Duke of York's army.[57]

Desertion was another reason to remove the Irish troops from the kingdom. The insatiable demand for soldiers led to a rapid expansion of the armed forces in Ireland in 1793, which ensured deterioration in the quality of recruits. In 1794 a memorandum on recruiting claimed that 'the worst kind of recruits' were being accepted into the army; either inexperienced young men' or the 'refuse of mankind.'[58] It was recruits such as these that caused the desertion rate to drastically increase, with Edward Cooke, the under-secretary at Dublin Castle, stating in June 1794 'Desertion is terrible at present … and we know not how to prevent it.'[59] Cooke's frustration was supported by the comments of the new lord lieutenant, Lord Fitzwilliam, a few months later: 'There is no keeping Irish troops in Ireland, they desert so abominably.'[60] An example of evidence supporting these claims is a report submitted by Lieutenant Colonel Eyre Power Trench of the 38th Foot in May 1794 where he states that when he inspected his regiment at Granard, County Westmeath, 233 men had deserted out of a total complement of 1,100 and he may have lost more while marching to their port of embarkation for Flanders.[61] The inability to adjust to the discipline and rigours of military life would certainly have affected many recruits who may never have ventured more than a few miles from their family home or village and chose to desert. However, there is evidence to suggest that desertion rates rose once the overseas destinations for departing regiments were announced.

Prior to 1798 most regular regiments raised in Ireland were sent for service in the West Indies. From 1794, Henry Dundas, as Secretary of State for War, constantly received requests for troops from generals commanding

---

57 Shepperd, *The Connaught Rangers*, p.8.
58 TNA: HO 100/47: ff.272–274, quoted in Thomas Bartlett, 'Indiscipline and disaffection in Ireland in the 1790s,' in Patrick J. Corish (ed.), *Radicals, Rebels & Establishments* (Belfast: Appletree Press,1985), p.116.
59 TNA: HO 100/47: ff.272–274, quoted in Thomas Bartlett, 'Indiscipline and disaffection in Ireland in the 1790s', p.116.
60 TNA: HO 100/48: f.429, quoted in Bartlett, 'Indiscipline and disaffection in Ireland in the 1790s,' p.117.
61 TNA: HO 100/48: f.306, quoted in Bartlett, 'Indiscipline and disaffection in Ireland in the 1790s,' p.117.

the various islands that extended throughout the region, where tropical diseases such as yellow fever and malaria continued to decimate the regiments stationed there, reducing the capacity to effectively defend British interests. Britain was highly protective of its possessions in the Caribbean as the revenue from raw materials produced on these islands, especially sugar, were essential in maintaining the booming British economy. Duties and taxes raised from these commodities were also essential in financing the war against Revolutionary France, not only for the maintenance of the Royal Navy and the British Army, but also to provide the subsidies that Britain was paying to its allies to help the fight against the French on the continent. There were never enough available troops to satisfy the insatiable demand for replacements in the Caribbean. The British government was forced to prioritise and juggle around what troops it had, including withdrawing regiments from its small army in the low countries. However, even this move proved insufficient and more drastic measures to find the required forces was needed. Pitt and Dundas were now forced to look to Ireland to help solve this issue.

Ireland proved to be a significant source of regular troops sent to the West Indies. Britain was determined to establish dominance in the Caribbean by not only retaining its own possessions, but also by depriving France of the islands under its control. To this end Dundas intended to commit a further 10,000 men to the West Indian campaign season of 1794–1795 to complete the conquest of Guadeloupe.[62] In 1793, Dundas had already ordered the flank companies of all the remaining infantry regiments in Ireland to embark for service in expeditions to Toulon and Gibraltar, as well as the West Indies. In November of the same year, he sent two regiments to the Caribbean from the Irish Establishment, followed by another 10 battalions the following year for the Guadeloupe campaign.[63] These units were initially sent to Gibraltar to acclimatise before heading to the tropical islands. According to Lieutenant General Sir Charles Grey, the officer commanding the British forces in the Windward Islands, these troops 'were the pick of the Irish army and … it was unlikely that such excellent soldiers could ever be assembled again in the war.'[64] Although this may be some exaggeration on Grey's part, there is no doubt that these troops were the most professional element of the Irish establishment and their overseas posting had a serious effect on the defensive capability of the army in Ireland. By the end of 1794, the 17th Foot was the only regular infantry line regiment remaining on the Irish establishment, with four light dragoon regiments also being ordered to prepare for service in the West Indies in April the following year.[65] Britain's focus on the Caribbean ensured that the cream of the Irish army was to quickly waste away through campaigning and tropical disease that ensured most of these Irish soldiers

---

62　Michael Duffy, *Soldiers, Sugar and Seapower: The British Expeditions to the West Indies and the War against Revolutionary France* (Oxford: Clarendon Press,1987), p.127.
63　Duffy, *Soldiers, Sugar and Seapower*, p.127.
64　Duffy, *Soldiers, Sugar and Seapower*, p.63.
65　Duffy, *Soldiers, Sugar and Seapower*, p.159.

never returned to their homeland. It was the military experience in the West Indies that also dramatically affected further recruiting in Ireland.

By the mid-1790s, the fear of serving in the Caribbean led to a reduction in Irish recruits volunteering for the regular army. News of the high mortality rate of troops serving in the West Indies had quickly filtered back to Britain and Ireland, so that by 1796, those cadres of British regiments sent to recruit in the kingdom were struggling to reach their full complement. Those units were usually seriously under strength and were shipped to Ireland to enlist recruits within the shortest time possible before embarking for foreign service. In July 1795, four English regiments were sent to Ireland to recruit to full strength and were secretly destined to be re-numbered before being sent to the West Indies. These intentions were kept from the troops to prevent any desertion.[66] However, the information was leaked resulting in the three-day mutiny of the 104th and 111th Foot in Dublin in August 1795 and the mutiny of the 105th and 113th Foot at Cork in September. The mutineers had taken to the streets fully armed in protest, declaring that their conditions of enlistment, which included not having to serve outside Ireland or Britain, had been broken.[67] And although these mutinies were quickly extinguished by militia, aided by small contingents of available regulars, news of the events and why they occurred spread throughout the country.

The demand for troops became so critical that Pitt turned to desperate measures. In 1794 he proposed the formation of an 'Irish Brigade' of six battalions of infantry to be raised from within the Catholic population of Ireland, specifically for service in the West Indies. This formation was to be officered by those members of the Irish Catholic peerage and gentry who had previously fought against Britain while serving in the Irish Brigade in French service, but who were now considered allies due to their continued allegiance to the French royal family.[68] These officers were to be given the rank that they had previously held in French service.[69] Remarkably, the most senior colonel of the proposed battalions was the Duke of Fitzjames, an illegitimate descendant of James II and thereby considered a senior Jacobite. However, by this stage of the century Jacobitism no longer posed a military threat to the Hanoverian dynasty, with most Irish Jacobites now willing to show allegiance to the British Crown. However, even these formations struggled to recruit to their full complement, with the Duke of Portland in February 1796 showing his concern at the inability of the officers to find sufficient recruits to bring their battalions to full strength:

> I am willing to hope that the zeal and gratitude of his Roman Catholic subjects will render it unnecessary [to reduce the regiments] and that their exertions to fulfil His Majesty's just expectations will correspond with the means which His Majesty's paternal goodness has afforded them of distinguishing themselves in the service of their country and of being placed in such honourable and advantageous

---

66 Duffy, *Soldiers, Sugar and Seapower*, p.173.
67 Duffy, *Soldiers, Sugar and Seapower*, p.173.
68 TNA: HO 100/55: Camden to Portland, 14 July 1795.
69 TNA: HO 100/55: Portland to Camden, 16 February 1796.

posts of trust and profit as their merits will entitle them to enjoy in common with the rest of their fellow subjects of every other religious persuasion.[70]

Even this direct threat by Portland proved powerless in raising the brigade to full strength. As a result, only the two numerically strongest regiments, Dillon's and Walsh's (commanded by Lieutenant Colonel Edward Stack, a Catholic), saw service in the West Indies. When they embarked from Cork in May 1796, the regimental return showed Walsh's battalion having only 495 rank and file, which was well below the official required strength of 600, although the troops were described as being a good body of men, some having long service and being more forward in discipline and drill than others.[71] However, by 1797 the Irish Brigade was disbanded due to the inability to muster sufficient recruits, with the rank and file being drafted into other regiments, while the officers were placed on half-pay.

There were also other factors that led to fewer Irish recruits 'taking the king's shilling' in the line regiments. The formation of the militia in 1793 had provided prospective volunteers with an alternative to joining a regular regiment. For many, especially married men, there were more incentives to enlist in a county militia battalion. By 1795, the experiences of the regular line regiments that had been decimated by disease through service in the West Indies were common knowledge throughout Ireland and the prospect of serving in a militia regiment that was to remain in the kingdom was more attractive. For married recruits, service in a line battalion would have meant overseas service and certain separation from family for an indefinite time, with any dependants facing destitution in the likely event that the recruit was killed in battle, died from wounds or disease, or was crippled from serious wounds. Home service with the militia offered soldiers more incentives such as limited service, a healthier climate, the option to have family remain with the battalion and live-in barracks, allowances for a spouse and dependent children, regimental schools provided for children, as well as only a small chance of having to face an enemy in open combat.[72] Also, by this period internal civil unrest was reaching a level previously unknown during the eighteenth century. Protestants felt threatened by the increasingly violent activities of the United Irishmen and the disaffected Catholic peasantry in rural areas.[73] This, coupled with the general lack of trust in the militia, ensured that many Protestants believed their military efforts were best served by falling back on their tradition of self-defence by forming local armed associations. Evidence of the effects of this can been seen in a letter from Camden to Portland in March 1796 where he stated that he had ordered cavalry recruiting parties to England due to the lack of recruits, which had previously enlisted from within Protestant communities, coming forward in Ireland.[74] Eventually thousands of prospective Protestant recruits, who

---

70   TNA: HO 100/55: Portland to Camden, 16 February 1796.
71   TNA: HO 100/55: Camden to Portland, 8 March 1796.
72   Nelson, *The Irish Militia*, pp.145–146.
73   Nelson, *The Irish Militia*, pp.145–146.
74   TNA: HO 100/60: Camden to Portland, 24 March 1796.

may have enlisted in the regular army, enthusiastically joined the newly established yeomanry in late 1796. Clearly, the threat of internal rebellion and the prospect of losing property and power was more important to the Protestant population in Ireland than any international politics.

Divided Defence Policies

The divided military defence policies for Ireland until 1798 determined the distribution and use of the armed forces in the kingdom. From the outbreak of war with Revolutionary France in 1793, the British government was mindful of an attempted invasion of Ireland by French forces at a time when the regular troops from the Irish establishment were desperately needed elsewhere. With the substantial reduction of regular infantry from the Irish garrison, heavy reliance was placed on the Royal Navy to intercept and defeat any French invasion force intended for Ireland.[75] Until 1796, the general attitude of the British government was that although an invasion attempt was possible, it was unlikely due to the poor state of the French navy.[76] This attitude was reflected in the inadequate defensive planning of the military in Ireland and the general poor state of the armed forces that was influenced by political interference. The army had always had the dual purpose in Ireland to assist the civil powers when called upon and to defend against invasion.[77] However, it was the political influence of the Protestant ascendancy that was determined to retain power and the increased fear of rebellion that saw the army being used more as a tool against insurgents. This ensured that most of the available troops of the garrison were distributed in small contingents throughout the kingdom rather than concentrated as an effective fighting force.

The problem that Dublin Castle faced in the 1790s was that it had insufficient forces to both effectively combat insurgency in the countryside and defend against invasion. During their terms as lords lieutenant, both Westmorland and Camden, were focussed on counter-insurgent measures. This ensured that the duties of the army changed so that it was vigorously used against the population that it was supposed to be defending. Some regiments, such as the Roscommon and Galway militias, remained in the same districts for the above period but were annually transferred to different locations within that district.[78] Until after the events of 1798, there appears to be no particular pattern to as to where militia regiments were posted, with the militia consisting of 77 percent of the armed forces in the southern district, 61 percent of the forces in the eastern district and 35 percent of the government troops in the northern district.[79] As the capital and seat of

---

75 TNA: HO 100/60: Camden to Portland, 24 March 1796.
76 Come, 'French Threat to British Shores, 1793-1798', pp.174–188.
77 S.J. Connelly, 'The defence of Protestant Ireland', in Thomas Bartlett & Keith Jeffrey (eds), *A Military History of Ireland*, (Cambridge: Cambridge University Press, 1996), p.241.
78 Ferguson, 'The army in Ireland from the restoration to the act of Union', p.181.
79 Nelson, *The Irish Militia*, p.182.

government, Dublin accounted for the largest concentration of troops as the security of the capital remained imperative. In 1796 its garrison consisted of one regiment of dragoons, one regiment of fencibles and three regiments of militia, while the nearby camp at Loughlinstown had a similar complement which also included several companies of artillery.[80] The low percentage of militia regiments within the garrison of Ulster was due to the battalions being predominantly Catholic regiments from southern counties, which Lieutenant General Lake feared would be susceptible to subversion from the United Irish.[81] This ensured that the majority of the security force in Ulster consisted of fencible regiments and some of the few regular units left in Ireland. However, every county in the kingdom had a militia regiment stationed in it, with most of the battalions being dispersed amongst small towns and villages.

Political interference further hindered the military command in Ireland during the 1790s. The nature of the Irish government was such that its civil and military affairs were integrated. The lord lieutenant's dual responsibilities as the senior civil and military leader led to Camden relenting to pressure from the Ascendancy, ensuring that the army was divided in its primary functions. This came to a head with the resignation of Abercromby in March 1798, mainly through his criticism of the state of the army, but also through his frustration with Camden's weakness in cowing to the constant appeals from the gentry for troops to provide protection for themselves and their property.[82] Abercromby had been critical of the dispersal of the army and believed that it could only be forged into an effective counter-invasion force by concentrating the regiments. This philosophy was in complete contrast to his predecessor, Carhampton, who was also a member of the Irish parliament, and Lake, who was to replace him. Both men were advocates of the Ascendancy cause and were applauded for their vigorous counter-insurgency operations in Connacht and Ulster prior to the rebellion.[83] Cornwallis had the same opinion as Abercromby when he became the lord lieutenant, and unlike Camden, he generally refused to bow to the constant demands of the Protestant oligarchy.[84] However, such change in policies and attitudes within the high command led to confusion within the lower levels of the army. Officers and soldiers who had actively been encouraged to administer severe punishments on disaffected populations were then expected to show more leniency for the months Abercromby was in command, only to revert to their previous tactics when Lake was appointed.[85] The counter-terror tactics were also advocated by many colonels of militia regiments, who as members of the Ascendancy were able to combine their military and political influence to protect their own interests. One example was Brigadier General John Knox, who as a member of the leading family in County Tyrone, used his political

---

80 TNA: HO 100/60: Camden to Portland, 21 March 1796.
81 Nelson, *The Irish Militia*, p.182.
82 Brownrigg, *The Life and Letters of Sir John Moore*, p.77.
83 Connelly (ed.), *The Oxford Companion to Irish History*, p.308.
84 Ross, *Correspondence of Charles, First Marquis Cornwallis*, pp.395.
85 Bartlett, 'Defence, counter-insurgency and rebellion: Ireland 1793–1803', p.276.

connections to promote the establishment of various yeomanry corps within the county when there were insufficient troops to protect his extensive estates.[86] Ultimately, the official use of 'terror' by the army was dictated by who was in command at the time, and the political influences and ideologies of those commanders. The underlying political subordination within the Irish establishment was lessened with the appointment of Cornwallis in 1798.

The counter-insurgent operations of the Irish army limited its effectiveness. In isolated locations where there were no established barracks, what discipline there was within regiments was soon eroded through troops being billeted in homes of the local population, which on occasions could be 20 to 30 miles from the company or battalion headquarters preventing supervision from officers.[87] There are insufficient contemporary records to establish every unit that attended the summer camps, but taking into consideration that there was only a small percentage of troops available to do so in 1796, and probably even fewer the following year due to the increase in insurgent activities, it is likely that a significant proportion of the Irish army had no more than basic musket and platoon drill at the time of the rebellion.

Counter-insurgent operations also had a negative effect on the discipline of the army in Ireland. Some troops became demoralised through the constant use in excessive policing roles within the communities they were required to live. Lord Carhampton, commander-in-chief of the army in 1795, directed a swift and ruthless campaign against Defenders in Connacht that year that set the tone of future operations. Draconian measures were taken where homes were indiscriminately burned, livestock slaughtered and many Defender suspects were imprisoned without trial, some being unlawfully pressed into service in the Royal Navy.[88] The inability or hesitance of the local magistrates to enforce the rule of law at the time, and later in some counties of Ulster in 1797, effectively saw martial law declared through the Insurrection Act. This provided the army with extended powers for search for arms and ability to impose curfews, with troops being authorised to act in dispersing unlawful assemblies if there was no magistrate present.[89] It is easy to see how the morale of the troops could be affected by such operations, especially the Irish Catholics who could have some empathy with the plight of the Defender suspects, when they were given orders such as those by Brigadier General John Moore. When conducting search and seizure operations for weapons in early 1798 he directed his men:

> ... to treat the people with as much harshness as possible, as far as words and manners went, and to supply themselves with whatever provisions were necessary to enable them to live well. My wish was to excite terror, and by that means obtain our end speedily. I thought this better than to act more mildly, and be obliged

---

86   Blackstock, *An Ascendancy Army*, p.93.
87   Blackstock, *An Ascendancy Army*, p.79.
88   Bartlett, 'Defence, counter-insurgency and rebellion: Ireland, 1793–1803', p.248.
89   NLI: 1013/352: Kilmainham Papers, General Order, 18 May 1797, quoted in Nelson, *The Irish Militia, 1793–1802*, p.137.

to continue for any time the real oppression; and, as I was present everywhere myself, I had no doubt of being able to prevent any great abuses by the troops.[90]

Moore's approach can be considered moderate compared to others, such as Brigadier General Richard Whyte who at the direction of Lake, ordered the Monaghan Militia to destroy the offices of the newspaper, the *Northern Star*, in Belfast because of its sympathies towards the republican cause.[91] It was such direction from senior officers that promoted excesses by the troops and fostered a breakdown in discipline.

The attempted invasion by the French at Bantry Bay in December 1796 exposed the incompetence of the army command at that time. Prior to this there had been no comprehensive defensive plan, as it was felt that the French navy was too weak to support a substantial invasion.[92] This false sense of security had ensured that only rudimentary plans had been formulated, which included the establishment of the training camps for the Militia, which also had the dual purpose of providing permanent reserves to defend Dublin in the event of a French invasion or internal rebellion.[93] The military thinking at this time was that the most likely areas the French would land would either be in the south, where there was a number of substantial harbours to help establish a bridgehead, or in the north that also had sizable harbours and where disaffection was strongest. It was thought unlikely that any landing would take place on the west coast due to its unforgiving coastline.

However, Camden's proposed changes to the garrison for the summer of 1796 showed that the size and experience of these reserves was limited. The Dublin garrison comprised 2,250 men from one fencible and three militia battalions, with the 9th Dragoons providing the only regular regiment.[94] A further 1,830 men were to provide support from the one fencible and three militia regiments stationed at nearby Loughlinstown. The reserves at Ardfinnin and Blaris camps only equated to 2,740 and 2,260 respectively and were comprised on a similar number of fencible and militia battalions such as that at Loughlinstown, although it is believed that small contingents of artillery were also based at these camps.[95] Significantly, there were no regular units to provide stability to these reserves. At this time there were only six cavalry and two infantry regiments of the line on the Irish establishment, and they had been posted throughout the kingdom. And although Camden's proposal shows he intended to have some concentration of forces at Cork, Belfast, and Dublin, generally the army was too dispersed throughout the country to allow for a substantial force to rapidly come together to meet any threat.

There also appeared to be a lack of planning on the part of the high command at this time. In October 1796, Ireland was divided up into five

---

90 Maurice, *The Diary of Sir John Moore*, p.289.
91 Bartlett, 'Indiscipline and disaffection in the armed forces in Ireland in the 1790s', p.127.
92 Paul M. Kerrigan, *Castles and Fortifications in Ireland, 1485-1945* (Cork: Collins Press, 1995), pp.150–151.
93 TNA: HO 100/60: Camden to Portland, 26 March 1796.
94 TNA: HO 100/60: Camden to Portland, 26 March 1796.
95 TNA: HO 100/60: Camden to Portland, 26 March 1796.

REBELLION, INVASION AND OCCUPATION

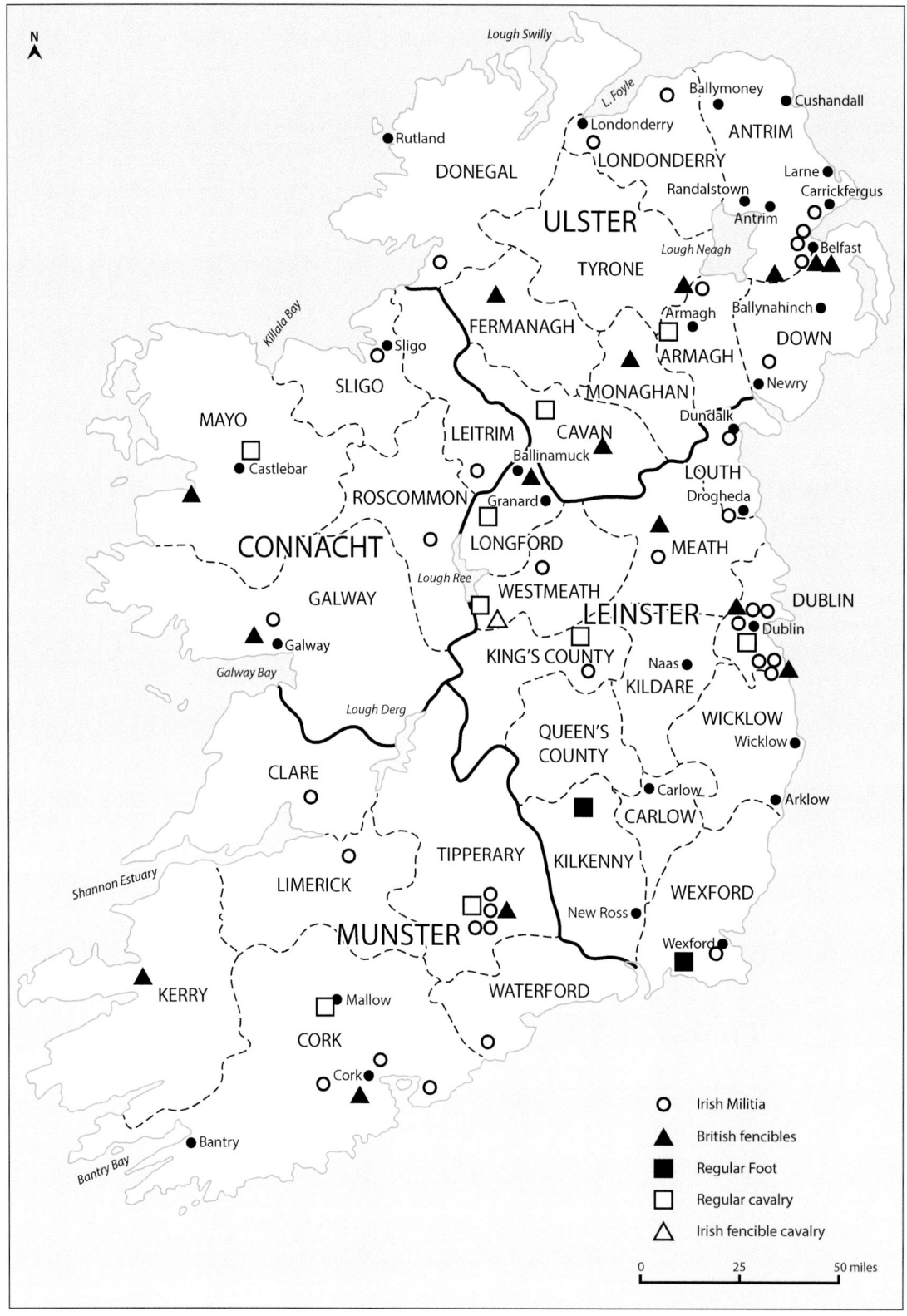

Proposed Distribution of the Irish Garrison, Summer 1796 (Source: Camden to the Duke of Portland, 21 March 1796 – TNA: HO 100/60)

military districts to simplify the management of the army. Each district, Northern (Ulster), Western (Connacht and part of Munster), Midland, Eastern (Leinster) and Southern (Munster and part of south-west Leinster) was to be commanded by a general who was responsible for the troops and military activities in his area. This was followed by a general order that directed the brigading together of regiments for training and emergencies, although it appears this only occurred on an ad-hoc basis.[96] Evidence of poor planning or incompetence on the part of the military leadership came from within the army itself. In early December, at a time when the government had intelligence of an impending French invasion, Brigadier General Eyre Coote had written to his superior, Lieutenant General William Dalrymple, indicating Bantry Bay as a suitable and likely strategic landing place for the French and that steps should be taken to plan for such eventuality.[97] However, Dalrymple, who was in command of the forces in the southern district, was not in a position to take such steps until any such landing was confirmed, although he did make a token gesture in ordering a detachment of the 5th Dragoons to the area.[98] His main priority was the defence of Cork and its harbour, which appeared to be a challenge with the insufficient resources available. This was outlined in a report submitted the same month by a Major Brown of the Royal Engineers, who stated that there were crucial problems in the defence of the city due to insufficient artillerymen and infantry, as well as incomplete defences.[99] Considering that Cork was regarded as the second city of the kingdom and its port was crucial to Britain's overall strategy, the lack of resources and poor planning for its defence gives some indication of the insufficient planning conducted for the defence from invasion for the rest of the Ireland.

Attempted French Invasion

The attempted invasion of Ireland by the French in December 1796 posed the most serious military threat to Ireland during the Revolutionary and Napoleonic wars. A substantial French fleet of 18 ships-of-the-line, 13 frigates, seven transports and eight smaller vessels had sailed from Brest on 16 December 1796 carrying 14,450 regular troops, 41,644 stands of arms and 5,000 uniforms.[100] This formidable force was under the command of *Général de division* Louis Lazare Hoche, an experienced officer who had recently defeated the Royalist uprising in the Vendee. Another French army of 14–15,000 men was assembling in Brest to reinforce Hoche's proposed

---

96 TNA: WO 68/221: f.28, General Order, 26 October 1796, quoted in Nelson, *The Irish Militia*, p.162.
97 PRONI: T 755/3/199, Coote to Dalrymple, 1 December 1796, quoted in Nelson, *The Irish Militia*, p.162.
98 Martin, 'Reform and Change within the Irish Army and Military System, 1763–1818', p.262.
99 PRONI: T 755/3/209: Report of Major Brown, RE, December 1796, quoted in Nelson, *The Irish Militia*, p.162.
100 Marianne Elliott, *Partners in Revolution: The United Irishmen and France* (New Haven & London: Yale University Press, 1982), p.111.

invasion.[101] The mouth of the River Shannon was the original proposed landing area for the French army. However, the fleet became dispersed due to a storm and unfavourable winds prevented it from reassembling. As a result, only 35 ships arrived off Bantry Bay on 21 December, excluding the ship carrying Hoche. The fleet then divided in two, with 19 ships remaining outside the bay while the rest entered it. Another storm several days later scattered the ships at the head of the bay, reducing the fleet to 16 ships. This ensured that the French now only had an available force of 6,500 troops and four artillery pieces to establish a bridgehead. Wolfe Tone was one of the senior United Irish leaders accompanying the part of the French fleet that made it into Bantry Bay and he recorded his despair in not being able to proceed with the landing in his diary:

> December 26 [1796]. Certainly we have been persecuted by a strange fatality… We have lost two commanders-in-chief; of four admirals not one remains; we have lost one ship of the line that we know of, and probably many others of which we know nothing; we have been now six days in Bantry Bay, within five hundred yards of the shore, without being able to effectuate a landing; we have been dispersed four times in four days; and at this moment, of forty-three sail, of which the expedition consisted, we can muster of all sizes but fourteen. There only wants our falling in with the English to complete our destruction…[102]

For a time, indecision prevailed amongst the French as Hoche and the naval commander, *Chef d'escadre* Justin Bonaventure Morard de Galles, who were together on the same frigate, had failed to rendezvous with the main fleet due to unfavourable winds.[103] However, although a decision was eventually made by *Général de division* Emmanuel Grouchy, the most senior army officer present, to land this force in an attempt to capture Cork, continued rough weather prevented a landing. The senior naval officer of the few ships of the scattered fleet that managed to make it into Bantry Bay, *Chef d'escadre* Francois Joseph Bouvet, fearing being trapped in the bay by the Royal Navy, decided to withdraw the fleet on 25 December and returned to France.[104] Had it not been for the unfavourable weather, the French could have landed and marched to Cork in four days, easily capturing the city and port, as the inadequate and inexperienced defending force of regulars, fencibles and militia would have been no match for the invaders.[105]

The military response to the arrival of the French in Bantry Bay was chaotic. The operation to mobilise a force to counter the expected landing was poorly run by army staff who had been surprised by the arrival of the sizable French force. Although any unlikely invasion was expected to be in

---

101 Martin, 'Reform and Change within the Irish Army and Military System, 1763–1818', pp.252–253.
102 Hewitt, *Eye-Witnesses to Ireland in Revolt*, p.63.
103 Kerrigan, *Castles and Fortifications in Ireland*, p.151.
104 Marianne Elliott, 'The Role of Ireland in French War Strategy, 1796–1798', in Hugh Gough & David Dickinson (eds), *Ireland and the French Revolution* (Dublin: Irish Academic Press, 1990), pp.209–210.
105 Kerrigan, *Castles and Fortifications in Ireland*, p.151.

the south, most of the military forces were stationed in Ulster and in the east to protect Dublin. This clearly indicates that the government's emphasis was more on countering insurgency which was presenting an immediate danger than preparing for an invasion that may never have happened. It was not until 1797 that Lieutenant General David Dundas, who believed that any French invasion would most likely occur along the southern coast or near the Shannon estuary in the west, formulated a plan of defence that focused on defending strategic geographical boundaries such as the River Shannon in the west and the rivers Lee and Blackwater in the south. Dalrymple admitted that he had not formulated any plan for the defence of Cork and that the insufficient and inexperienced force that he had gathered to meet the French was only a diversion to allow time for a sizable army to be concentrated.[106]

At the time he had no more than approximately 5,600 troops, comprising mostly of militia and fencibles, to defend the whole southern district, but believed he could only muster around 2,000 to challenge the French near Bandon. Confusion reigned amongst the military hierarchy, which lacked inspiration from the commander-in-chief, Carhampton, who conceded that Cork and Limerick might be captured by the French. Regiments were ordered south to establish a concentrated force near Cork, but Carhampton wrote to Pelham stating that he believed no more than 8,000 men could be collected together in time to defend the city and that it might be better to form a strong defensive line at Fermoy on the River Blackwater, where a force of 12,000 infantry supported by cavalry and artillery would be more effective.[107] Thirty-one of the 38 militia regiments were mobilised and moved south, leaving the policing of most of the country to the fledgling and inexperienced yeomanry.[108] However, no proper system had been adopted for troop movements which saw many regiments making disorganised forced-marches in the middle of winter. There had been little or no provision made for feeding the troops on the march, with most having to improvise by buying their own food or by relying on the generosity of the civilian population.[109] The important part the population played during this time was emphasized by Dalrymple in a letter published in the *Dublin Journal* where he stated that the inhabitants were 'displaying every proof of loyalty and attachment' to the troops.[110]

The military authorities had been anxious about a possible invasion from September 1796 and had taken some measures. Supply depots were established at Clonmel, Bandon, Galway, Banagher, Portumna, Omagh, Hillsborough, Newry, and Dundalk, while ovens had been built at Athlone, Birr and Omagh.[111] However, these proved insufficient during the emergency. There were deficiencies evident in medical services and artillery supplies, with the commissariat being incapable of providing enough food and fodder

---

106 Bartlett, 'Defence, counter-insurgency and rebellion: Ireland, 1793–1803', p.269.
107 Martin, 'Reform and Change within the Irish Army and Military System, 1763–1818', pp.262-263.
108 McAnally, *The Irish Militia*, p.98.
109 McAnally, *The Irish Militia*, pp.97–98.
110 *Dublin Journal*, 17 October 1782–12 December 1799, *Dublin Journal*, 31 December 1796.
111 McAnally, *The Irish Militia*, p.100.

for the troops and horses.[112] Clearly, the Bantry Bay crisis highlighted the complacency of the leadership and inadequate planning that the Irish army and government needed to address.

However, the condition of the army in Ireland prior to the rebellion in 1798 remained poor. Lord Carhampton had lost the confidence of the majority of his subordinate officers, as well as Camden, who eventually was to replace him with Lieutenant General Sir Ralph Abercromby. This was after a number of experienced senior generals had refused to serve in Ireland due to the well-known difficulties the position posed. Abercromby, who had a reputation as a credible, capable, and experienced general officer, had arrived in the kingdom in early December 1797 to commence his duties. However, he resigned in March 1798 as a result of his unpopular criticism of the state of the army in Ireland and the government policies affecting its use. Little had been done to improve the organisational faults highlighted 12 months earlier despite Carhampton's attempted reforms that included strengthening the garrisons of Cork and Limerick, along with the formation of four new battalions of light infantry created from the detached elite companies from each militia regiment.[113] On his arrival Abercromby found that the logistical requirements for the army had not been sufficiently attended to: 'On my arrival here … I found an army of upwards of 40,000 without any arrangement made for their subsistence.' He also considered the cavalry unfit for service, with the infantry officers showing little ability in commanding their troops: 'In their present state they are exposed to be corrupted, to be disarmed and made prisoners.'[114] He also told his friend, Brigadier General John Moore, 'No artillery was in a condition to move. Even the guns attached to the regiments were unprovided with horses. No magazines were found for the regiments and there was little or no order or discipline.'[115]

The army had been dispersed to protect the gentry in disaffected areas which made it difficult to quickly assemble a sizable and effective field army to meet any possible French landing. Abercromby was of the belief that policing duties should be left to the yeomanry, that the dispersed nature of the army was 'ruinous to the service.'[116] He argued that the gentry needed to attend to their own protection through service in the yeomanry, while the army should be used for garrison duty and to provide a substantial reserve. By ordering the withdrawal of the troops from their current deployment he hoped to restore discipline, as well as establish a number of permanent formations at strategic points.[117] At this time Camden fully supported his new commander-in-chief and reported to Portland that he would follow through with Abercromby's suggestions to enable the army to regroup.[118] However, although Abercromby was successful in improving the logistical

---

112 McAnally., *The Irish Militia*, p.100.
113 TNA: HO 100/67: Carhampton to Camden, 10 June 1797.
114 Abercromby to Lake, 13 December 1797, quoted in Pakenham, *The Year of Liberty*, p.61.
115 Maurice, *The Diary of Sir John Moore*, p.271.
116 BL: Pelham Manuscripts, Add MSS 33/105/334, Abercromby to Pelham, 23 January 1798, quoted in Pakenham, *The Year of Liberty*, p.61.
117 Pakenham, *The Year of Liberty*, p.62.
118 TNA: HO 100/75: Camden to Portland, 24 February 1798.

requirements for subsistence of the army by establishing a chain of supply depots for arms, ammunition and provisions, as well as strengthening the forts guarding the along the south-west coastline, the general concentration of the army was not implemented.

Internal Irish politics determined the state of the army prior to the rebellion. On 26 February 1798 Abercromby wrote, 'The very disgraceful frequency of courts martial, and the many complaints of irregularities in the conduct of the troops in this kingdom having so unfortunately proved the army to be in a state of licentiousness which must render it formidable to everyone but the enemy.'[119] Abercromby's intentions were for the improvement of the military situation in Ireland; however, the wording of the order created a political backlash. The commander-in-chief immediately lost the support of a vast number of officers within the army, who took the order as direct criticism against them. The British government also saw the order as a criticism of its policies in Ireland and feared the Whig opposition would use it to gain political points. However, it was pressure from the Irish parliament that led to Abercromby's resignation in late March. The Ascendancy, led by such Protestant hard-liners such as Lord Clare and John Beresford, believed that Abercromby had been too lenient on the disaffected population by employing less harsh measures to ensure the seizure and surrender of arms. Although his policy of threatening 'free-quartering' of troops in the disaffected counties of Kildare and King's and Queen's had been successful in increasing the number of weapons surrendered to authorities and restoring peace, his rejection of counter-terror tactics had created bitterness within the gentry who were the main targets of the insurgents.[120] This led to a united move from the Irish parliament to lobby Dublin Castle for Abercromby's dismissal.[121] Although backed by a small core of professional officers, Abercromby had lost the support of the army and parliament, forcing Camden to seek his resignation.

The change in command of the army had a direct link to the rebellion. Camden was now forced to make Lake the commander-in-chief as he was the most senior general willing to accept the position. He had not been his first choice as he was not of great intellect and Camden was not in favour of the excessive actions he had promoted towards the civilian population, especially in Ulster.[122] From the time Lake took command in April, Ireland was set for general insurrection due to his reckless and ill-coordinated disarming policy. Counter-terror was reintroduced with vigour, especially when martial law and free-quartering was declared in the disaffected counties. The declaration of the Insurrection Act throughout the country on 30 March saw the government actively encourage excesses against suspected insurgents, with Pitt directing Camden to make a 'speedy and well-concerted effort for crushing the rebellion by the most vigorous military exertions in all the disturbed provinces,' and that he was not to

---

119 TNA: WO 68/221: General Order, 26 February 1798, quoted in Nelson, *The Irish Militia*, p.176.
120 Bartlett, 'Defence, counter-insurgency and rebellion: Ireland, 1793-1803', p.276.
121 Pakenham, *The Year of Liberty*, p.64.
122 Pakenham, *The Year of Liberty*, p.64.

REBELLION, INVASION AND OCCUPATION

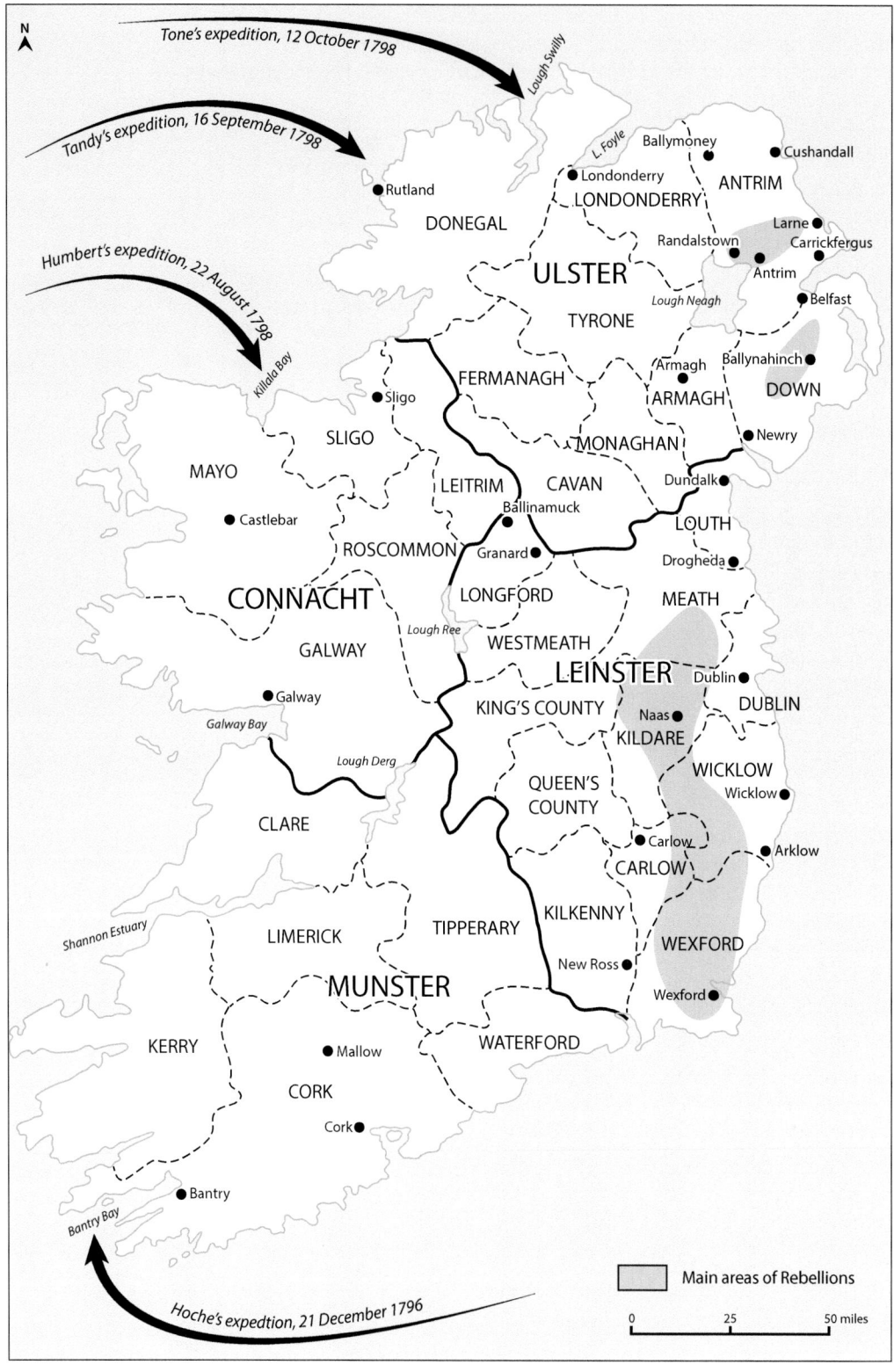

Locations of Rebellion actions and French expeditions
(Source: Pakenham, *The Year of Liberty*, revised edition, abridged by Toby Buchan, p.112)

concern himself unduly with army discipline.[123] Although the policy proved fruitful in gaining rebel arms and the arrests of the majority of the United Irish executive, the excesses of flogging, house-burning, 'pitch-capping', murder and torture occurred on a large scale. The army was now seen as an oppressive tool of the Ascendancy that had become increasingly fearful of the Catholic peasantry, leading to large-scale confiscation and destruction of agricultural produce that people relied on for income and sustenance. The excesses committed by the military and fostered by the government only led to further alienation of sectors of the population that had previously been neutral, but who were now forced to defend themselves and their property. Such actions polarised the kingdom and led to open rebellion, although this was confined to certain parts of the country.

---

123 Bartlett, 'Defence, counter-insurgency and rebellion: Ireland, 1793–1803', p.275.

5

The 1798 Rebellion

The year 1798 was a watershed in Irish history. The rebellion that erupted in May of that year, followed by the invasion of a small French force in August, not only led to a change in the dynamics of the army in Ireland but also led to lasting political and social structures within the kingdom. The British and Irish governments had feared popular rebellion throughout the country for many years; however, they had failed to make sufficient military preparations for the simultaneous insurrection and French invasion that had been the long-term goal of the United Irish. The bulk of the fighting against the rebels and the French had to be conducted by the Irish militia, British fencibles and Irish yeomanry.

Contrary to the historiography surrounding these events, the inexperienced and semi-trained Irish militia generally proved their loyalty and fought well, leading to the eventual defeat of their foes. However, the government victories during the year also came about due to the lack of organisation and leadership within the rebel armies, as well as the limited size of the French invasion force. The Royal Navy also played a major role in the defence of the kingdom by intercepting and defeating a series of French fleets carrying troops intended for Ireland. Ultimately, the rampant militant republicanism and militant loyalism that had polarized the Irish population and had reached crisis point that year, led to atrocities typical of civil wars and the estimated deaths of 25,000 rebels and non-combatants, along with hundreds of soldiers.[1] However, although the rebellion spread the length of the country and was an extremely bloody affair, it was successfully and quickly dealt with, and lead to Britain imposing greater control over the troubled land.

According to the official return of the government forces in Ireland submitted in January 1798, there were a total of 41,068 rank and file troops serving in the kingdom at that time. This included 3,493 regular line cavalry, 1,816 fencible cavalry, 1,830 regular line infantry, 10,751 fencible infantry, and 22,728 Irish militia. There was no further return made until July of the same year, which was after the rebellion had been smothered and the

---

[1] Bartlett, 'Defence, counter-insurgency and rebellion: Ireland, 1793-1803', p.287.

garrison, boosted by reinforcements from Britain, had been increased to 48,332.²

It is probable that when the rebellion erupted in May the number of troops in Ireland would have been similar to numbers given in the January return. Although Lieutenant General Sir Ralph Abercromby had improved the concentration of some regiments in an effort to provide reserves and improve training, the majority of troops were now mainly dispersed to defend against a French invasion, ensuring that regiments were either posted to garrison strategic cities, towns and coastal forts, such as Dublin, Belfast, Cork and Limerick, or stationed at one of the permanent camps to provide reserves.³ Those individual units that were scattered throughout rural Ireland were commonly dispersed into small troops or companies to protect the local gentry and to assist in the search and seizure of arms. An example of this was the North Cork Militia which was the only regiment stationed in the county of Wexford on the eve of the uprising. This battalion had been divided into small detachments and companies that were stationed in Wexford town and several smaller provincial towns, such as Enniscorthy and Ferns, not only to assist in counter-insurgent operations but also to assist local magistrates and yeomanry in maintaining the law.⁴ This ensured that when the rebellion broke out in Wexford, there were less than 500 troops between the Wicklow/Wexford border and Duncannon Fort near Waterford.⁵ Few troops had been stationed in County Wexford as rebellion was unexpected there due to the prosperity within the county and the lack of known United Irish activity.

The Beginning of the Rebellion

The year 1798 also marked a turning point in the fortunes of the Irish militia, which from this time had lost the confidence which the British government had previously placed in it to defend Ireland. A better understanding of the rebellion and the events immediately leading up to it provides an insight as to how this occurred. The increasingly violent counter-insurgent operations being carried out by government forces, which included the bulk of the militia, created tension within the disaffected counties and had an impact on the military capabilities of United Irish. The continual arms seizures and arrests of senior rebel leaders had reduced the effectiveness of the organisation. Months of fruitless waiting for French action had a corrosive effect on rural supporters who had been the subjects of military oppression during April and May. This had damaged revolutionary morale and heightened religious tensions.⁶ Arthur O'Connor and Father James Quigley, a Catholic priest from Dundalk, were the first of the United Irish executive to be captured when

---

2   Ferguson, 'The army in Ireland from the restoration to the act of Union', p.147.
3   Daniel Gahan, 'The Rebellion of 1798 in south Leinster', in Bartlett (ed.), *1798: A Bicentenary Perspective*, p.111.
4   Nelson, *The Irish Militia*, pp.186–188.
5   Gahan, 'The Rebellion of 1798 in south Leinster', p.111.
6   David Dickson, *New Foundations: Ireland 1660–1800* (Dublin: Irish Academic Press, 2000), p.211.

they were arrested in Margate, Kent, on 28 February 1798 after being sent to negotiate with the French Directory for military support in the proposed insurrection.[7] This was followed by the mass arrest of 16 of the most senior United Irish executives, including the Leinster leadership, at Oliver Bond's Dublin address on 12 March. Wolfe Tone summed up how devastating this was to the United Irish cause:

> I have read news of the most disastrous and afflicting kind, as well for me individually, as for the country at large. The English Government has arrested the whole committee of United Irishmen for the province of Leinster, including almost every man I know and esteem in the city of Dublin. It is by far the most terrible blow which the cause of liberty in Ireland has yet sustained. I know not whether in the whole party it would be possible to replace the energy, talents, and integrity, of which we are deprived by this most unfortunate of events. I have not received such a shock from all that has passed since I left Ireland.[8]

Such disasters urged those of the executive still at large, such as Lord Edward Fitzgerald, John Lawless and John Sheares, to attempt a *coup* before the government had succeeded in destroying the rebel infrastructure.[9] The lukewarm response of their allies led to the new United Irish leadership determining to raise a rebellion on their own in the hope that it would prompt the French to send an invasion force once the revolt had begun.[10]

The fundamental purpose of the United Irish rebellion was the overthrow of the Irish administration in Dublin. The primary military objective was the capture of the capital. This was dependent on participation of rebels over a wide area. The success of the United Irish uprising was reliant on a three-stage strategy. Central to this plan was the capture of key sites in Dublin, such as the Customs House and Four Courts, in the belief that depriving the government of such buildings would cripple the established infrastructure of the kingdom. The second priority was to secure the regions immediately outside the capital to establish a defensive ring around the city. A letter from an informer, Francis Higgins, sent to Edward Cooke on 20 May indicated that the insurgents had intended to occupy positions from Garretstown, Naul, Dunboyne, taking a circuitous route around the city to Dunleary. The third phase of the operation revolved around establishing sufficient forces to defend against the inevitable counter-attack from the government army.[11] It was determined that the uprising would begin on 24 May, to be signalled by the stopping of the overnight mail coaches on the outskirts of Dublin on the evening of 23 May. It was hoped that such tactics would spread panic to the

---

7   Nancy J. Curtain, *The United Irishmen: Popular Politics in Ulster and Dublin, 1791–1798* (Oxford: Clarendon Press, 1988), p.64.
8   Hewitt, *Eye–Witnesses to Ireland in Revolt*, p.66.
9   Curtain, *The United Irishmen*, pp.257–258.
10 Curtain, *The United Irishmen*, pp.11–12.
11 NAI: 620/18/14: Rebellion Papers, Francis Higgins to Edward Cooke, 20 May 1798, quoted in Liam Chambers, 'The 1798 Rebellion in North Leinster', in Thomas Bartlett et al (eds), *1798: A Bicentenary Perspective* (Dublin: Four Courts Press, 2003), pp.122–123.

garrison towns and help paralyse the government.¹² The executive believed that victory would be obtained through superior numbers provided by the thousands of Catholic Defenders and the support of disaffected members of the militia.¹³

The success of the uprising was jeopardised before it began through the loss of its operational leader. The arrest and fatal wounding of Lord Edward Fitzgerald in Dublin on 19 May was a disastrous blow for the United Irish cause. Higgins had informed Dublin Castle that this revolutionary Irish peer was to be the commander-in-chief of the rebel forces, due to his high profile and that he was the only executive member to have had any military experience.¹⁴ His capture ensured that there was a lack of coordination and leadership which prevented an effective rising in Dublin. Fitzgerald's name had given credibility to the planned revolt, and his arrest had persuaded many in the capital that the cause was already lost.¹⁵ Not only did the United Irish now lack any central leadership, but thanks to informers such as Higgins and planted spies within the insurgent organisation, such as Francis Magan and Captain John Armstrong, the government was fully aware of the plans of the rebels. Troops, which mainly consisted of militia regiments together with several regiments of fencibles and regular cavalry, were wisely concentrated in and around Dublin where measures were taken to discourage insurgent attacks on government buildings within the capital by increasing armed patrols and strengthening the guards at strategic points, such as Dublin Castle.¹⁶ Camden ensured that the streets of the city were saturated with troops who were employed in arresting suspects and searching for arms, with the summary burning of all buildings where pikes were found.¹⁷ And although Pakenham claims that confusion reigned amongst the Dublin garrison when the alarm was called and that there had been insufficient steps taken to secure vital bridges, the show of force was enough to persuade the estimated few hundred leaderless rebels within the city on 23 May not to take any action.¹⁸ Such activities discouraged a general uprising in the city, which was necessary for the United Irishmen to achieve their first objective. The seizing of Dublin was imperative for the success of the rebel strategy and the failure to do so ensured the revolt was no longer a *coup d'état,* but a series of uncoordinated local actions that lacked direction.

The rising in the surrounding counties of Dublin met with some success due to the rebels having the initiative. Although the government had been aware that the mail coaches were to be targets of the insurgents, officials believed the rising had been planned for a later date and it was a shock to them when they received a letter from an informer on the afternoon of

---

12 Pakenham, *The Year of Liberty*, pp.123–124.
13 Pakenham, *The Year of Liberty*, pp.123–124.
14 NAI: 620/18/14: Rebellion Papers, Francis Higgins to Edward Cooke, 20 May 1798, quoted in Chambers, 'The 1798 Rebellion in North Leinster', pp.122–123.
15 Curtin, *The United Irishmen*, p.258.
16 Curtin, *The United Irishmen*, p.258.
17 Pakenham, *The Year of Liberty*, pp.112–113.
18 Pakenham, *The Year of Liberty*, p.119.

REBELLION, INVASION AND OCCUPATION

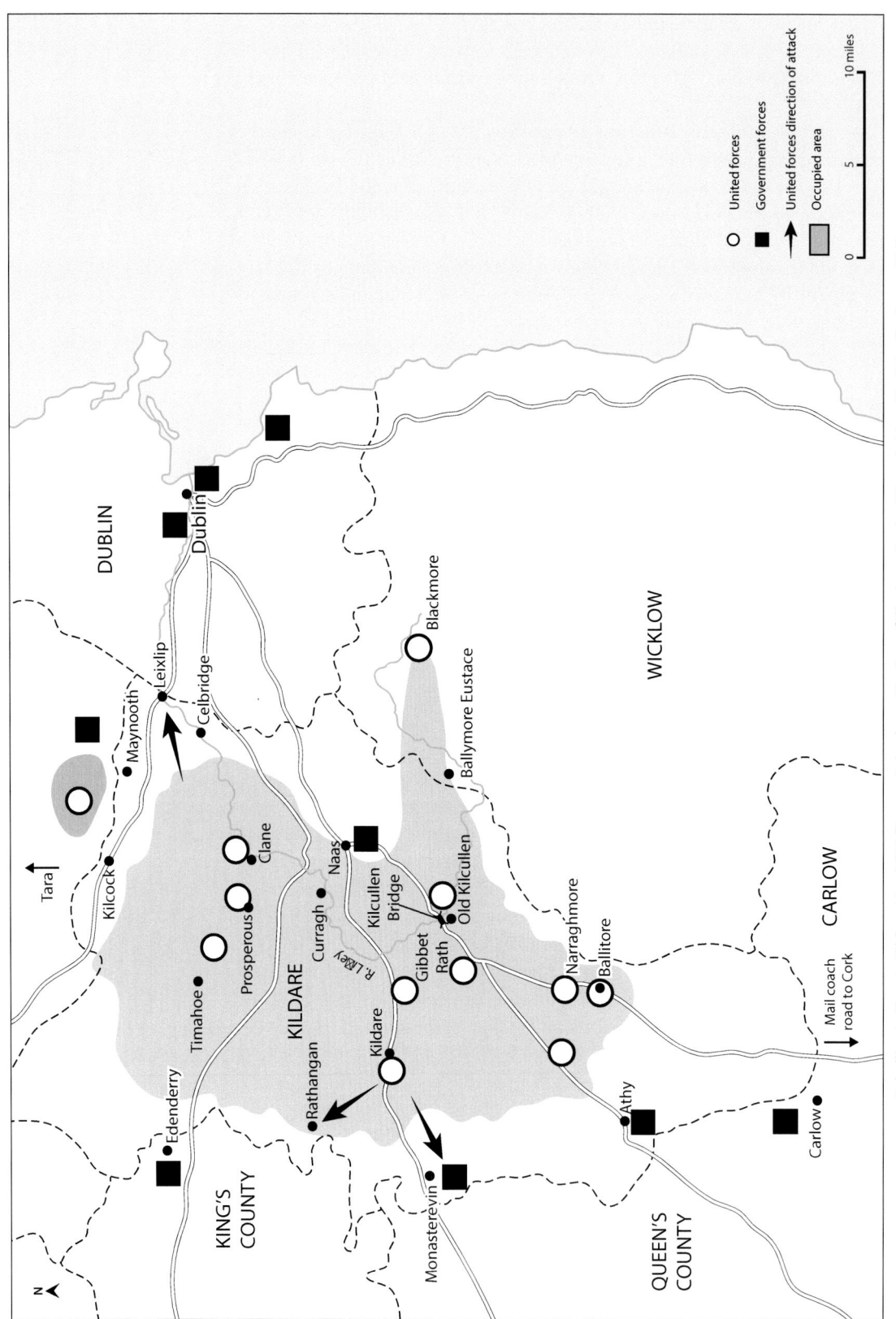

Rebellion in County Kildare, May 1798 (Source: Pakenham, *The Year of Liberty*, revised edition, abridged by Toby Buchan, p.114)

23 May stating that the revolt was to begin that evening.[19] Couriers were immediately dispatched to Colonel Lord Gosford commanding at Naas and Major General Richard Wilford at Kildare, however, the numerous smaller detachments scattered in towns and villages surrounding Dublin could not be informed in sufficient time to prevent them being surprised by the United Irishmen.[20] Subsequently, that night cells of United Irishmen in counties Dublin, Meath, Kildare, King's, Queen's and Wicklow gathered along the main roads leading from Dublin on which the various mail coaches travelled. Roadblocks were established not only to seize the coaches but also to sever communications between the high command at Dublin Castle and the government forces in the provinces. The rebels were able to quickly gather substantial forces that ensured superior numbers when launching surprise attacks on small garrisons of government troops. Near Naul 2,000 rebels surrounded the Westpaltown barracks, while at Curragh around 1,000 insurgents marched down the village street armed with pikes and muskets.[21] Roadblocks were formed along the Navan road, the Galway road, as well as the main road leading south to Cork, and it is estimated that by the morning of 24 May up to 10,000 rebels had formed a secure crescent around the capital.[22]

The isolated garrisons of militia and yeomanry were the first targets of the rebels. The excessive counter-insurgent operations that had been directed by the government and carried out with much vigour by the army and yeomanry, had resulted in numerous atrocities that alienated the local populations. One of the most famous examples was that of Captain John Swayne who commanded a detachment of the City of Cork Militia in the town of Prosperous, County Kildare, and who was notoriously known for advocating the torturous practice of 'pitch capping'– pouring hot tar on the heads of suspected rebels. On the night of 23 May when the rebellion began, Swayne was murdered in his bed and his troops were surprised and locked in their barracks, where they all perished after it was set alight.[23] The policy of free quartering also proved disastrous for some troops who were separated from their officers when the revolt erupted. In Clane, County Kildare, soldiers from the Armagh Militia were still in their billets when the rebels attacked the village. They had to desperately fight their way to their officer in small groups, losing two killed and five wounded, before they could form an effective defence.[24] On the same night a detachment of Tyrone Militia stationed at Ballymore Eustace, County Wicklow, fought off a determined rebel attack but lost an officer and four men in doing so.[25] The insurgents proved successful in capturing a number of small towns, forcing the surprised garrisons to flee, while any army officers, such as Lieutenant William Giffard

---

19   Pakenham, *The Year of Liberty*, pp.115–117.
20   Pakenham, *The Year of Liberty*, p.129.
21   Pakenham, *The Year of Liberty*, pp.123–124.
22   Pakenham, *The Year of Liberty*, pp.123–124.
23   Nelson, *The Irish Militia*, pp.183–184.
24   Nelson, *The Irish Militia*, pp.183–184.
25   Nelson, *The Irish Militia*, pp.183–184.

REBELLION, INVASION AND OCCUPATION

of the 82nd Foot, who had the misfortune of travelling by coach and being stopped by the rebels, were usually murdered.[26]

At Prosperous the rebel force comprised of 500 men who were mainly farmers and cotton mill workers led by Dr John Esmonde, an officer in the local yeomanry.[27] This mob marched to the town barracks and forced their way into the guard house where the 12 militiamen present were all dispatched. A detachment of the Ancient Britons stationed at the cotton factory was subsequently attacked and overwhelmed. Of the 57 soldiers who had formed the garrison, only 19 managed to escape with their lives.[28] Ironically, most of those killed were Catholic. Synchronized attacks had also been launched at the nearby towns of Clane and Naas where the surprised government troops had managed to beat off the first attacks, but with some losses. However, the small, combined garrison of local yeomanry and Armagh Militia at Clane was forced to retreat to Naas due to the large number of rebels who threatened to surround them. At Naas the garrison of around 220 men was attacked by three separate columns of rebels, amounting to several thousand, who were intent on capturing the town barracks and gaol. Only after repeated charges by the mounted Ancient Britons, but mainly through the telling fire of the militia artillery, were the insurgents forced to retreat.[29] At the village of Old Kilcullen, Kildare, the aged Lieutenant General Sir Ralph Dundas, commander of the Midland district, was unable to organise a counter-attack as he himself was beleaguered by 300 rebels who had occupied the local churchyard. With only a mixed force of 20 fencible infantry and 40 cavalry of the Romney Fencibles and 9th Dragoons, Dundas ordered the mounted element of his force to repeatedly charge the fortified rebels. This was disastrous for the government force, in that the cavalry proved ineffective against the insurgent pikemen, resulting in the heavy loss of 23 soldiers killed.[30] Dundas was then forced to fight his way out of the village in an attempt to concentrate the dispersed troops in the county. The rebel cause was further helped by an order for the government troops in County Kildare to initially withdraw and concentrate at Kildare town to create a sufficient counter-attack force. This

Caricature of Captain Swayne, City of Cork Militia, pitch capping Irish civilians. (National Library of Ireland Free Collection)

---

26   Nelson, *The Irish Militia*, pp.183–184.
27   BL: Add MSS 33,106/10: R. Griffith to Pelham, 13 July 1798, quoted in Pakenham, *The Year of Liberty*, pp.134–136.
28   BL: Add MSS 33,106/10: R. Griffith to Pelham, 13 July 1798, quoted in Pakenham, *The Year of Liberty*, pp.134–136.
29   Pakenham, *The Year of Liberty*, pp.134–136.
30   Pakenham, *The Year of Liberty*, pp.134–136.

enabled the United Irish to establish a small enclave that was successful in severing communications to the south and west of the capital in a time of confusion and uncertainty.

However, the United Irish success in most of Leinster was limited and short-lived. There had been 14 engagements in the first 24-hours of the rebellion, of which only two had been victories for the insurgents. In most cases small government garrisons had been able to repel rebel attacks, and in some cases rout the ill-disciplined mobs. The rebels had managed to occupy several towns and villages, but mainly through them not being garrisoned or through the government troops being strategically withdrawn. Those villages that had been seized were soon recaptured, such as Rathangan, County Kildare, which had been secured by the insurgents on 23 May but subsequently recaptured by the City of Cork Militia the following day.[31] The abortive rebel attacks on Lucan, County Dublin, Kilcock, County Meath, and Leixlip, County Kildare on 25 May led to insurgents withdrawing to a defensive camp at Dunboyne. Lack of leadership then led to indecision, resulting in the rebel army being attacked and routed at the battle of Tara in Meath two days later. The uprising in the counties of the Pale was effectively over with the surrender of 3,000 rebels at Knockallan Hill, Kildare on 28 May, with only a few small bands of ineffectual United Irish remaining scattered throughout the countryside. Thomas Pakenham convincingly argues that those locations that the United Irish had occupied were of no strategic value and that no military threat to the capital ever materialised.[32] However, news of this localised rebellion had quickly spread throughout Ireland and had inspired thousands of other disaffected Irishmen in Wexford to take up arms against the state.

The Uprising in Wexford

The government had not expected any trouble in the south-east of Ireland, but this was where the rebellion was to pose the greatest threat, either from the United Irish or their French allies. This is evident by analysing the concentration of the Irish garrison at the time. In May 1798 half of the Irish establishment was stationed in Munster and concentrated along a short defensive line from Limerick to Cork due to the belief that any French attack would most likely occur in the south.[33] The rest of the Irish army was clustered in the Midlands to protect Dublin, while there was a sizable force maintained in Ulster where the United Irish where perceived to be strongest. The North Cork Militia had only recently been sent to Wexford, either in late April or early May, to assist in the search and seizure of arms. According to Sir Richard Musgrave, the battalion headquarters was established in the town

---

31 NAI: 620/37/208: Rebellion Papers, Lieutenant Colonel Longford to Lieutenant General Dundas, 29 May 1798, quoted in Nelson, *The Irish Militia*, p.184.
32 Pakenham, *The Year of Liberty*, p.137.
33 D.A. Chart, 'The Irish Levies during the Great French War', *English Historical Review*, vol.32 (1917), pp.497–516.

of Wexford, where around 19 officers and 369 rank and file were stationed.[34] Only three companies were distributed elsewhere in the county, with Captain Snow's company and 30 men from Captain de Courcy's company posted at Enniscorthy, one subaltern and 30 men stationed at Gorey, as well as the same number billeted at Ferns.[35] The only other armed forces immediately available in the county to assist the militia were the yeomanry. The nearest available reinforcements were scattered in neighbouring counties, with the Antrim Militia at Arklow, County Wicklow, the Meath Militia and 86 soldiers of the 13th Foot in Waterford City, along with the 9th Dragoons stationed in Carlow.[36] The distance these units had to march to support the North Corks, coupled with uncertainty and the necessity to maintain the peace and security of the areas in which they were garrisoned ensured that the sole militia regiment in Wexford was initially forced to confront the numerically superior rebel forces on its own.

It was the rebellion in Wexford that posed the most serious threat to the Ascendancy in Ireland. It was the only county where the United Irish were able to raise armed civilian mobs that were large enough to overwhelm the limited government forces in south Leinster. The exact number of disaffected who joined the uprising in Wexford will never be known as the rebel columns consisted of clusters of localised forces of volunteers or impressed civilians that were never formed into formal regiments. An army in name only, these assemblies had no structure and were mostly led by individuals who had no military experience, relying on the fervour of the crowd to obtain success. Pikes, which were made locally and readily available, were the most common weapons of the rebels and proved effective against yeoman cavalry, while agricultural implements were also weapons of necessity due to the scarcity of firearms.[37] The number of rebel 'volunteers' remaining in the field was fluid and determined by the successes or defeats of the insurgents. Nevertheless, some indication of the size of the rebel forces can be established from contemporary accounts of the rebellion. The first encounter between government troops and United Irishmen in Wexford occurred at Oulart Hill on 27 May, where Cornwallis claims the rebel force consisted of 5,000 men.[38] The figures given for the rebel army that attacked New Ross on 5 June were greater; the figure of 30,000 quoted by Sir Richard Musgrave, can be disregarded as a gross exaggeration due to his obvious bias in his attempt to magnify the Catholic threat.[39] However, the numbers of 10–15,000 given by Miles Byrne, a United Irish officer who fought in the uprising, seem more likely, indicating that the rebel army was 10–15 times the size of the defending government force.[40] He claims that the insurgent

---

34 Myers & McKnight, *Sir Richard Musgrave's Memoirs of the Irish Rebellion of 1798*, p.306
35 Myers & McKnight, *Sir Richard Musgrave's Memoirs of the Irish Rebellion of 1798*, pp.326, 370 & 409.
36 Chart, 'The Irish Levies during the Great French War', p.508.
37 Pakenham, *The Year of Liberty*, p.136.
38 Ross, *Correspondence of Charles, First Marquis Cornwallis*, p.345.
39 Myers & McKnight, *Sir Richard Musgrave's Memoirs of the Irish Rebellion of 1798*, p.331.
40 Thomas Bartlett, 'Miles Byrne: United Irishman, Irish Exile and Beau Sabreur', quoted in Daire Keogh & Nicholas Furlong (eds) *The Mighty Wave: The 1798 Rebellion in Wexford*

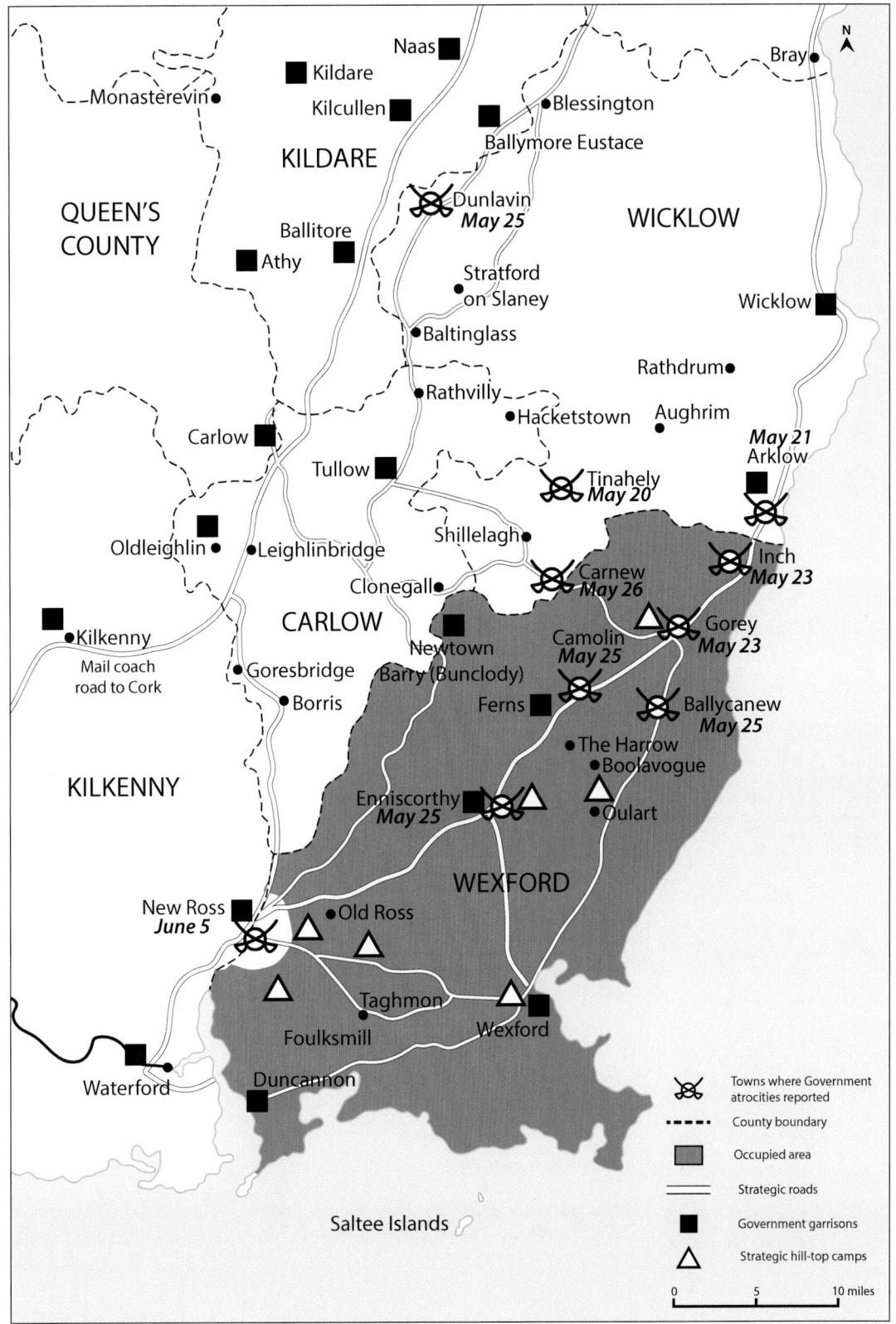

Rebellion in County Wexford, May–June 1798 (Source: Pakenham, *The Year of Liberty*, revised edition, abridged by Toby Buchan, p.115)

force that attacked Arklow on 9 June consisted of 20,000 rebels, but that their defeat was due to only 2,000 men having muskets for which there was very little ammunition.[41] What these figures indicate is that the United Irish were able to muster a horde of 30–40,000 men in a very short time. It was imperative for Dublin Castle that the rebellion be contained before it could spread throughout the kingdom.

Contrary to the historiography of a Catholic crusade promoted by contemporary historians such as Musgrave, the rising in Wexford gained popular support due to localised economic depression. This had caused some disaffection amongst the middle-classes, as well as the Catholic peasantry, ensuring the membership of prominent Protestant and Catholic gentry, such as Bagenal Harvey, who provided leadership amongst the United Irish in the county.[42] Intelligence gained from government spies, informers and from the arrest of United Irish leaders, such as Anthony Perry of Inch, had led to an increase in counter-terror activities in northern Wexford.[43] These increasingly violent activities of search, seizure and arrests, coupled with propaganda sponsored by the rebel leadership and local magistrates, had polarised the community. Protestants were fearful of Catholic insurrection, while the Catholic peasantry was continually being exposed to floggings, house-burnings and 'pitch-capping' by the yeomanry.[44] A wave of hysteria swept through the county, with stories of atrocities committed by the yeomanry encouraging those who had previously sworn allegiance to the crown to take up arms against the local government agents. On 26 May news of the murder of rebel prisoners by the garrison at Dunlavin, Kildare, along with the same plight of 28 prisoners at Carnew on the Wicklow border, convinced many that the rumours of the planned extermination of the Catholic population had begun.[45] At this same time news of the rebellion in Kildare and Meath had spread throughout Wexford. Ultimately, it was the fear of torture, death, and destruction of property, together with the stories of rebel successes that convinced thousands to join the armed resistance.[46]

The character of the rebellion was more of a peasant *jacquerie* than of a revolution. With the arrests of the senior leaders within the Leinster United Irish movement, the subsequent rebellion became a spontaneous and disorganised revolt. The rebels lacked any central direction once they rose against the local garrisons, with any further action being determined by local leaders who were not privy to any grand strategy proposed by the imprisoned rebel executive. This ensured that many rebels only rose after hearing of similar actions occurring elsewhere, while others quickly surrendered once it became clear the rebellion would fail.[47] The support that the uprising did

---

(Dublin: Four Courts Press, 1996), p.121.
41   Thomas Bartlett, 'Miles Byrne: United Irishman, Irish Exile and Beau Sabreur', p.122.
42   T.W. Moody & W.E. Vaughan, *A New History of Ireland: Vol.4 – Eighteenth Century Ireland, 1691-1800* (Oxford: Clarendon Press, 1986), p.357.
43   Pakenham, *The Year of Liberty*, pp.164–167.
44   Pakenham, *The Year of Liberty*, pp.164–167.
45   Pakenham, *The Year of Liberty*, pp.164–167.
46   Hewitt (ed.), *Eye-Witnesses to Ireland in Revolt*, p.69.
47   Pakenham, *The Year of Liberty*, p.217.

gain was fuelled more by resentment than politics. In Wexford the rebel leadership was comprised of disaffected Protestant and Catholic landed gentry, including at least one retired British Army officer, Captain Matthew Keogh, who were suffering from an economic downturn due to poor grain prices and resented the indifference of the government towards their plight. The peasantry gave their support due to resentment of the oppressive nature of the government counter-insurgent operations rather than from any desire for shared political power, with leadership provided at parish level by local Catholic priests, such as Fathers John and Michael Murphy and Philip Roche.[48] Thomas Cloney, a young Wexford farmer who joined the rebels at Vinegar Hill only took up the cause as he felt he had no alternative due to coercion from the insurgents and tactics of the government:

> The innocent and the guilty were alike driven into acts of unwilling hostility to the existing government; but there was no alternative; every preceding day saw the instruments of torture filling the yawning sepulchres with the victims of suspicion or malice; as a partial resistance could never tend to mitigate the cruelty of their tormentors, I saw no second course for me, or indeed for any Catholic in my part of the country, to pursue.[49]

By holding the initiative, the United Irish were able to initially defeat the inadequate government forces in Wexford and take control of the county. The rebellion erupted in Wexford on the evening of 26 May when a party of insurgents led by a local parish priest, Father John Murphy, intercepted a patrol of the Camolin yeomanry near the village of the Harrow, near Ferns. An attempt to disarm the mob by a Lieutenant Bookey, the officer-in-command of the patrol, led to him and another member of the local gentry attached to the corps being killed.[50] This incident ignited rebellion in the county, with the yeomanry seeking revenge by indiscriminately killing suspects and burning houses in the area, while thousands of the peasantry joined the insurgents in attacking isolated yeoman garrisons and the homes of Protestant magistrates, who were seen as agents of the government and gentry, in an effort to gain firearms. With the yeomanry mainly based in various towns, the United Irish were able to effectively mobilise in the countryside unhindered.[51] News of a large force of insurgents having gathered at Oulart Hill, 15 miles north of Wexford town prompted Lieutenant Colonel Richard Foote of the North Cork Militia to march against them on 27 May. A force of 109 militiamen and 19 mounted yeomen met the estimated 500 rebels who had strategically placed themselves at the top of the hill.[52] At this time, a Major Lombard of the militia instigated an uphill charge on the rebel position without the permission of Foote, who had wisely determined not to attack due to the

---

48 Pakenham, *The Year of Liberty*, p.217.
49 Hewitt, *Eye-Witnesses to Ireland in Revolt*, p.69.
50 Pakenham, *The Year of Liberty*, pp.164–167.
51 Blackstock, *An Ascendancy Army*, p.149.
52 Pakenham, *The Year of Liberty*, p.175.

superior numbers of the insurgents and the likelihood of being outflanked.[53] As a result, after firing their muskets, the inexperienced and outnumbered government force was indeed outflanked and annihilated, with only Foote and three soldiers managing to escape with their lives.[54] Victory in this skirmish was crucial to the rebel cause in that it not only gave the insurgents confidence in facing government troops, but led to thousands more joining the revolt.

It was the rapid rise of the disaffected populace, coupled with the shock of defeat, that dramatically reduced the morale of the government forces in the county. The superior number of rebels eventually forced the inadequate and isolated militia and yeomanry garrisons to retreat from Ferns, Gorey and Enniscorthy where they had concentrated. On 28 May Father Murphy led 6,000 rebels in an attack on the 300-man garrison at Enniscorthy, which included 80 North Cork militiamen and over 200 yeomen from three local corps.[55] And although the garrison was able to successfully withdraw from the town, it was at the cost of 74 men killed and 17 wounded.[56] Confusion and lack of experience within the officer corps of the local government forces initially aided the rebel cause.

With most of the county under rebel control, Wexford town was besieged. At this time the garrison was approximately 1,000 strong which included the remnants of the North Cork Militia, various yeomanry corps, as well as 200 soldiers of the Donegal regiment that had marched to the town from their post at Duncannon Fort. The officer now commanding in the town was Lieutenant Colonel Richard Maxwell of the Donegal Militia who had called for more reinforcements. A force comprising the Meath Militia, a severely under strength battalion of the 13th Foot and several pieces of artillery, had reached Taghmon about 12 miles west of Wexford town on 30 May. However, the advance guard of the column, including the artillery, was ambushed, and annihilated at Three Rocks. The commander of the main column, Major General William Fawcett laid the blame on a Captain Adams, a company officer of the Meath Militia: 'Owing to extreme ignorance, and a total inexperience of any service or his duty as an officer, instead of waiting to receive any orders from me, proceeded. Adams, with no precaution taken, or weapons loaded, was ambushed and cut to pieces.'[57] This proved disastrous for the relief of Wexford in that Fawcett then chose to retreat due to the overwhelming number of rebels, further reducing the morale of the besieged garrison. An English–born resident of Wexford, Charles Jackson wrote of what he witnessed at the time:

> On Wednesday, May 30, in the morning, the troops (the Donegal and [North] Cork Militia, nearly six hundred in all), went out to meet the rebels, who were

---

53 Pakenham, *The Year of Liberty*, p.175.
54 Nelson, *The Irish Militia*, p.187.
55 Pakenham, *The Year of Liberty*, p.178.
56 Nelson, *The Irish Militia*, pp.188–189.
57 PRONI: MIC 67/43: Lake–Hewitt Correspondence, Major General Fawcett to Lieutenant General Lake, quoted in Nelson, *The Irish Militia*, p.190.

now supposed to be fifteen thousand strong. About three miles from Wexford, at a place called Three Rocks, there was some firing, when the militia, finding them so powerful from numbers, and in possession of the artillery taken the day before, retreated to the town… A council was called, and it was resolved, that it was impossible to defend the town, as the greatest part of the Catholics who had taken up arms [to defend the town] had deserted. The proportion of the Catholic inhabitants of Wexford I believe to have been about three to one Protestant, but only bout two hundred had taken up arms; on the remainder, however, no dependence could be placed…In the meantime, the troops, accompanied by all the unmarried yeoman, effected their escape to Duncannon Fort, about twenty-three miles off.[58]

As to be expected, at this time the United Irish had no formal uniform, but many did openly display their allegiance to the cause through numerous adornments. Jackson recorded that at the capture of Wexford by the rebels:

The whole of the rebels wore white bands around their hats. Some of a higher order had the Irish harp drawn in gold leaf on a green ground, encircled with the words '*Erin ga braugh!*', signifying 'Ireland for ever!' Others, of a more desperate turn, had a broad green ribbon bound entirely round their hats, with 'Liberty and Equality' in large letters in the front.[59]

The loss of so many of their comrades at Oulart Hill and Enniscorthy had caused a collapse in morale of the North Cork Militia, and it was the regiment's perceived unreliability and reduction to only 273 rank and file that led to its evacuation of Wexford town on 30 May.[60] Once the town was abandoned by the militia, the United Irish occupied it and proclaimed the creation of the Republic of Wexford. In effect, mass support for the rebellion ensured that the United Irish quickly gained control of the whole county, with the government forces now having to prevent the rebellion from spreading.

A similar incident to that at Three Rocks occurred at Tubberneering, near Ballymore, on 4 June where a column of militia, commanded by the inexperienced Lieutenant Colonel Lambert Walpole and sent from Dublin to reinforce Major General William Loftus in his advance from Arklow into Wexford, was ambushed and routed. Walpole had been a staff officer more concerned with fame and glory, who had not only disregarded superior orders by taking an alternative route but had also failed to place advance guards and flankers on the march.[61] This event proved crucial in that it caused panic amongst the government force commanded by Loftus that had gathered at Gorey for an advance into the rebel held county. Confusion then led to the whole force abandoning Gorey to the insurgents and a general retreat of government troops through Arklow to Wicklow.[62] These incidents allowed

---

58   Hewitt, *Eye–Witnesses to Ireland in Revolt*, pp.72–72.
59   Hewitt, *Eye–Witnesses to Ireland in Revolt*, p.73.
60   Nelson, *The Irish Militia*, p.187.
61   Myers & McKnight, *Correspondence of Charles, First Marquis Cornwallis*, p.373.
62   Nelson, *The Irish Militia*, p.195.

REBELLION, INVASION AND OCCUPATION

time for the United Irish to form their rapidly increasing army of disaffected civilians into three sizable columns, with the intention of marching into neighbouring counties to spread revolution. The suffering of such reverses also provided the Ascendancy with evidence to support their questioning of the competence of the militia.

However, once Dublin Castle had recovered from the initial shock of the uprising, the military hierarchy in Ireland effectively contained and extinguished the rebellion. The government reaction to the revolt revolved around three priorities: firstly, the protection of Dublin, then the defeat of the rebels in Kildare and Meath, and finally the recapture of Wexford.[63] Dublin had remained secure from the outset of the uprising and by 1 June the army had regained the initiative in the counties surrounding Wexford. By 28 May many of the rebels in Kildare had seen the futility of further resistance with 3,000 surrendering to Lieutenant General Sir Ralph Dundas at Knockallan Hill, while Duff had relieved the beleaguered garrison in Kildare town on the same day. On 1 June the Crown forces prevented the rebellion from spreading into Carlow by defeating a large insurgent army that had launched an attack on the garrison at Newtownbarry.

'Portrait of an Irish Chief' by James Gillray. (Anne S.K. Brown Military Collection)

The Battle of New Ross

The Battle of New Ross on 5 June 1798 proved pivotal in preventing the rebellion spreading from Wexford, and with the successful defence of the town by the Crown troops the military initiative swung against the Irish republicans The United Irish leader, Bagenel Harvey, was a Protestant landlord and United Irishman who lived at Bargy Castle in the south of Co. Wexford. He had no military experience, no burning revolutionary zeal and, coming from the middling classes, had little understanding of the plight of the Catholic peasantry.[64] It was Harvey's decision to allow a two-day delay in camping at Carrickbyrne Hill while marching on New Ross that gave Major General Henry Johnson, commander of

---

63 Daniel Gahan, 'The Military Planning of the 1798 Rebellion in Wexford', in Daire Keogh & Nicholas Furlong (eds), *The Mighty Wave: The 1798 Rebellion in Wexford*, p.101.
64 Pakenham, *The Year of Liberty*, p.221.

THE 1798 REBELLION

Battle of New Ross, 5 June 1798. The militia uniforms portrayed in this caricature were only introduced after 1800. (New York Public Library)

the government forces in the town, much needed time to plan and mount his defence.

New Ross lies on the River Barrow, which flows north to south. At the time the main part of the town lay on the east bank of the river with the small suburb of Rosbercon on the west bank, with a wooden bridge connecting the two. Both sides of the town were built on steep slopes that led down to the river. The streets were narrow and winding which proved ideal for defence with cannon; otherwise, they proved equally difficult for attack and defence.[65]

Prior to 3 June New Ross had been virtually undefended, with only the troops available for its defence being the 150-strong Ross Yeomanry commanded by the local landlord, Charles Tottenham. He had attempted to put the town in a state of defence hoping to be reinforced before any rebel attack. This occurred on 3 June when Johnson, accompanied by Major General Charles Eustace, arrived with a force consisting of a detachment of the 4th Light Infantry (a composite battalion of Irish Militia light companies from various regiments), the Clare, Donegal, and Meath militia regiments, along with small elements of artillery and regular cavalry consisting of troops from the 4th and 5th Dragoons. Johnson was an Irishman who had led the 17th Foot during the American War of Independence and Cornwallis had a

---

65   Pakenham, *The Year of Liberty*, p.221.

low opinion of him due to his being surprised and captured at Stony Point, New York.[66]

Despite receiving intelligence that indicated that the rebel force advancing towards him was estimated as being at least 20 times greater than the garrison of 1,400 troops available to him, and despite the difficulties he faced mounting the defence of the town, Johnson remained confident that with disciplined troops supported by artillery and who would be properly led, that he would defeat the rebels, no matter how large their numbers.[67] Musgrave estimated the rebel force to be up to 30,000, but this is regarded as an exaggeration and it is generally accepted a figure of 10–15,000 is more likely.[68]

On 4 June Johnson had been reinforced by a contingent of the Dublin militia, commanded by Lord Mountjoy, along with several artillery pieces, giving a total of six cannon for the defence.[69] He had also predicted the main rebel attack on the walled town would be made from the east on the Three Bullet Gate, which was directly below the insurgents' camp on Corbet Hill overlooking the town. To this end he set his forward position consisting of a flank battalion of regular and militia infantry, supported by two cannons, outside the Three Bullet Gate. He then established a similar second defensive position outside the Bishop's Gate, while he placed the rest of the infantry and artillery around a series of strongpoints within the town itself, as well as at the wooden bridge across the river Barrow.[70] The Clare regiment was placed in defence of Irishtown, the Dublin County regiment defended the Three Bullet Gate, and either the Donegal or Meath battalions were placed at the Priory Gate. It is possible that elements of the Light Infantry battalion were scattered in support of these defensive positions based on the reported casualty returns after the battle. The return showed that the light companies of the Antrim, North Mayo, Kilkenny, Queen's County and Clare Militias, that made up the 4th Light Battalion, had been heavily engaged, suffering 65 casualties between them.[71] Getting a totally accurate account of the dispositions of the defending units is difficult as no participants have left a record of the overall description of the battle.

The rebel attack was launched at dawn on the morning of Tuesday 5 June after one of Harvey's mounted aides had been shot and killed a few minutes earlier when he approached the position with a note urging the garrison to surrender or face destruction.[72] The attack comprised of three separate rebel columns; one column led by John Boxwell attacked the Priory (south) Gate near the river, a second attacked the adjacent Three Bullet Gate at the south east of the town, while a third led by John Colclough assaulted the Market Gate at the north east area of the town's defensive wall. It was estimated that several thousand rebels armed with muskets, blunderbusses and pikes attacked the Crown troops dug in at the Three Bullet Gate where Johnson

---

66 Nelson, *The Irish Militia*, p.197.
67 Pakenham, *The Year of Liberty*, pp.222–225.
68 Musgrave, *Rebellions*, p.384.
69 Pakenham, *The Year of Liberty*, pp.222–225.
70 Pakenham, *The Year of Liberty*, pp.222–225.
71 Nelson, *The Irish Militia*, p.199.
72 Pakenham, *The Year of Liberty*, pp.225–226.

A private of the Downshire Regiment of Militia, 1793. This was the standard uniform worn by the Irish militia from 1793 until 1800. The only distinction between regiments was the facing colour on the collars, cuffs and turnbacks. (Original artwork by Christa Hook (www.christahook.co.uk) © Helion & Co.)

16th Light Dragoons, 1784. This provides an example of the standard British regular light cavalry uniform worn during the Revolutionary and early Napoleonic period. The Irish yeomanry replicated this but tended to wear red jackets instead. (Anne S.K. Brown Military Collection)

Officer, 6th Dragoons, 1800. This is the standard uniform of regular British cavalry regiments in the 1790s. (Anne S.K. Brown Military Collection)

'Henry Munro chief of the Irish rebels', by Thomas Rowlandson. (Anne S.K. Brown Military Collection)

Trooper of the 1st Regiment Fencible Cavalry (Light Dragoons), 1798. The unit was known as Roden's Fox Hunters and was present at Castlebar. (Anne S.K. Brown Military Collection)

This image shows the typical uniform of French infantry during the Revolutionary period. (Anne S.K. Brown Military Collection)

'The Scots Guards', by Richard Simkin. This image is an example of the uniform worn by the Foot Guards in Ireland in 1798. (Anne S.K. Brown Military Collection)

Watercolour by Johann Heinrich Ramberg showing a variety of British uniforms of the 1790s, from the East India Company, to Highlanders, the Guards, the Royal Navy and more. (Anne S.K. Brown Military Collection)

Another watercolour by Johann Heinrich Ramberg showing a further selection of 1790s British uniforms. (Anne S.K. Brown Military Collection)

Officer of the 2nd (Queen's Royal) Regiment of Foot, 1807. This image provides an example of the standard regular and militia officers dress from the period. (Anne S.K. Brown Military Collection)

personally directed the position. The defence included trenches outside the gate manned by soldiers from the Light Battalion. However, by around 7:00 a.m. the thin defensive line broke due to the overwhelming numbers and tenacity of the insurgents, forcing the Crown troops to retreat into the town, followed by hundreds of rebels who swarmed through the gate. The rebels attacking the Priory and Market Gates had been held in check by the defenders and it was only the rebel success at the Three Bullet Gate that saw the insurgents enter the town. The confusion that occurred when the United Irish gained entry was explained by Thomas Cloney, who was given command of 500 rebels attacking the gate:

> … it was resolved to send the intrepid Colonel John Kelly forward with five hundred men, to drive in the out-posts of the King's troops, who had occupied the fields and ditches between our camp and the town … Colonel Kelly had now advanced with five hundred men of his battalion of Bantry men, and I had orders …to advance with five hundred men of my battalion of Bantry me to support him. The men of the barony of Bantry, which is by far the largest in the county of Wexford, were divided into two battalions, each consisting perhaps of about fifteen hundred men…To such a young hero as Kelly … he but too successfully performed his duty, for having drove his opponents in full flight before him, the enthusiasm of the main body could no longer be restrained; they all poured down in and in the same direction, without order or control … Lord Mountjoy, who had advanced in front of his regiment, the County of Dublin Militia, to remonstrate with the people, fell by a rash hand … Having advanced near the Three Bullet Gate, parties of the King's troops still retained their positions at both sides of the road, and we were exposed to cross fire from both, while Colonel Kelly and his men were endeavouring to force an entrance to the town … In about half-an-hour the King's troops were dislodged from the fields, and after an obstinate resistance, driven back from the Gate.[73]

It appears that Harvey, who did not personally lead the attack and had initially remained behind in the camp, was surprised by the rebel success as he had only ordered that the garrison outposts be driven in, with strict orders not for the town itself to be attacked. Once in the town, the rebels broke into two separate columns; with one capturing the lightly defended barracks, along with the muskets and ammunition stored within the building, while a second column attacked the garrison position at the Main Guard next to the courthouse. This defence consisted of about 15 men of the Donegal militia, commanded by a Sergeant Hamilton, manning a pair of swivel guns. As the rebels approached the position several cannons were wheeled in to bolster the defence, and canister was then used to blunt the rebel attack.[74] Another defensive position that stopped the progress of the rebels was at the churchyard where Captain Benjamin Bloomfield of the Royal Artillery made use of several cannons to good effect. This caused a large number of casualties among the insurgents, and they began retreating back along the

---

73 Hewitt, *Eye-Witnesses to Ireland in Revolt*, pp.80–81.
74 Pakenham, *The Year of Liberty*, pp.230–231.

street, followed by the government troops. At this point there was much hand-to-hand fighting in the streets of the town, with the rebels slowly being pushed back towards the town gate.[75] Johnson had shown great initiative in rallying the troops from across the river and led a counterattack along the narrow streets which the rebels were unable to withstand.

The confused nature of the battle had a detrimental effect on both sides. The repulse of the rebel attacks on the Priory and Market Gates led to many insurgents panicking and fleeing, while others joined the attack on the town through the Three Bullet Gate only to find themselves confronted by their compatriots fleeing through the narrow streets back to the gate to escape Johnson's counterattack. It was around this time that Pakenham argues that Johnson made a fatal blunder by thinking that all the rebels had lost their fighting spirit after seeing them fleeing back through the gate and away from the town. The small number of cavalry available to Johnson – about 50 troopers of the Midlothian Fencibles Cavalry and around the same number of the 4th and 5th Dragoons – had been held in reserve on the quayside. They were ordered to move and support Johnson's counterattack to recapture the Three Bullet Gate. The regular dragoons rode through the gate attempting to attack the fleeing rebels in the open. However, the United Irishmen turned on their pursuers with their pikes and dispatched the commanding officer of the dragoons and 28 of his men.[76]

The victory over the cavalry gave the United Irishmen a renewed vigour to their morale and they once again charged back through the Three Bullet Gate into the town. It was now the turn of the Crown troops to flee through the town, with many escaping across the bridge to safety. At this stage only the Main Guard and a strong point manned by the Clare militia at the Market Gate, along with a small contingent under Johnson's direct command positioned between the Three Bullet Gate and eastern wall were still holding out in the town. The rebels poured through the town, setting light to many buildings as they progressed towards the river, but at the point of success their attack lost momentum. Dispersed into small groups by the winding streets and becoming exhausted from hours of intense hand-to-hand fighting leading to heavy casualties, the rebels lacked fresh reserves to take advantage of their success, and many began plundering buildings. They were also lacking in effective leadership; Harvey had remained at the Three Bullet Gate and there was no one to order the burning of the wooden bridge to prevent another counterattack from Crown troops across the river.

In the end it was the courageous leadership of Johnson that led to the government troops recapturing the town. Seeing his troops fleeing across the bridge he stopped the rout by crossing over the river and appealing to his men's patriotism not to desert their countrymen still defending the town. This action appears to have rallied the troops and inspired them, with the Dublin militia in the vanguard, to follow him back across the bridge in a second counter-attack. The rebels lacked the experience to effectively use the cannon they had captured, and the battle was reduced to bitter street

---

75   Pakenham, *The Year of Liberty*, pp.228–231.
76   Pakenham, *The Year of Liberty*, pp.228–231.

THE 1798 REBELLION

fighting. An unknown artillery officer who fought in the town wrote of what he saw and experienced:

> Major Vesey, of the Dublin County [Militia], the next in command to Lord Mountjoy, again led his men over the bridge, exhorting them to revenge for the loss of their colonel. The whole brigade ... being led by General Johnson – as brave a commander as ever drew sword – were determined to retake the town, to conquer or to die. Again, we opened a tremendous fire on the rebels, which was as fiercely returned. We retook the cannon which had been taken from the King's forces in a former engagement and turned them on the enemy. The gun I had the honour to command being called to the main-guard, shocking was it to see the dreadful carnage that was there; it continued for half an hour obstinate and bloody: the thundering of the cannon shook the town, the very windows were shivered in pieces with the dreadful concussion. I believe six hundred rebels lay dead in the Main Street; they would often come within a few yards of the guns. One fellow ran up, and taking off his hat and wig, thrust them up the cannon's mouth the length of his arm, calling to the rest, 'Blood-an-'ounds, my boys, come and take her now, she's stopt, she's stopt!' The action was doubtful and bloody from four in the morning to four in the evening, when they began to give way in all quarters, and shortly after fled in every direction.[77]

The courage and zeal of the United Irishmen was not enough to defeat the discipline and military training of the militia and regular troops, and by 4:00 p.m. the rebels had been driven back to the Three Bullet Gate. By 6:00 p.m. most of majority of the surviving rebels were exhausted and had retreated back to their camp or dispersed into the countryside.[78] Thousands of insurgents lost heart in the revolt and simply returned to the homes, while many others flooded back to Wexford town with exaggerated stories of defeat.

Victory proved costly for the government with the death of Lord Mountjoy, commander of the Dublin Militia, along with 86 soldiers killed, 58 wounded and five officers and 76 men reported missing.[79] The loss to the rebels was immense, with one eye witness stating that 62 cart-loads of bodies were dumped into the local river, in addition to 3,400 that were buried in a mass grave.[80] However, this may have been an exaggeration, with James Alexander, a prominent loyalist who was tasked with arranging the disposal of the bodies estimating a total of 2,600 deceased rebels, including 1,010 bodies removed from within the town streets. The battle had also been costly to the United Irish in loss of *materiel,* with a large quantity of muskets and pikes, as well as 19 field guns, being left behind.[81] Although not routed, the southern United Irish army of Wexford withdrew back towards Wexford

---

77   Hewitt, *Eye–Witnesses to Ireland in Revolt*, p.85.
78   Pakenham, *The Year of Liberty*, pp.228–231.
79   *Faulkner's Journal*, 9 June 1798, quoted in Nelson, *The Irish Militia*, p.200.
80   Pakenham, *The Year of Liberty*, p.328.
81   BL: Add MSS 33/105/400, Alexander to Pelham, 10 June 1798, quoted in Pakenham, *The Year of Liberty*, p.328.

town, where under the new leadership of Father Philip Roche, its main focus was now on the defence of the republic capital and raiding operations.

The importance of the successful defence of New Ross cannot be overestimated when considering the failure of the United Irish rebellion spreading from Wexford. Although certain elements of the militia wavered under the vastly superior numbers of the attacking rebels, they were not defeated and had shown some considerable mettle when well led. In fact, most of the fighting had been conducted by the Irish militia, together with the artillery, while the cavalry proved ineffective, and the yeomanry appear not to have been engaged. The militia had proven itself by fighting with spirit, while the rebels had suffered a traumatic defeat, losing valuable leaders, weapons, and men. The defeat also ensured that the United Irishmen of Kilkenny chose not to join the rebellion, with the military initiative in western Wexford now in favour of the Crown forces.

The Rising in Ulster

Two days after the battle of New Ross in the south, rebellion broke out in Ulster in the north. In comparison to the rising in Wexford, the rebellion in Ulster failed to gain sufficient popular support and was quickly extinguished. The dragooning of the province by government forces in 1797 and early 1798 ensured that there was little chance of any such rebellion succeeding. The counter-terror activities may have inspired some to take up arms against the government, but the fear of reprisals also persuaded many to remain at home when the uprising broke out in Antrim on 7 June. There was dissention within the United Irish leadership in Ulster over the limited chance of success of any uprising without military support from the French, which ensured confusion and lukewarm responses to the call-to-arms.[82] Active popular support for the rebellion was restricted to isolated disaffected locations within counties Antrim and Down, where the traditional democratic philosophies of the dominant, but politically repressed, Presbyterian population led to support for a revolution. Such fractions within the United Irish movement ensured that the rebel forces were easily contained and defeated.

In contrast to the military situation in Wexford, the Irish army was in a stronger position to deal with any rebellion in Ulster in 1798. The province had been the birthplace of the United Irish movement and it was here that the government expected open rebellion to occur. From the time that the militant republican organisation had been outlawed in 1795, Dublin Castle had been generally supportive of the counter-revolutionary measures taken by the army in the north of the kingdom, although the severity of such steps was questioned at times. The policy of disarming Ulster had been in place from March 1797 when Lieutenant General Lake had launched a series of search and seizure operations that had critically weakened the military effectiveness of the insurgents through arrests and seizure of weapons. This

---

82 Curtain, *The United Irishmen*, pp.65–66.

THE 1798 REBELLION

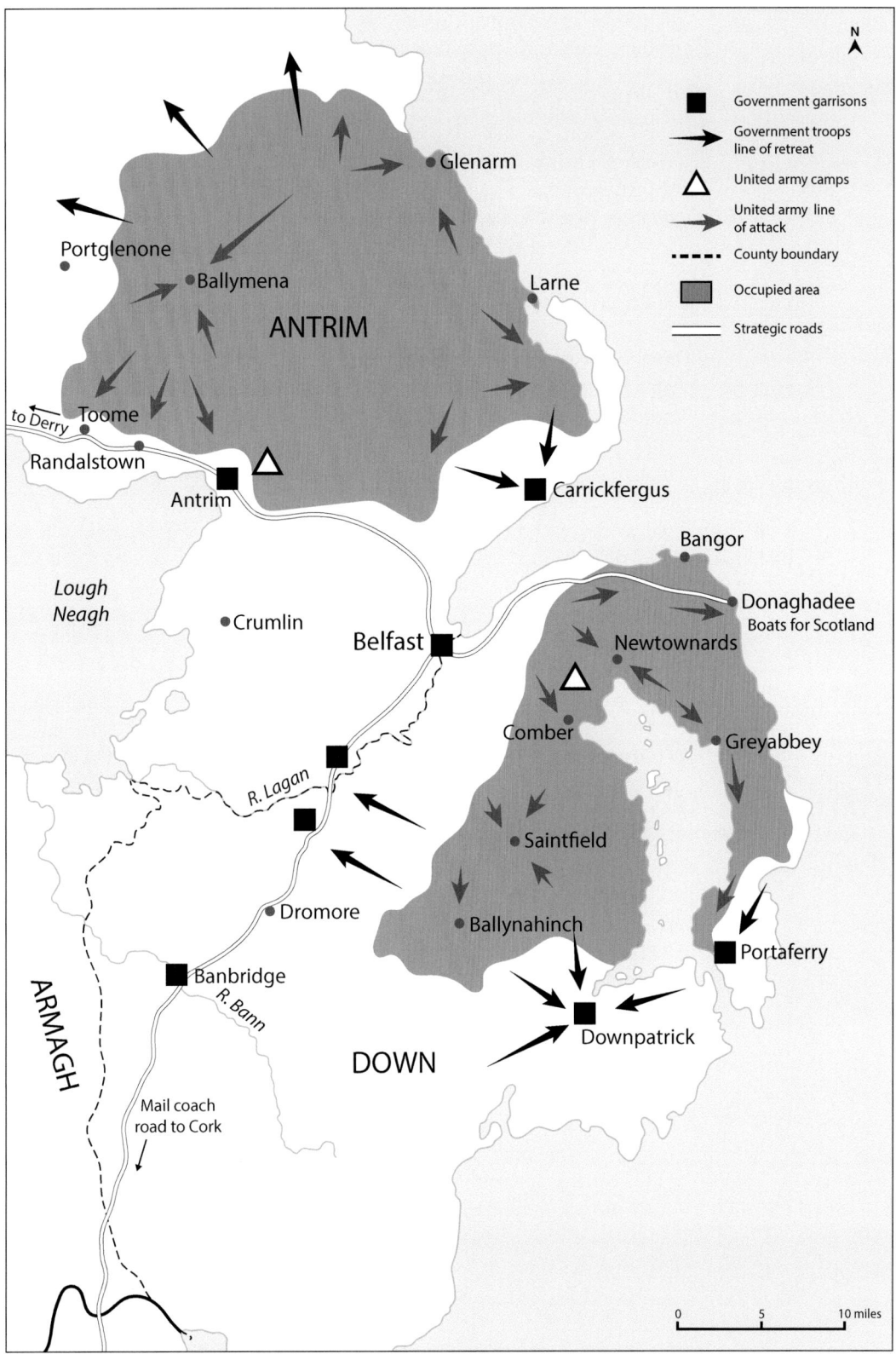

Rebellion in Ulster, June 1798 (Source: Pakenham, *The Year of Liberty*, revised edition, abridged by Toby Buchan, p.116)

seriously disrupted the United Irish executive in Ulster, where a 'period of sullen quiescence' within the revolutionary movement remained until the uprising in Antrim and Down the following year.[83] The fear of an uprising in Ulster also ensured that there was a concentration of troops to counter such action, as well as a strategic plan to contain any rebellion. Major General George Nugent, an experienced and competent officer, commanded the government forces in the north. In June 1798 he had at his disposal approximately 9,000 soldiers, which were mostly Irish militia and British fencibles, along with 5,000 yeomen.[84] He had formulated a sound strategy of placing company and troop-sized garrisons of infantry and yeomanry in disaffected locations whilst maintaining a substantial reserve at Blaris Camp, near Belfast. Nugent had also fostered an effective network of informants and spies to provide essential intelligence to counter any insurgent moves. This ensured that when the rebellion did erupt the government forces could quickly regain the military initiative.

The rebellion in Ulster was also easily defeated due to confusion and lack of co-ordination within the United Irish leadership. The leadership of the Ulster insurgents was in disarray due to the number of arrests carried out by the government troops. Many of those who had escaped such action were disillusioned by the absence of any French military support and showed little enthusiasm for rebelling, with some even becoming informants for the Crown. James Hope, a northern United Irishman, wrote after the uprising:

> The organisation of the north being thus deranged, the colonels flinched, and the chief of the Antrim men [Robert Simms] not appearing, the duty fell on Henry J. McCracken; he sent fighting orders to the colonels of Antrim, three of whom sent the identical orders to General Nugent, and the messenger he sent to [County] Down proving unfaithful, the people of Down had no correct knowledge of affairs in Antrim, until they heard of the battle of 7 June.[85]

This led to Henry Joy McCracken assuming the responsibility of commander-in-chief of the rebel forces in Antrim. The rebellion in Wexford had inspired him to launch simultaneous attacks on Antrim and Randalstown, County Antrim, on 7 June in an attempt to seize the local magistrates who were meeting in Antrim on that date. He mistakenly assumed similar attacks would be conducted by United Irishmen in County Down on the same day. However, poor communications within the organisation ensured that the risings in Antrim and Down became uncoordinated isolated rebellions that were defeated in turn. Had McCracken and Henry Munro, leader of the Down rebellion, been able to conspire to simultaneously launch their attacks, they may have had more success by forcing Nugent to fight on two fronts. However, this was not the case, with the uprising in Down erupting on 9 June at a time when the rebellion in Antrim was effectively spent.

---

83 R.G. Morton, 'Plans for Ulster Defence, 1795-1797', *The Irish Sword*, vol.2 (1956), pp.270-274.
84 Morton, 'Plans for Ulster Defence, 1795-1797', p.272.
85 Hewitt, *Eye–Witnesses to Ireland in Revolt*, p.99.

The rebels found little success in Ulster. The insurgents were divided, even before the attack on Antrim town was carried out, due to the defection of 5,000 Catholic Defenders who had previously promised to rise. Many other contingents failed to arrive at the rendezvous point arranged by McCracken, but he eventually gathered a force of 6,000. However, by the time he launched his attack on the small garrison of the town of Antrim around 2:00 p.m., unbeknown to him, a reinforcing column of government troops were also entering the town. Prior to the rising Major General Nugent had received a copy of McCracken's orders from a defecting United Irish colonel by the name of Magin.[86] This ensured that he could dispatch a sizable force to locate and destroy the main rebel army, as well as relieve the smaller garrisons that had been targeted in McCracken's orders. The rebels had some success with the brief occupation of Randalstown and Ballymena, but their attacks on Larne and Antrim was repulsed due to determined defence by the small garrisons, allowing time for relief columns to arrive.

The clash at Antrim was a confused bloody affair, typical of street fighting, which ultimately led to panic amongst the rebels and their retreat from the town, leaving 300 dead.[87] The government garrison comprised 70 light dragoons, 50 yeoman infantry and about 30 armed loyalist civilian volunteers, with this force having occupied two strongpoints; the market house and Lord Massereene's castle.[88] When McCracken launched his attack on Antrim he had no thought of providing any defensive positions against the possibility of approaching government reinforcements. At the time that he led his force of around 6,000 insurgents to storm the town from the east, a relief force of government troops from Blaris camp galloped into the town from the opposite direction. This force consisted of 150 of the 22nd Light Dragoons, supported by two small curricle light artillery pieces. The cavalry made the mistake of charging directly at the rebel column surging up the main street which resulted in many dragoons being brought down by pikemen, leading to about a third of the force being killed or wounded. The cavalry quickly retreated and left the artillery behind.

The United Irish now had the initiative, but this was short lived. Thirty minutes later the main reinforcements arrived from Belfast, which consisted of more dragoons, 250 militia infantry and two 5-inch howitzers. Before advancing on the rebels the town was bombarded for half an hour, causing confusion and heavy casualties among the United Irish. A small group defending the churchyard put a determined fight for a short time, but the rest of McCracken's force fled. The rebels lost about 300 casualties, almost all killed; either in the fighting itself or in the dispatch of the wounded and prisoners that followed the Crown victory. The casualties for the Crown and Loyalists were much lighter; around 60 killed or wounded.[89] Although the rebels had succeeded in seizing control of most of the county, except for

---

86   A.T.Q. Stewart, *The Summer Soldiers: The 1798 Rebellion in Antrim and Down* (Belfast: The Blackstaff Press, 1995), p.89.
87   Pakenham, *The Year of Liberty*, pp.251–254.
88   Pakenham, *The Year of Liberty*, p.252.
89   Pakenham, *The Year of Liberty*, p.254.

Carrickfergus and Belfast, the defeat at Antrim had broken the confidence of the insurgents. Wary of possible risings in Belfast and Down, Nugent then successfully negotiated the surrender of rebel arms by offering a general amnesty.

The defeat of the rebels in County Down effectively extinguished the rebellion in the north. On 9 June a mixed force of York Fencibles and local yeomanry were surprised by a large rebel force that had gathered at Saintfield, 10 miles east of Belfast. This force was led by Henry Munro, a young draper from Lisburn with no military experience, who had been chosen to lead the United Irish in the absence of those leaders who had been arrested or chose not to join the rebellion. After defeating the government troops, Munro marched his army of 7,000 rebels to the important market town of Ballynahinch where they encamped in a wooded park, 'Montalto,' in the demesne of the local magnate, Lord Moira. The rebel army then largely remained inactive, with indecision amongst the inexperienced leadership. At this time the United Irish controlled all the north-east area of County Down and had established camps at Ballynahinch, Saintfield, Newtownards and Kilgobbin – along with numerous small garrisons in other places. However, the rebels were no position to actively seek an engagement with the Crown forces; like the rebels in Wexford, only a few were armed with muskets or pistols, and ammunition was in short supply, while the rest had pikes, old swords, or pitchforks.[90]

The initiative now belonged to the Crown forces. By 12 June Nugent had advanced on Ballynahinch from Belfast with a force of 1,500 men, which included the Monaghan Militia, part of the 22nd Dragoons, a detachment of artillery and 600 fencibles.[91] The rebels had stationed their front line on Windmill Hill on the Saintfield side of the town, but they were easily dislodged from this position by an attack by the Argyll Fencibles. This was followed by an artillery barrage that affected the morale of the rebels, some of whom chose to sneak off in the night rather than face fighting in the coming battle.[92]

The following morning, 13 June, Munro led the rebel attack against Nugent's force that held the centre of the town. He was aware his strength lay in the massed companies of pikemen and that they would be exposed to heavy casualties by the Government artillery if they remained on the open hillside of their current position. He thought the best chance of success for the United Irish would be to attack the Government held town where the effect of the artillery would be less and where the use of pikes and the superior number of rebels could lead to victory. This initially led to some success, with the defending militia unit being driven back, losing 30 casualties. However, this was short lived by a reverse on the rebel flank where the Argyll Fencibles, supported by artillery, attacked the encampment at Montalto. A young

---

90 Pakenham, *The Year of Liberty*, p.260.
91 NAI: 620/33/129: Rebellion Papers, Nugent to Lake, 13 June 1798, quoted in Nelson, *The Irish Militia*, p.207.
92 Pakenham, *The Year of Liberty*, pp.262–264.

United Irishmen who escaped the Government reprisals after the uprising, wrote of his experience during the battle:

> When we mustered on a hill south-west of the town our number was much augmented that I though it impossible that we could be conquered. But, alas! On the approach of the enemy, all those thoughts vanished. The firing of their cannon no sooner commenced than our men fled in thousands, and when night came on we had not more than a third of our force remaining. Few men were killed on Tuesday evening; but few minds were unclouded by fear. We were reduced to a handful, ill appointed, and undisciplined, exposed to attack of a regular body of military, well-armed, and led by experienced officers … We received orders from Munroe, our general, to go foremost into the town, but we refused. Three parties were then sent before us, but before reaching the town they all found means to flinch, and we were obliged to go up in the face of a party of the Monaghan Militia, who did not fail to salute us with a brisk fire. We ran like bloodhounds, and the Monaghans fled into the town, where they kept up a kind of broken fire, which we returned, although only about twenty of us were armed with muskets. We obliged them to take shelter in the houses twice, but when we attempted to pursue our victory, a cannon which raked the street with grapeshot compelled us to retire. Our ammunition being spent, and the army receiving fresh supplies, we at last gave way, the 22nd Light Dragoons pursuing us, and killing all they could overtake.[93]

There were numerous rebel counter attacks, but they were repeatedly repulsed, suffering heavily from the artillery, with one eyewitness describing the rebels as being 'blown from the mouth of the cannon like chaff.'[94] Nugent's official report to Lake give a clear picture of how the rebels were defeated:

> Accordingly about 3 o'clock in the morning having previously occupied two hills on the right and left of the town to prevent the rebels from having any other choice than the mountains in their rear for their retreat I sent Lt. Col. Stewart to post himself with part of the Argyll Fencibles and some yeomanry, as well as a detachment of the 22nd Lt. Dragoons, a situation where he could enfilade the rebel line; whilst Col. Leslie and part of the Monaghan Militia, some cavalry and the Yeoman infantry should attack them on the flank … The rebels poured down with impetuosity upon Col. Leslie's detachment and even jumped into the road from the Earl of Moira's demesne to endeavour to take one of his guns but were repulsed with slaughter. They attacked Lt. Col. Stewart's detachment with the same activity but he repulsed them also and the fire from his howitzer obliged them to fly in all directions.[95]

---

93   Hewitt, *Witnesses to Ireland in Revolt*, p.106.
94   NAI: RP/620/33/129: Madden MSS S.3.690, James Witherspoon's account, quoted in Nelson, *The Irish Militia*, p.207.
95   NAI: RP/620/33/129: Madden MSS S.3.690, James Witherspoon's account, p.207.

Nugent estimated that 300–400 insurgents were killed out of a force of 4,000–5,000, while his casualties were considerably lighter with one officer and eight soldiers killed, along with 13 wounded.[96]

With the capture and execution of Munro the rebel army in Down dissolved, thus effectively ending the rebellion in Ulster. The uprising in the north had lasted only one week and had been a complete failure in attempting to inspire a general rebellion in the province. Ultimately, what resulted was the complete destruction of the United Irish movement in the north, where the failure of the rising, coupled with the following reprisals ensuring there was little support for any future republican revolts.

Rebel Defeat at Arklow

At the Battle of Arklow fought on Saturday 9 June, four days after the failed rebel attack on New Ross, the militia again accounted for most of the government troops that stoutly defended the town with disciplined musketry. This, coupled with the artillery, ensured the eventual rout of the northern division of the United Irish army of Wexford that was attempting to march on the capital. With rebel defeat at New Ross, the hopes of the rebellion in Wexford now lay with this northern column whose leaders intended to march through County Wicklow and on to Dublin. At the time this force was encamped at Gorey, but it had no single overall commander. The three senior leaders – Father Michael Murphy, Anthony Perry, and Billy Byrne – decided that the best course of action was to attack and defeat the Government force at Arklow, Co. Wickford, which they believed would then open their way to the capital. However, Lieutenant General Lake had been marshalling the units available to him so that a concentrated force of disciplined troops blocking the most likely routes to Dublin available to the rebels would stop the rebellion from spreading.

To this end, on Wednesday 6 June he ordered Major General Francis Needham, who was then encamped at Loughlinstown, to advance on Arklow and reoccupy the town after it had previously been abandoned after the United Irish victory at Tubberneering.[97] Similar to New Ross, Arklow was another town built on a rise that leads down to a river, with the town being on the southern bank. Needham had a force of 1,335 infantry and 500 cavalry to defend the town. He placed his force in a crescent formation to the south of the town, with the Antrim militia regiment and the grenadier company of the Londonderry regiment (commanded by Colonel Richard Maxwell) on his right flank to the west of the town, with Colonel John Skerrit commanding the Durham and Dunbarton Fencibles regiments in the centre. Lieutenant Colonel Robert Cope had command of the Armagh regiment and the light infantry battalion on the left flank to the end of the position, with the cavalry also on the left flank protecting the bridge across the Avoca

---

96   NAI: RP/620/33/129: Nugent to Lake, 12 June 1798, p.207.
97   Nelson, *The Irish Militia*, pp.204–205.

THE 1798 REBELLION

'The memorable Battle of Arklow.' (Anne S.K. Brown Military Collection)

River.[98] There were also five field artillery pieces positioned throughout the defensive ring to support the infantry.

Like New Ross, at Arklow the rebel leadership relied heavily on revolutionary zeal and superior numbers to defeat the Crown forces, but this was not enough to gain the victory they needed. The United Irish plan was to launch two simultaneous attacks of two disorderly columns, that Pakenham estimated together to be around 19,000 insurgents. One of the columns had marched to the east of the town and attacked an area known as the 'Fisheries.' The other column, personally led by Father Murphy, attacked to the west of the town where Needham had anticipated the rebels would strike and where his defences were strongest. The fighting was intense, and the rebels suffered greatly from the canister shot of the artillery – tins packed with musket balls that were very effective at short range. However, the rebels repeatedly attacked the Crown troops who were dug in around the perimeter and gained the respect of Needham: 'Their perseverance was surprising and their efforts to take the guns on our right were most daring, advancing even to the muzzles, where they fell in great numbers.'[99] Some of the rebels did manage to break through the defender's line and set part of the town alight, causing panic among some of the troops who fled across the bridge. But these rebels were not in sufficient numbers to make a serious difference to the overall defence of the town.

Archibald MacLaren, a sergeant in the Dumbarton Fencibles, wrote of his experience during the engagement, highlighting the strength and reliance

---

98   Nelson, *The Irish Militia*, pp.204–205.
99   Pakenham, *The Year of Liberty*, p.281.

on trained, disciplined, and well-led troops compared to the zeal of a much larger force of ill-disciplined armed civilians:

> [We were] ordered out about a quarter of a mile to line the ditches on each side of the main road where the enemy was advancing. When the Croppies [United Irish] appeared with their green flags fixed to pole-heads in imitation of colours; they fired, which compliments we returned. As I did not think my Halbert [sic] a proper weapon to annoy the enemy at a distance, I exchanged it for a firelock … When we had exchanged about a dozen rounds, an aide-de-camp from the General ordered us to retreat to join the Armagh [Militia] in the street. This we did in seeming confusion, and the rebels (no doubt), thinking that we fled, came on with great vaunting, setting up a loud huzza. One fellow, an officer, inspired with spirits and whisky (of which they had drank very copiously at a village called Coolgreene), galloped in front, having something resembling a stand of colours in his hand … and waving his hat, called out, 'Blood and wounds my boys! Come on, the town is ours!' But here the foolhardy hero was aware, he turned the corner of a house which brought him almost to the mouth of a field-piece, surrounded by some hundreds of soldiers ready to fire or receive him on the points of their bayonets.[100]

MacLaren also emphasizes the important role artillery played in the battle for both sides, especially when served by trained soldiers:

> Two field pieces taken from the Londonderry [Militia] at Gorey were played upon us from the eminence opposite the Durham and Cavan [Militias]; but as the chief management of these pieces was entrusted to a sergeant of the Antrim [Militia] who had been made their prisoner, we sustained no damage for some time, for at every shot he pointed with so much elevation that the balls whistled over our heads; but being observed by one of his officers, he was so far obliged to rectify this seeming mistake that they very next shot struck one of the Durham [Militia] field pieces and smashed the carriage to pieces, which pleased the croppy officer so well that he cried out, 'A hundred pounds for the soldier!' meaning I suppose that one trained soldier was better than many of his rude followers.[101]

Sustained superior firepower of artillery and musketry won the day for the Crown forces at Arklow. After around two and a half hours of fighting the column attacking the east side of town was the first to retreat, having sustained heavy losses. Again, in a repeat of what happened at New Ross, the cavalry rode after the retreating rebels and lost a few men to some rebel pikemen who turned on their attackers. The rebel attack to the west also faltered shortly afterwards and Needham reported they withdrew back to Gorey leaving up to 300 dead behind.[102]

Arklow was the turning point in the rebellion in Wexford. Lacking any effective experienced military leadership, the rebels had thrown themselves

---

100 Hewitt, *Eye-Witnesses to Ireland in Revolt*, p.89.
101 Hewitt, *Eye-Witnesses to Ireland in Revolt*, p.90.
102 Pakenham, *The Year of Liberty*, p.281.

at an entrenched defensive position manned by trained and disciplined troops, supported by artillery, and who were reinforced prior to the rebel attacks. The rebels were also inferior in firepower, relying heavily on fowling pieces, pikes, and other agricultural implements for engaging in hand-to-hand fighting. And although they had captured many cannons and muskets in previous actions, they were lacking in ammunition and sufficient people with the knowledge and experience to operate them. It was the rebel defeat at Arklow that directly led to destruction of the United Irish army at Vinegar Hill.

The Subjugation of Wexford: Vinegar Hill and Enniscorthy

Lieutenant General Lake's plan to extinguish the Wexford rebellion was simple. It involved an advance on the rebels, which were now concentrated around Enniscorthy, with five columns approaching from different directions to surround the insurgents and ensure that they had no opportunity to escape. However, the breakout of rebellion in Ulster on 7 June, the risk of possible attacks on Dublin from isolated United Irish groups still roaming outside the city, and the constant threat of a French landing to support the rebellion, left Lake concerned that until he received reinforcements, he had insufficient troops to commit to a following up his plans in Wexford. Lord Camden had already requested 10,000 reinforcements from England, but there had been some delay as Westminster had originally deferred in sending so many. The rising in Ulster created some panic in the British government and eventually the requested number of men were provided, but not before both rebellions in Wexford and in Ulster were defeated.[103]

Lake had planned to take personal command of the operations in Wexford and had given word to his subordinates to remain on the defensive until he gave the orders to advance. His greatest fear was that the rebels would break through the cordon of Crown forces and spread rebellion into other counties. This ensured that his priority was to destroy the rebel army in the field. To achieve this his plan involved dividing his army, the majority of which consisted of Irish militia battalions, into three columns that would move south to converge on the rebel camp near Enniscorthy; Lieutenant General Sir Ralph Dundas would be in overall command of the columns with Major General Needham advancing from Arklow, Major General William Loftus advancing from Gorey and Major General Sir James Duff leading a column from Newtownbarry. These columns were to be supported by Major General Johnson from New Ross who had been ordered to proceed to Old Ross and join with Brigadier General John Moore (later Lieutenant General Sir John Moore of Corunna fame) who was progressing from Duncannon to Foulkes Mill with his small force of light infantry.[104]

It was only at Foulkes Mill that the United Irish made any serious attempt to challenge the converging Crown forces. Moore's small column of around

---

103 Pakenham, *The Year of Liberty*, p.283.
104 Nelson, *The Irish Militia*, p.208.

2,000 men consisted of the 2nd Battalion of the militia light infantry, two companies of the 5th Battalion of the 60th Foot (a rifle battalion of mainly Germans dressed in green jackets and commonly known as 'Jagers'), 50 Hompesch Mounted Riflemen (another German unit), together with six pieces of artillery On 20 June Moore's column was attacked by a force of rebels estimated at five times their numbers at Taghmon, on the road between Foulkes Mill and Wexford town. The rebels, who had been sent from Wexford town, made a frontal attack along the road that initially broke the morale of the inexperienced, poorly trained and led light infantry, resulting in his centre wavering and his left flank breaking. However, this engagement provided another example of how well the Irish militia could fight when effectively led. Moore's diary records how, through his leadership, the situation was turned from a possible rout into victory:

> The companies of light infantry, being unaccustomed to fire, hesitated a little. I was obliged to get off my horse to put myself at their head … I met the light infantry … all in the woods mixed and retreating. The enemy following close and firing. I succeeded in stopping some immediately and got them to jump out of the road and make a front on each side of it. I then encouraged the rest first to halt, then to advance, and when I saw them ready for it, I took off my hat, put my horse into a trot, gave a huzza, and got them to make a push. The tide immediately turned.[105]

This failed rebel attack was the last offensive United Irish operation in County Wexford and left the disjointed leadership with the realisation that the rebellion was now doomed.

The following day, 21 June, saw the complete destruction of the main rebel force at Vinegar Hill outside Enniscorthy. Lake had massed a combined force of around 10,000 men, with 20 pieces of artillery and an estimated 400 wagons loaded with ammunition and supplies to take on the 20,000 rebels (including women and children) who were encamped on the summit of the hill. Pakenham argues that Lake had always intended the result to be a massacre as he gave no consideration of offering terms of surrender to the rebel leadership. Extermination was his answer to the risk of the rebels surrendering and later continuing to spread rebellion that may have led to an extended guerrilla war throughout Ireland.[106] The actions of the Crown forces during the engagement gives some credence to Pakenham's view.

Lake's battle plan was devised to ensure the rebel force was surrounded and that none could escape. The plan involved an attack on the hill from the River Slaney by two columns led by Major Generals Loftus and Duff, with Major General Johnson attacking the town of Enniscorthy. Lieutenant General Dundas was to lead a column against the rebel camp from the east side of the hill, while Major General Needham on the left flank of the Lake's attack was directed to move around to the south of the hill to cut off any rebel retreat. The battle began at 7:00 a.m. with a cannon and howitzer

---

105 Maurice, *The Diary of Sir John Moore*, p.297.
106 Pakenham, *The Year of Liberty*, p.293.

'Rebel Defeat at Vinegar Hill, 21 June 1798' by George Cruickshank. (New York Public Library Free Image Collection)

bombardment on the exposed and unfortified rebel encampment. This lasted for about an hour, followed by a successful infantry attack, supported by a cavalry charge up the exposed east side of the hill. The rebels, who had suffered heavy casualties, were unable to sustain a defence against the onslaught, with many choosing to escape south along the road to Wexford. Lake had ordered the battle to commence before Needham had time to complete the encirclement. A gap in the perimeter, later to be known as 'Needham's Gap,' provided an opportunity for numbers of insurgents to escape. One group led by Father John Murphy headed towards Kilkenny intending to rekindle rebellion there, while another escaped to the relative safety of the Wicklow Mountains to continue a campaign of guerrilla warfare; exactly what Lake had tried to avoid.

The fiercest fighting took place in Enniscorthy between Johnson's troops and rebels defending the bridge. Miles Byrne, a United Irishman who fought at Arklow and Vinegar Hill, and who later commanded the Irish Legion in Napoleon's army, wrote in his memoir of the rebel defence of the town:

> The town of Enniscorthy and its outlets were splendidly defended by Mr William Barker and Father Kearns, who, with the corps they commanded, were at the advanced posts beyond the Duffrey gate at daylight, where they had been skirmishing the evening before with the English forces, under the command of General Johnson. Mr Barker had one four-pounder mounted on a car [cart], which was of little use, except from the moral effect it might have had on his men. His military acquirements and the knowledge of tactics, which he had learned in

REBELLION, INVASION AND OCCUPATION

'Father John Murphy and the Heretic Bullets' by George Cruickshank. (New York Public Library Free Image Collection)

the service of France, were now of the greatest advantage, and turned to the best account of the defence of the place confided to his charge. Mr Baker first began by placing a strong guard in reserve on the bridge, and then advanced with the main body to meet the enemy, having each flank covered with his gunmen. In this order of battle he commenced a most desperate attack on the enemy's line and kept his ground until it was perceived that our forces had retreated from the hill; still he defended and disputed every position, and held his post of the bridge with a valour beyond description, until he lost his arm and was carried away from the field of battle ... at this critical moment the undaunted [Father] Kearns replaced Mr Barker in command, but he, too, soon received a wound which the division of our army of two trustworthy chiefs. Now, the retreat from the town, as well as the hill, became inevitable. [107]

The United Irish pikemen put their weapons to good use, and although forced to make a fighting withdrawal along the cobbled streets, they inflicted heavy casualties of the Government troops who suffered about 20 killed and 60 wounded, including two militia colonels.[108] However, despite the courage and zeal of the rebels, their position was hopeless and they eventually broke, leading to an estimated 500 fugitives being pursued and cut down.[109] A

---

107   Miles Byrne, *Memoirs of Miles Byrne* (Dublin: Maunsel, 1907), vol.1, pp.129–130.
108   Pakenham, *The Year of Liberty*, p.294.
109   Pakenham, *The Year of Liberty*, p.294.

number of atrocities were committed by the Government troops after the battle had been won, but none worse than the setting fire to the makeshift rebel hospital in Enniscorthy while the patients and staff were still inside. This action was later attributed to the indiscipline of the Irish militia, but it does raise questions as to the direct part Lake and his senior subordinates played in the massacre of non-combatants. Despite any criticism against the behaviour of the militia after the battle at Vinegar Hill, the Irish militia provided the bulk of Lake's and Johnson's forces in their victory and were engaged in most of the fighting: Lake commanded the Armagh, Cavan, Antrim, Londonderry, and Tyrone regiments, along with the 1st and 4th Light Battalions, while Johnson commanded the Donegal, Sligo, Meath, Roscommon, and Dublin County regiments.[110]

Again, in Kildare and Meath the militia had provided the bulk of the forces used to surround and defeat the insurgents before the rebellion could spread further. In Ulster, the Monaghan Militia, whose loyalty was under question due to the high number of Catholic rank and file, as well as the recent executions of a small number of disaffected militiamen, proved to be most reliable at Ballynahinch where their discipline and doggedness saw them rout the rebels who had mounted a surprise attack with superior numbers.[111] These events all proved to be decisive in the defeat of the rebellion before reinforcements could be mobilised and sent from Britain. The criticism aimed at the militia during the uprising appears to be regarding the behaviour towards civilians and property after battles had been won. However, it is easy to understand how any such conduct occurred when it had been actively encouraged in previous operations led by Carhampton and Lake.

The firepower of the government artillery, plus no attempt by the rebels to fortify the position, ensured that the United Irish army was routed with great loss at Vinegar Hill and Enniscorthy. Miles Byrne later wrote of the poor state of defence of the rebel position:

> At break of day the different corps began to quit their bivouacs. Each to repair to the position assigned to them on the hill and on all the roads leading into the town of Enniscorthy. Our wounded men that we had transported on cars [carts] with us from the county of Wicklow, in order to have them placed in the hospital, we left at Drumgold, one of the suburbs of the town under Vinegar Hill; we also had to leave there a vast number of women and young girls who had followed their husbands and brothers, to escape from the English monsters who were devastating their homes … Skirmishing at all our advanced posts commenced with the day; however battle did not become general on the whole line before seven o'clock, but at daybreak several cannon shots were heard in different directions from the enemy's camp. These were signal guns, which proved to us that we were now surrounded on all sides, except the Wexford one … I had not seen Vinegar Hill since the morning after the battle of Newtownbarry, the 2nd of June, and I was surprised to find that scarcely anything had been done to make

---

110   Nelson, *The Irish Militia*, p.209.
111   Pakenham, *The Year of Liberty*, pp.206–207.

it formidable against the enemy; the vast fences and ditches which surrounded it on three sides, and which should have been levelled to the ground, for at least a cannon shot, or half a mile's distance, were all untouched. The English forces, availing themselves of these fences, advanced from field to field, bringing with them their cannon, which they placed to great advantage behind and under cover of the hedges and fences; whilst our men were exposed to a terrible fire from their artillery and small arms, without being able to drive them back from their strongholds in those fields.[112]

Although a number of rebels, including Byrne, managed to escape the encirclement and withdrew to the Wicklow Mountains where they continued a campaign of guerrilla warfare until 1803, the serious military threat in Wexford had been extinguished. On the same day Wexford town was recaptured by Moore. The series of defeats and subsequent government reprisals ensured that the popular support that the United Irish needed for the rebellion to spread and succeed had quickly dissolved, ensuring that the rebel forces were now reduced to a few small, isolated bands that were easily accounted for in the following mopping-up operations.

Quality, or lack of it, in leadership determined the behaviour of the militia and the officer corps must be held responsible for any valid criticism against their troops. There was a measure of political expediency in attributing the few defeats to the poor quality of the militia and disaffection in the regiments, since this proved to contemporaries that the defence of Ireland was best handled by the British government in London.[113]

The End of the Rebellion

The defeat of the rebellion in Ireland in 1798 was due to many factors, which included the failure to co-ordinate Presbyterian discontent and Catholic disaffection with a simultaneous French invasion, and the flawed rebel strategy of fighting against government troops in open battle. The decision to launch an uprising without French military support was a gamble that proved disastrous for the revolutionary cause. The rebel strategy of relying on overwhelming the government forces with superior numbers had some merit but was basically flawed. They may have had the initiative when the rebellion was first launched, but once the government forces were able to concentrate, the United Irish armies lacked any trained and disciplined formations needed to successfully confront the government army in open linear-style battle. The counter-terror operations of the government had seriously depleted the number of firearms available to the insurgents, ensuring that the rebel troops had to rely heavily on the use of pikes, which although lethal, were most effective as defensive weapons, such as when attacked by cavalry. This was evident at New Ross where elements of the 4th and 5th Dragoons charged a mob of retreating rebels, only for the pikemen to turn and dispatch the

---

112 Byrne, *Memoirs of Miles Byrne*, pp.126–128.
113 Pakenham, *The Year of Liberty*, p.217.

cavalry commanding officer and 28 of his troopers.[114] The limited number of firearms ensured that the United Irishmen were reliant on the tactic of a shock charge, similar to the tactics used by Jacobite infantry in the 1745 rebellion in Scotland, to engage with the enemy.[115] This proved successful against poorly trained and numerically inferior formations, such as the North Cork Militia at Oulart Hill. However, as with the Jacobite charge at Culloden in 1746, it proved disastrous against a force of disciplined troops who could maintain superior fire power, such as the government defence of Arklow.[116] What also proved significant was that the rebels lacked trained artillerists to put the captured field guns to good use. The rebels' need for such experience was so desperate that at New Ross they forced captured artillerymen to load and fire the cannons at gun point.[117] The sections of Royal Artillery and Royal Irish Artillery that accompanied the government forces were the best trained and most professional corps within the Irish establishment and it was their ability to maintain constant accurate fire against the rebels that inflicted high casualties on the insurgents and reduced their morale. It was the effect of artillery fire that ensured the defeat of the insurgents at New Ross, Arklow and Vinegar Hill.[118] By waiting for the landing of a French army the rebellion would have had a greater chance of success. Not only would the French have provided the republican cause with the experienced troops and *materiel* necessary to achieve victory against the Irish army, but Dublin Castle would have had to withdraw regiments from parts of the kingdom to consolidate its forces to face the French in open battle, thus leaving the defence of large areas of rural Ireland to the inexperienced yeomanry.

The lack of effective leadership within the United Irish movement, which had passed from Ulster to an executive committee in Dublin, was significant in the defeat of the rebel armies. The arrest of the Leinster executive in March of 1798 effectively crippled the United Irish movement, ensuring command and organisational structures were limited to local control, fostering confusion and lack of direction amongst the rebel cells within Dublin and surrounding counties, some who chose not to act without orders from the executive.[119] This was evident in every separate uprising, where indecision prevailed once the rebels had failed to achieve their goals. In Meath the isolated rebel bands drew together at an encampment at Tara and remained there inactive until surrounded and routed.[120] The republicans responded similarly in Wexford, when they converged on Vinegar Hill and were destroyed after failing to break out of the county. Insufficient military experience amongst the

---

114 Pakenham, *The Year of Liberty*, p.231.
115 Kevin Whelan, 'Reinterpreting the 1798 rebellion in County Wexford', in Daire Keogh & Nicholas Furlong (eds), *The Mighty Wave: The 1798 Rebellion in Wexford* (Dublin: Four Courts Press, 1996), p.27.
116 TNA: HO 100/68: Needham to Camden, 10 June 1798.
117 Pakenham, *The Year of Liberty*, p.235.
118 G.A. Hayes-McCoy, 'The Government Forces Which Opposed the Irish Insurgents of 1798', *The Irish Sword*, vol.4 (1959), pp.16–28.
119 Whelan, 'Reinterpreting the 1798 rebellion in County Wexford', p.23.
120 NAI: 620/18/14: Rebellion Papers, Francis Higgins to Edward Cooke, 25 May 1798, quoted in Chambers, 'The 1798 Rebellion in North Leinster', p.125.

leadership also limited the chance of success, with Fitzgerald being the only member of the executive to have served as an officer in any capacity. There were a small number of deserters from the officer corps of the militia and yeomanry that joined the insurgents, such as Doctor Esmonde at Prosperous, but the prominent leaders of the rebellion were mostly inexperienced civilians.[121] In Wexford local Catholic parish priests, such as Fathers John and Michael Murphy, as well as Father Philip Roche, were inspirational in leading their disaffected parishioners but were ignorant of military tactics. The same can be said of Anthony Perry and Bagenal Harvey, who as local gentry provided traditional leadership but whose lack of military knowledge seriously jeopardised the success of the revolt. Similarly, the leadership in Ulster was lacking in military experience, with Henry Joy McCracken being a prosperous cotton manufacturer, while Henry Munro was a draper.[122] It was this lack of military experience and knowledge amongst the leaders that ensured the rebels armies were decimated on repeated murderous frontal attacks that not only weakened the rebel numerical advantage but eventually broke the morale of the disaffected population.

Another factor in the failure of the rebellion was the lack of active support from the general populace throughout other counties within Ireland. The French revolution had polarised the Irish population and that there was large-scale support amongst liberal Protestants, Presbyterians and Catholics for a similar uprising in Ireland to provide male suffrage and Catholic emancipation.[123] This may have been true amongst the educated middle-classes but not so for the Catholic peasantry, most of whom could not read.[124] The revolutionary ideology fostered by the United Irish was a foreign concept to the uneducated Irish peasantry and the idea of a democratic nation governed by the people was alien to the peasantry that had traditionally relied on the aristocracy for leadership and protection.[125] They had always been ruled by kings and the Irish Catholics had generally remained loyal to the exiled House of Stuart throughout the eighteenth century. The French revolutionary philosophies were extremely secular and critical of the influence the Catholic Church had over the state.[126] Any such propaganda distributed by the United Irish would have discouraged many Catholics from participating in a rebellion that threatened the continuation of their religious practice. The fact that the Catholic bishops in Ireland, together with the Catholic Committee, had actively discouraged their flock from supporting any insurrection would most certainly have accounted for the general lack of popular support. This was evident in the open displays of loyalty and support by the peasantry in the south of the kingdom towards

---

121 Pakenham, *The Year of Liberty*, p.127.
122 Nelson, *The Irish Militia*, pp.206–207.
123 R.F Foster, *Modern Ireland, 1600–1972* (London & New York: Penguin Press, 1988), pp.264–266.
124 Gerard O'Brien, 'Francophobia in later eighteenth-century Irish History', in Hugh Gough & David Dickinson (eds), *Ireland and the French Revolution* (Dublin: Irish Academic Press, 1990), p.49.
125 Mike Cronin, *A History of Ireland* (Basingstoke, Hampshire: Macmillan, 2001), pp.107-111.
126 O'Brien, 'Francophobia in later eighteenth-century Irish History', p.49.

the Crown forces marching to counter Hoche's invasion in 1796.[127] They had a basic fear that the United Irish were in league with the French to drive Catholics off the land.[128] This suspicion is understandable when considering that the United Irish was mainly based in Ulster amongst educated young radicals of the middle classes who saw Catholicism as an oppressive religion based on superstition.

One point that historians agree on is that as viceroy, the Earl of Camden was ineffective in providing decisive leadership in a time of national crisis. As lord lieutenant, Camden was also head of the military establishment in Ireland, although at the time he had a designated commander-in-chief of the army, Lieutenant General Lake, who served under him and was responsible for the administration and operational control of the armed forces. However, although Camden openly displayed a lack of confidence in Lake and the troops under his command, believing their quality and numbers were inadequate to deal with the rebels, he encouraged Lake to carry out counter-terror campaigns knowing that such measures would lead to more disaffection amongst the population.[129] He saw rebellion as an opportunity to crush dissention in Ireland, however, once the uprising had begun, he faltered when he became infected with the panic that quickly spread throughout Dublin and the Ascendancy.[130] This panic was fuelled by the numerous reports received from panic-stricken gentry and magistrates throughout the kingdom, with Camden writing to the British Home secretary demanding troops be sent from Britain to help end the revolt:

> Unless Great Britain pours an immense force into Ireland, the country is lost. Unless she sends her most able generals those troops may be sacrificed ... from the delay in sending the reinforcements which were promised, the rebellion has much extended itself, that it now assumes so formidable a shape that I think it my duty to state ... the country is lost, unless a very large reinforcement of troops is landed.[131]

This comment is significant in that by the time he wrote this letter on 11 June, the rebels in Meath and Kildare had been defeated and had surrendered, while the rebellion in Wexford had been contained with the United Irish defeats at New Ross and Arklow. The government forces had seized the initiative, forcing the insurgents to withdraw to Vinegar Hill and at this stage it was only in two counties in Ulster that the rebels had any chance of overwhelming the Irish army. Camden also came under attack from members of the Ascendancy for his inertia and was heavily criticised for preventing Lake from marching out of Dublin with a column to reinforce Dundas in Kildare. He repeatedly argued that the security of the capital was paramount,

---

127 William O'Connor Morris, 'Ireland, 1793-1800', *The English Historical Review*, vol.6, no. 24 (October 1891), p.713.
128 Cronin, *A History of Ireland*, p.110.
129 Bartlett, 'Defence, counter-insurgency and rebellion: Ireland, 1793-1803', p.270.
130 Bartlett, 'Defence, counter-insurgency and rebellion: Ireland, 1793-1803', p.270.
131 TNA: HO 100/77: Camden to Pelham, 11 June 1798.

stating that no such mission could take place until reinforcements arrived in the city from Britain.[132] This led to the rural gentry of the county claiming that they had been abandoned by the army and government, resulting in many being unnecessarily murdered in their homes by rebel mobs.

The actions of some senior army officers fostered a contemporary belief that the military hierarchy proved ineffective during the revolt. This perception was initiated by Abercromby's comments earlier that year and reinforced by later criticism from Camden and others within the army, such as John Moore. Camden had little confidence in his commander-in-chief, which may have contributed to Lake's actions against the rebels: 'General Lake is not fit to command in these difficult times … He has no arrangement, is easily led, and no authority … I am sure you must be aware how very unpleasantly circumstanced I am without a commander-in-chief upon whom I have the most perfect reliance.'[133] Other generals were berated for their lack of aggression against the insurgents, especially by loyalists who suffered at the hands of the rebels. Sir Ralph Dundas was heavily criticised by the Ascendancy for his strategic decision to withdraw his scattered detachments in Kildare to concentrate at Naas when the rebellion first erupted.[134] This ensured that the whole of the county was abandoned to the rebels who were able to target the unprotected Protestant gentry. With the benefit of hindsight, the criticism against Dundas was understandable. However, at the time he was not aware of the general failure of the United Irish and had prudently decided to concentrate his troops rather than leave them exposed in isolated positions where they could have been annihilated by overwhelming superior numbers, especially as Camden had refused to send reinforcements from Dublin. His greatest censure came when on 28 May he negotiated generous, but unauthorised terms for the surrender of 6,000 insurgents at Gibbet Rath.[135] He was ridiculed for such humane actions by Lake, who on 24 May had ordered no prisoners to be taken, as well as the vengeful Ascendant population who were clearly seeking a more brutal end to the uprising.[136] Other officers to suffer public criticism were Major General Fawcett, who led a column from Duncannon Fort to relieve Wexford town, but was ambushed and hastily retreated, making no further advances into rebel-held territory, while Major General Johnson was described by Cornwallis as being 'no soldier'.[137] However, the comment regarding Johnson seems somewhat unjustified considering it was he who rallied the panicking militia at New Ross and inflicted a major defeat on the United Irish.

Ultimately, the high command of the Irish establishment proved competent enough to crush the rebellion. Justified criticism has been aimed at Lake for causing much disaffection amongst the population prior to the uprising through his brutal disarming campaigns, as well as encouraging

---

132   Pakenham, *The Year of Liberty*, p.154.
133   TNA: HO 100/77, Camden to Pelham, 6 June 1798.
134   Nelson, *The Irish Militia*, p.186.
135   Nelson, *The Irish Militia*, p.186.
136   Bartlett, 'Defence, counter-insurgency and rebellion: Ireland, 1793–1803', p.279.
137   Andrew P.R. Martin, *Reform and Change within the Irish Army and Military* (M.A. thesis, University of Canterbury, 1990), p.298.

many rebels to continue to fight by authorising atrocities during and after the uprising. However, he managed to formulate the successful strategy of containment that led to the defeat of the revolt in Wexford, using mainly the inexperienced and semi-trained militia and fencibles that made up the majority of the military force in Ireland at the time. Some of his subordinates forged admirable military reputations during the rebellion, especially Brigadier General John Moore who was later knighted and promoted for his recapture of Wexford town. Cornwallis was so impressed with Moore that he gave him independent command of the elite force used to combat the small insurgent groups who had retreated into the Wicklow Mountains once the main rebel army had been destroyed in Wexford.[138] Major General George Nugent also proved himself worthy of high praise with his swift and total destruction of the United Irish armies in Antrim and Down within a week. Others, such as General Sir James Duff and General Sir James Craig were commended by Lake and members of the Ascendancy for their zeal in leading counter-insurgent operations, which although merciless, proved effective in extinguishing the rebellion in the areas they commanded.[139]

The British government proved effective in preventing the revolt of 1798 from becoming as widespread as a similar insurrection mounted by the Royalists of the *Vendee* in France. The eighteenth century British Army was generally not well-suited or equipped for counter-insurgent operations, being numerically small and with training restricted to musket and formation drill specific to linear warfare. Nonetheless, Dublin Castle had succeeded in weakening the military potential of the United Irish through mass arrests and the seizure of arms during the counter-insurgent operations of 1797–1798, especially in Ulster where weapons had been retained by previous members of volunteer associations. Dublin Castle had also succeeded in penetrating the United Irish movement by cultivating an intelligence network that provided details of planned actions.[140] This ensured that pre-emptive strikes could be made against the cause, such as the arrest of the Leinster executive committee, which would seriously hinder rebel success. Information regarding the planned uprising also ensured that government troops could be concentrated in strength at locations targeted by the insurgents, such as prominent government buildings in Dublin. Certainly, the failure of United Irish to gain widespread active support throughout the country limited the chance of the rising to becoming a national revolution, thus limiting its likelihood of success. When the rebellion came the government troops quickly isolated and defeated the rebel forces, thus preventing the revolt from spreading and discouraging others from rising in support. The ability to make good use of secure internal sea links through the Irish Sea ensured reinforcements available from Britain could be sent within a short time, although only two Fencible regiments, the Durham and Lancashire Fencibles, had arrived in the Dublin area prior to the rebellion being effectively crushed

---

138 Ross, *Correspondence of Charles, First Marquis Cornwallis*, p.277.
139 Bartlett, 'Defence, counter-insurgency and rebellion: Ireland, 1793–1803', p.279.
140 Pakenham, *The Year of Liberty*, pp.89–90.

at Vinegar Hill.[141] However, the rapid influx of units from Britain ensured that Cornwallis had a large enough army to easily surround and defeat the small French invasion force led by *Général de brigade* Humbert at Ballinamuck, County Longford, on 8 September the same year.

The rebellion was characterised by atrocities committed by both the rebels and government forces, contributing to thousands of deaths of surrendering antagonists and non-combatants. The precise number of people killed during the uprising and the subsequent invasion by the French could never be established due to the high number of civilians involved. The nature of the United Irish peasant armies meant that there were no regular military formations where muster roles would have provided an exact number of combatants and casualties. Therefore, the most accurate estimation of the number of lives lost during the conflicts is provided by contemporary records and observation made by those who witnessed the events. The estimation of the total number of those killed varies from 20,000–30,000, although many historians now tend to accept a figure of 25,000 as being realistic.[142] This became the bloodiest civil conflict in Ireland since the Civil Wars of the 1640s and 1650s, and the Williamite War of 1689–1693. When comparing the official casualty figures provided for the Irish government forces to the estimated total deaths during the uprising and French invasion, it appears the majority of those killed were either civilian insurgents or non-combatants. The number of those killed in battle is easily accounted for by the number of bodies recovered and disposed of. However, it is impossible to account for the thousands of civilians, both Catholic and Protestant, who were slaughtered indiscriminately while attempting to escape from the conflict or who had the misfortune of living in the location where the rebellion erupted.

Numerous atrocities during the uprising were initially inspired by the actions of government troops during the disarming campaigns, as well as religious fervour and fear promoted by both the Ascendancy and the republicans.[143] News of such events quickly spread, fostering a hardening of attitudes, and promoting a sense of desperation amongst the belligerents. Heinous acts were repeatedly committed by factions who now saw the conflict as a struggle for survival, typical of civil wars where the normal rules of society are disregarded. The temporary eviction of government troops from Wexford allowed many rebels to seek vengeance for past oppression by attacking and murdering loyalist gentry and citizens who had been held prisoner in the town gaol.[144] News that troops at New Ross had hanged or shot every rebel they had found created hysteria in Wexford that led to the massacre of 97 loyalist men and women prisoners at the town bridge by a republican mob.[145] The other most notorious rebel atrocity occurred at Scullabogue on the day the United Irish were defeated at New Ross, where more than 100 loyalist prisoners, including women and children, and some

---

141   NLI: MS 464: Paymaster General's Office Register.
142   Bartlett, 'Defence, counter-insurgency and rebellion: Ireland, 1793–1803', p.287.
143   Pakenham, *The Year of Liberty*, p.174.
144   Pakenham, *The Year of Liberty*, pp.296–297.
145   Hewitt, *Eye-Witnesses to Ireland in Revolt*, pp.91–92.

Catholics, were burned in a barn after 35 men had already been shot in front of their families.¹⁴⁶ Such incidents only promoted further murderous activity which ensured that the majority of deaths were suffered by non-combatant from both sides.

However, some atrocities committed by government troops had been given official sanction. Lake's order of 24 May that no rebel prisoners were to be taken during the military operations became common knowledge throughout the kingdom ensuring that quarter was seldom given by either side. The rebellion now became a conflict where only the complete eradication of the enemy forces would ensure victory. The eighteenth century was dubbed as the 'age of reason' where unwritten rules of war were accepted by civilised European states.¹⁴⁷ The voluntary 'laws of nations' that were the accepted rules of conduct of between warring European states, prohibited measures that were themselves unlawful, including the massacre of an enemy who had surrendered.¹⁴⁸ In the 1798 rebellion these rules were ignored by many within the Irish military establishment, especially the yeomanry, who zealously followed Lake's lead. An example was Major General Duff who authorised the massacre of 350 rebel prisoners at Gibbet Rath on 31 May after they had already negotiated terms with Lieutenant General Dundas.¹⁴⁹ This was followed by the standard practice of dispatching all rebel wounded found on the battlefield, as well as the indiscriminate execution of insurgent suspects.¹⁵⁰ Such actions were vigorously carried out by government troops at Vinegar Hill, where the rebel hospital in nearby Enniscorthy was burned while the wounded were still inside.¹⁵¹ These practices that were promoted by Lake were considered ruthless by many of his contemporaries, with Cornwallis giving a clear indication of the state of affairs in a letter to the Duke of Portland on his arrival in Ireland: 'The accounts that you see of the numbers of the enemy destroyed in every action, are, I conclude, greatly exaggerated; from my own knowledge of military affairs, I am sure that a very small proportion of them only could be killed in battle, and I am much afraid that any man in a brown coat who is found within several miles of the field of action, is butchered without discrimination.'¹⁵²

The responsibility for the atrocities committed by the government forces, including the militia, during the rebellion and subsequent French invasion lies with the high command. Lake's orders, especially the order to refuse quarter to surrendering rebels at Ballinamuck where the French force was captured, were certainly in breach of these principles and it could be argued that his directive removed all culpability from his subordinates and troops for their murderous actions. According to these rules of war, a general had

---

146 Pakenham, *The Year of Liberty*, pp.226–227.
147 E. Vattel, *The Law of Nations or Principles of the Law of Nature Applied to the Conduct and Affairs of Nations and Sovereigns*, new edition by Joseph Chitty (London: S. Sweet, 1834), pp.369–370.
148 Vattel, *The Law of Nations*, pp.369-370.
149 Chambers, 'The 1798 Rebellion in North Leinster', p.126.
150 Dickson, *New Foundations: Ireland 1660-1800*, p.214.
151 Pakenham, *The Year of Liberty*, p.2.
152 Ross, *Correspondence of Charles, First Marquis Cornwallis*, pp.354–355.

the right to sacrifice the lives of his enemy to ensure his safety and that of his own men if he was dealing with an inhumane foe who frequently commits 'enormities'.[153] This authorised him to refuse quarter to some of his prisoners and to treat them as his people have been treated. However, unlike the earlier United Irish uprising, the discipline of the French forces during the failed invasion had ensured very few atrocities were committed by their rebel allies.[154] It is clear that Lake certainly believed that the rebellion seriously threatened the survival of the Ascendancy, and that the uncivilised actions of some of the rebels placed him in such a position: 'I really feel most severely being obliged to order so many men out of the world; but I am convinced, if severe and many examples are not made, the Rebellion cannot be put to a stop.'[155] Certainly, the generals were within their rights to order the destruction of homes and property of known insurgents and supporters if by depriving them of their property they were weakening the enemy in order to render them incapable of supporting unjust violence and depriving the rebels of means of resistance.[156]

However, the deaths of so many women, children, and sick and feeble old men, who were either camp followers or had the misfortune of living in areas of insurrection, was unjustifiable. Lake's attitude towards the rebels reflected the belligerent sentiment of the Ascendancy which had resulted from insurgent activity prior to the uprising, with his order to refuse quarter to rebel prisoners being made before the alleged atrocities of the rebel mobs had been committed. There is no doubt that the indiscipline of some of the government troops, as well as that of the insurgent armies, would have led to some atrocities being carried out by both sides. However, although much blame was conveniently aimed at the ill-discipline of the Irish militia, the ultimate liability lies with their commander-in-chief. During this period the 'Law of Nations' removed any accountability from the officers and soldiers as they were considered as instruments of war for the sovereign and state, where they executed his will and not their own.[157] However, in the case of the Irish Rebellion of 1798 the responsibility of the systematic butchering of rebel suspects and prisoners lies directly with Lake. The orders that he issued were of his own volition and had not been sanctioned by the Crown. It could be argued that Camden must share some responsibility, as his weakness at preventing such measures resulted in both he and Lake being replaced by Lord Cornwallis in late June before the rebellion had finally been extinguished.

The opposite approach taken by Cornwallis towards the insurgents led to a less blood-thirsty end to the rebellion. When he took office as the lord-lieutenant and commander-in-chief of the armed forces in Ireland on 22 June 1798 he was convinced the actions promoted by Lake had left the rebels

---

153 Ross, *Correspondence of Charles, First Marquis Cornwallis*, pp.354–355.
154 Richard Francis Hayes, 'An Officers Account of the French Campaign in Ireland in 1798', *The Irish Sword*, vol.2, issue 6–7 (1955), pp.161–171.
155 Charles, Marquis of Londonderry (ed.), *Memoirs and Correspondence of Viscount Castlereagh* (London: Henry Colburn, 1848), vol.1, pp.223–224, Lake to Castlereagh, 22 June 1798.
156 Vattel, *The Law of Nations*, pp.299 & 361.
157 Vattel, *The Law of Nations*, p.293.

with no other option but to remain fighting: 'The violence of our friends, and their folly in endeavouring to make it a religious war, added to the ferocity of our troops who delight in murder, most powerfully counteract all plans of conciliation.'[158] By this time the rebellion was restricted to guerrilla-style warfare in the Wicklow Mountains. In an attempt to end hostilities he directed Moore and a force of regular troops that he could depend on to confront the rebels to 'try either to seduce them or invite them to surrender, for the shocking barbarity of our national troops would be more likely to provoke rebellion than to suppress it.'[159] However, Cornwallis firmly believed that the system of counter-terror carried out by the government forces was led by the Protestant Ascendancy who were adverse to all acts of clemency. This belief was reinforced during the French invasion, when Lake who as a firm supporter of the Ascendancy, ordered that no quarter be given to the Irish rebels who were attempting to surrender with their French allies at Ballinamuck on 8 September.[160] It was his belief that principal members of both houses of parliament were willing to pursue measures that would see an attempt to exterminate the Catholic peasantry who made up 80 percent of the population, leading to irreconcilable rebellion and the destruction of the country.[161] Ultimately, it was Cornwallis's humane and just treatment of those insurgents remaining under arms after Vinegar Hill and Ballinamuck, but who had later surrendered, that convinced many insurgents to lay down their arms.

The role of the Irish militia in the suppression of the 1798 rebellion and the defeat of the French invasion later that year has been marginalised in traditional historiography of the era. The initial defeat of the North Cork Militia at the hands of the Wexford rebels during the uprising and the rout of the British forces by the French at Castlebar have been perpetually used by British historians as examples of the poor quality of the Irish militia that necessitated the augmentation of the British forces in Ireland after 1798. However, accounting for the government forces available to suppress the rebellion, together with an appreciation of the actions in which militia regiments were involved, provides quantitative evidence that the Irish militia was crucial in the defeat of the insurgents before the bulk of reinforcements were sent from Britain. Furthermore, there is compelling evidence to show that contrary to the traditional view, the Irish militia regiments performed well at Castlebar during the French invasion and that the British defeat was due more to the decisions of the senior commanders present. In general, although there were serious weaknesses within the Irish establishment at the time of the uprising, the military forces proved adequate in quickly dealing with the insurrection. However, if the rebellion had spread throughout the country and had been simultaneously supported by a large French invasion

---

158 Ross, *Correspondence of Charles, First Marquis Cornwallis*, Cornwallis to Major General Ross, 1 July 1798, p.355.
159 Ross, *Correspondence of Charles, First Marquis Cornwallis*, Cornwallis to Major General Ross, 28 July 1798, p.377.
160 Pakenham, *The Year of Liberty*, p.373.
161 Ross, *Correspondence of Charles, First Marquis Cornwallis*, p.357.

Table 5.1 – Irish militia involvement in the 1798 rebellion

Date	Action	Proportion of Militia in infantry engaged
24 May 1798	Naas	100 percent
	Kilcullen	None
	Prosperous (defeat)	100 percent
25 May 1798	Carlow	60 percent (estimate)
27 May 1798	Oulart Hill (defeat)	100 percent
28 May 1798	Enniscorthy	27 percent
1 June 1798	Newtownbarry	61 percent
4 June 1798	Tubberneering (defeat)	100 percent (estimate)
5 June 1798	New Ross	100 percent
7 June 1798	Antrim	100 percent
9 June 1798	Arklow	64 percent
12 June 1798	Ballynahinch	33 percent (estimate)
21 June 1798	Vinegar Hill	65 percent (estimate)
26 June 1798	Kilconnell Hill	100 percent
5 July 1798	Whiteheaps	100 percent (estimate)

Source: Nelson, *The Irish Militia, 1793–1802*, p. 214

force, then the ability of the government to deal with these dual threats would have seriously stretched military resources. Ultimately, the poor reputation of the militia proved politically expedient for the Ascendancy and the British government in arguing for a greater reliance on the yeomanry and the augmentation of British forces in the kingdom.

The Irish militia deserves more credit for the suppression of the rebellion and the recapture of Wexford than the traditionally acknowledged. Militia regiments provided the bulk of the government forces in all of the crucial actions that led to the containment and defeat of the rebels: including Newtownbarry with 61 percent; New Ross with 100 percent; Arklow with 64 percent; and Vinegar Hill with 65 percent.[162] These battles were crucial in the defeat of the insurrection: at Newtownbarry the insurgents were prevented from advancing into County Carlow; at New Ross they were stopped from moving into counties Kilkenny and Waterford; and at Arklow the rebels were prevented from advancing on Dublin. Defeat in these actions greatly demoralised the United Irish forces and forced them to concentrate at Vinegar Hill where they were destroyed on 21 June. Even in Ulster, where there were only a few militia regiments in 1798, the militia provided one-third of the government infantry at the principal battle of Ballynahinch which saw the defeat of the rebels and the end of the uprising in the province.[163] The serious reverses at Oulart Hill and Tubberneering, where the militia provided 100 percent of the infantry force, most certainly added to the unfavourable reputation of the militia. However, these defeats were not due to the poor quality of the troops, but more to the inexperience and over-confidence of the commanding officers. At Oulart Hill a single company of the North Cork militia was ordered to charge up hill in a position where their left was

---

162 Nelson, *The Irish Militia*, p.214.
163 Nelson, *The Irish Militia*, p.214.

exposed to a flank attack, while at Tubberneering a column of militia led by an inexperienced regular officer, Colonel Walpole, was ambushed in a defile due to Walpole failing to deploy scouts.[164] What is evident is that these actions which resulted in the defeat of the rebellion within five weeks, all took place before any significant reinforcements could be sent from Britain.

Ultimately, the Irish militia proved an effective and loyal force during the turbulent year of 1798. To be sure, the militiamen were prone to bouts of ill-discipline, especially when let loose on the defeated rebels, but in general the militia regiments proved their worth in battle when well led. Without the militia the rebellion could have spread throughout Ireland, threatening the defence of Britain.

---

164 Pakenham, *The Year of Liberty*, pp.207–208.

6

Defeat of the French Invasion

Although the French invasion of August that year came too late to support the United Irish and proved nothing more than an ill-advised 'forlorn hope', the defeat of the government forces at Castlebar led to the permanent tainting of the reputation of the Irish militia and thus, ultimately determined the future composition of the Irish military establishment. The prelude to the battle began with the landing of the small French expeditionary force, led by *Général de brigade* Jean Joseph Humbert, which landed on the west coast of Ireland at Cill Chuimin (Kilcummin) Strand, County Mayo, on 22 August 1798. Humbert only had 1,100 men under his command, but the remote location of the landing ensured they were unopposed by any Crown forces.[1] At this time most Government troops were being used to mop up the remaining pockets of rebels in Leinster in the east of the kingdom.

The element of surprise ensured initial success for the French invasion. On 22 August 1798, a fleet of three frigates and one corvette carried a small French army into Killala Bay, County Mayo. Initially meant more as a reconnaissance force for an intended larger army that was still gathering in France, the number landed was certainly insufficient to pose a major threat to the Irish government. Under the experienced command of Humbert, the French force comprised 888 infantrymen (mainly of the 70e demi-brigade), 42 artillerymen, 57 cavalry troopers (mostly of the 3e chasseurs à cheval) and 35 staff.[2] The French had been militarily unprepared to offer substantial support when the United Irish had risen in May; their navy was weak, finance was limited and a large number of their available forces were already earmarked for Bonaparte's expedition to Egypt. Due mainly to the promises of the Irish republican, Wolfe Tone, that a French invasion would be supported by a general uprising, plans were hastily formulated for an 8,000 man expedition to be led by *Général de brigade* Jean Hardy.[3] However, political intrigue within the French Directory, possibly promoted by Count d'Antraigues who was receiving payments from Pitt's secret service, ensured the withholding

---
1   Hayes, *The Last Invasion of Ireland*, pp.16–25.
2   Murtagh, 'General Humbert's Futile Campaign', p.177.
3   Murtagh, 'General Humbert's Futile Campaign', p.176.

of the necessary funds to mount the large-scale operation.⁴ Subsequently, Humbert embarked without waiting for Hardy's troops and after escaping detection by the Royal Navy successfully landed unopposed at the isolated coastal village of Killala. Humbert's rash actions jeopardised the success of the whole venture, with the news of his landing leading to the forfeiture of surprise and tightening of the naval blockade of the French coast that hindered Hardy from providing the necessary reinforcements.

The nearby small town of Killala was the first settlement to be captured by the French after a brief, but futile, resistance had been made by a small company-size mixed force of about 80 Crown troops, consisting of a small detachment of the 6th Dragoon Guards cavalry and yeomanry. This force had originally deployed on a ridge on Mullaghorn Hill near the outskirts of the town but evacuated the position when the French advanced on them. The Crown troops then withdrew into Killala and took up a defensive position in a side street. In an attempt to cut off any retreat from the town, Humbert sent a detachment of French and United Irishmen to the south of Killala, while United Irishman, Captain Henry O'Kane, rode into the town to reconnoitre the enemy defences. After shooting a local yeoman who had challenged him, O'Kane rode back to report his findings, whereupon *Chef de brigade* Jean Sarrazin who was in command of the French advanced guard, ordered a general advance into the town. When Sarrazin and his troops reached the centre of Killala they received an ineffective volley from the small Crown force that then fled in disorder when the French presented their bayonets ready to charge. The yeoman retreated to the grounds of the local castle, where they surrendered a short time later, while the dragoons took flight along the road to Ballina. Humbert and the small group of United Irishmen who had travelled from France with him, such as O'Kane and Bartholomew Teeling, who was an aide-de-camp to the French commander, had achieved their first victory, albeit only a skirmish. They had taken 25 prisoners for the loss of only one wounded lieutenant.⁵

News of the French landing had caused extreme panic among the Protestant Ascendancy in the west of Ireland. Those yeomanry who had escaped Killala raised the alarm among the local Crown forces, resulting in cavalry units of yeomanry, Orangemen and 'other Cromwellian gentry'

French *Général de brigade*, 1796. (Anne S.K. Brown Military Collection)

---

4 Hayes, *The Last Invasion of Ireland*, p.9.
5 Hayes, *The Last Invasion of Ireland*, p.9.

(Protestants) hurrying to Ballina the night of the landing. By the following morning the Crown force at Ballina amounted to more than 1,000 men, which also included a small garrison of regular troops.[6]

By this time news of the invasion had also spread among the local Catholic population, resulting in a large number of disaffected Irish making their way to the town to join the force of United Irishmen, led by Captains Neil Kerrigan and Henry O'Kane, supporting the French invasion. A French landing in Connacht had been considered by Cornwallis as one of the least likely places for this to occur due to the rising only having occurred in the north and east of Ireland, and that there had been no indication of active popular support for the United Irish in the west. When news of the invasion in Connacht reached Dublin, it came as a surprise to Cornwallis who then officially placed the whole kingdom under martial law for fear of an expected larger French force being landed elsewhere where the United Irish had been more active.

However, there was significant support for the United Irish cause in the west, especially among the Catholic peasantry. This is not surprising when considering the miserable existence many of them were suffering. An example of this can be found in the writing of *Capitaine* Jobit, a French officer in Humbert's force, who wrote of his impressions of the local population after the landing at Kilcummin:

> We were surprised at the poverty which we saw at the first part of our journey; never did a country present a more mournful appearance. The men, women and children were almost naked and have no other shelter than the small wretched cabin, which gives no protection against the severity of the weather and which they share with poultry. When we passed the miserable cabins, which we entered only to look around, those inside prostrated themselves at our feet and, with their faces against the ground, chanted long prayers for our success.[7]

Support for the French expedition also came from the disaffected Catholic gentry. Upon landing, the United Irish leaders sent out riders throughout the country to tell of the landing in the hope of raising the population to their cause with the password, *T a do caraid ag Cill Eala* ('Your friends are at Killala'). This led to a quick response, with large numbers of recruits and sympathisers arriving at Killala, some of which had previous military experience. One such person was Colonel Matthew Bellow, a former officer in the Austrian army and who was also the younger brother of the Catholic bishop of Killala. Eleven of his maternal uncles had been officers in the French Irish Brigade, which was proof of his family's distinguished military service. In view of this, Humbert immediately appointed him as general in command of the Irish auxiliaries that continued to gather at Killala.[8] Catholic priests were also active in recruiting support for the expedition, with locals such as Father David Kelly of Ballycroy, Father Monnelly of Backs, Father

---

6   Hayes, *The Last Invasion of Ireland*, pp.24–25.
7   Hayes, *The Last Invasion of Ireland*, p.18.
8   Hayes, *The Last Invasion of Ireland*, p.22.

DEFEAT OF THE FRENCH INVASION

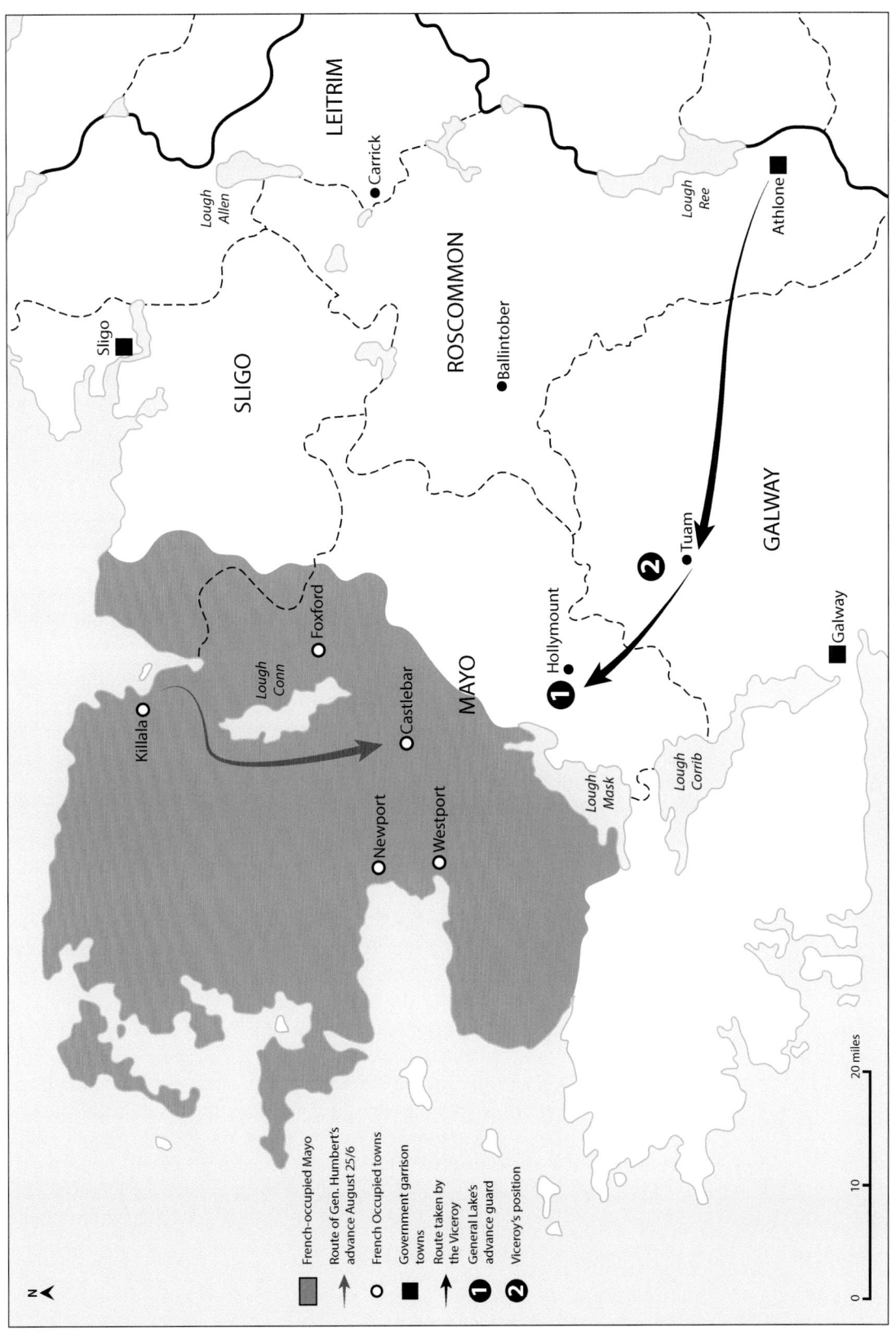

French invasion of County Mayo, August 1798 (Source: Pakenham, *The Year of Liberty*, revised edition, abridged by Toby Buchan, p.117)

James Conroy of Adragoole and Father Owen Cowley bringing in recruits from their parishes.[9]

Although the exact number of local recruits is unknown, there is evidence that groups were arriving at Humbert's headquarters at Killala Castle in their hundreds on an hourly basis and amounted to over 1,000 within 24 hours of the French landing. Once there they were issued with items of French uniforms and were formed into companies under local leaders who had been commissioned by Humbert. Muskets, ammunition, and pikes were distributed to the recruits, while swords and pistols were issued to the new officers. They were subsequently paraded and underwent rudimentary drill and marching; but there were no illusions regarding their military effectiveness against trained regular troops, which these raw levies could never be expected to match.

Humbert's next success came with the capture of Ballina, a few miles south of Killala, two days after the landing. His immediate objective was the capture of Castlebar, the administrative centre of County Mayo and to do that he first had to take control of Ballina. To this end, following the day of the landing and seizure of Killala, he dispatched Sarrazin with a force of 250 men to do a reconnaissance along the road to Ballina that led along the river Moy. Sarrazin was accompanied by a young United Irishmen named Duffy who was a local of the district, but who had travelled to France two years previous and had joined the French army due to his patriotic zeal. It was Duffy who led the advanced guard, dressed in a green coat of the United Irish.[10]

However, when Sarrazin and his small force approached Ballina, he discovered that the town was occupied by a much larger force, including two pieces of artillery. He decided to withdraw back towards Killala to report to Humbert. This was in view of the Crown force, whose commanders were of the opinion the French were withdrawing in panic. Several hours later a cavalry force of regulars and yeomanry advanced up the same road and got to within a mile of Killala before they were challenged by 100 French dragoons who had ridden out from the town. A small firefight occurred resulting in the Crown force making a hasty retreat after they had been outflanked by a small detachment of Irish rebels led by Colonel Fontaine. The Ballina garrison then withdrew all the way to Foxford, 10 miles south of Ballina, abandoning the town altogether.[11]

Humbert began moving the main Franco-Irish force from Killala to Ballina on Saturday 25 August after Sarrazin had taken possession of it the day before. However, on the same day he received intelligence that a large British garrison at Sligo was intending to move south to recapture Killala. He could not afford to lose the town as it was his supply base where he had stored 280 barrels of gunpowder, and his intended point to retreat to for embarkation if the expedition should fail.[12] To counter this he sent *Chef de*

---

9   Hayes, *The Last Invasion of Ireland*, p.22.
10 Hayes, *The Last Invasion of Ireland*, p.22.
11 Pakenham, *The Year of Liberty*, p.352.
12 Pakenham, *The Year of Liberty*, p.352.

DEFEAT OF THE FRENCH INVASION

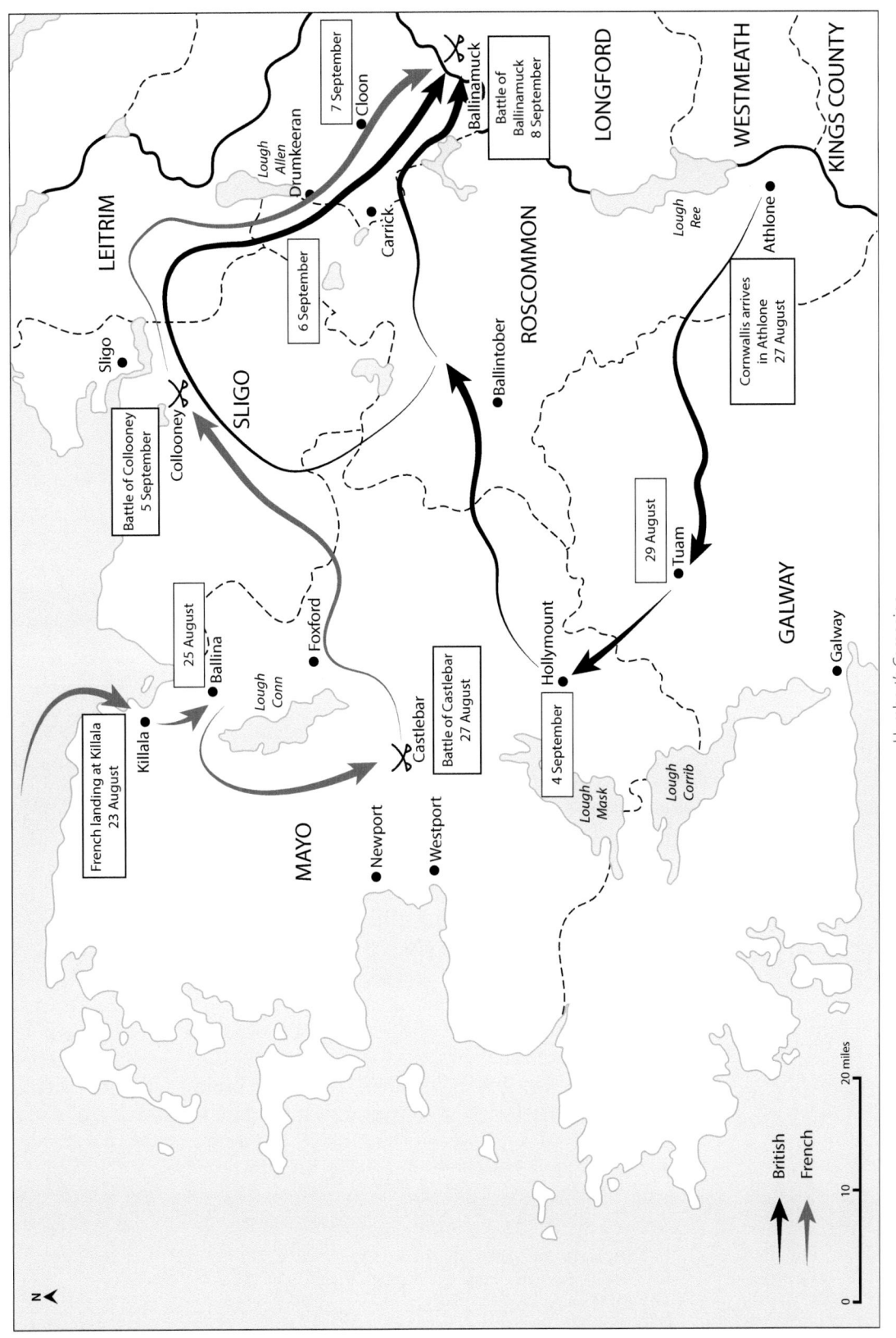

Humbert's Campaign

brigade Charost with 200 French soldiers, along with a company of Irish auxiliaries, back to Killala to defend the town.[13]

The French were well received by the population of Ballina and, according to Thomas Pakenham, the number of Irish insurgents volunteering joining the Franco-Irish force had reached around 5,000. The majority of these were Catholic peasants who had no military experience, or knowledge of how to load and fire muskets, and were of little value militarily. However, there were a number of Catholic gentry who had previously served as officers in the French army that came to offer their service to the cause at this point. Notable among these was Colonel Austin O'Malley who had brought with him other family members and retainers from his estate. However, the most notable of all was George Blake of Garracloon who had previously served as an officer in the British army and was reputed for his courage and military efficiency; Humbert immediately offered him a commission as a general to command all of the Irish insurgents.[14]

Humbert's position was precarious, and he was forced to maintain the initiative if he was to succeed in the venture. Apart from the British force threatening his base at Killlala, he had also been advised that there were 3,500 regulars advancing towards him, which included a substantial force established at Castlebar.[15] He decided his best chance of success was to defeat the enemy at Castlebar before the Crown forces could fully unite and defeat him by superior numbers. A victory at Castlebar could also inspire a greater uprising of the Irish population, which was the main reason for the expedition in the first place.

The Battle of Castlebar

On Sunday 26 August Humbert advanced from Ballina towards Castlebar with 700 French infantry and cavalry, along with a similar number of Irish levies and a single cannon. The obvious route to take was via the main coach road through Foxford and then on to Castlebar. However, a local parish priest reported that a strategic bridge at Foxford was blocked by a substantial garrison of 1,000 Crown troops and that an alternative route via an undefended mountainous cart track could be used without alerting the enemy. Although this 25-mile route proved difficult, especially as it was a night march, Humbert was able to avoid a costly clash at Foxford and surprise the Crown forces when he arrived outside Castlebar the following morning.[16]

The Crown force at Castlebar was led by Major General John Hely-Hutchinson who was in command of all Government forces in Connacht at this time. He had 1,700 troops available to him in defence of the town, the majority of which were Irish militia (Kilkenny and Longford regiments), along with four companies of Fraser's Scottish Fencibles, a detachment of

---

13 Hayes, *The Last Invasion of Ireland*, p.31.
14 Hayes, *The Last Invasion of Ireland*, p.33.
15 Pakenham, *The Year of Liberty*, p.353.
16 Pakenham, *The Year of Liberty*, p.353.

Lord Roden's 1st Irish Fencible Cavalry, a troop of the 6th Dragoon Guards, a single understrength company of the 6th Foot, the Galway Yeomanry Infantry, together with 10 light artillery pieces and a single howitzer.[17] If managed effectively, this force should have been sufficient to successfully defend the town and Hutchinson was confident that the plans he had devised would result in victory. His confidence was further boosted with the arrival of Lieutenant General Lake from Dublin who brought additional troops with him.[18]

As it turned out, Hutchinson had been advised by a local yeoman who had come across Humbert's advance in the early hours of the morning that the French had taken an unexpected route. He immediately sent out one of his senior subordinate commanders, Brigadier General Trench, along with an escort of 200 mounted troops to investigate the situation. After proceeding for about three miles, they reached Mount Burren where they observed Humbert's force rapidly approaching. Upon receiving a volley of musketry Trench and his troops quickly retreated to Castlebar to confirm the situation. This allowed Hutchinson sufficient time to take up a well-placed defensive position with his force of around 5,000 infantry and 1,500 cavalry on Sion Hill to the north of the town before the Franco-Irish force arrived. He had chosen the position the evening before as it commanded the rising country up to 1,000 yards away in the direction that he anticipated the French force would attack.[19]

In theory Hutchinson's conventional defensive line in depth should have defeated the inferior enemy force. The Government troops were formed up in two irregular lines running south-west to north-east, with the flanks secured by two lakes, Tucker's Lake and Lake Rathbawn.[20] The forward line consisted of four curricle (light mobile) guns, including two manned by experienced gunners of the Royal Irish Artillery, and from left to right, the under-strength regular battalion of the 6th Foot, several hundred infantry from the Kilkenny Militia Regiment under the command of Lord Ormonde, and the Prince of Wales Fencibles.[21] Most of the artillery was dispersed along this first defensive line, including a small battery of three guns under the command of Captain James Shortall placed forward on the extreme right of the line. The second line consisted of infantry from the Fraser Fencibles, along with two battalion guns and a corps of the Galway Yeomanry Infantry and was placed to cover an area of rough ground known as the 'Rocks of Rathbawn.'[22] Behind these two lines was a defensive reserve of four companies of the Longford Militia commanded by Lord Granard. According to convention, the cavalry, consisting of Lord Roden's 1st Fencible Cavalry (known as Roden's Foxhunters), several squadrons of the 6th Dragoon Guards, and corps of mounted local yeomanry were held in reserve in between the two

---

17 Reid, *Armies of the Irish Rebellion 1798*, p.44.
18 Hayes, *The Last Invasion of Ireland*, pp.38–39.
19 Hayes, *The Last Invasion of Ireland*, p.41.
20 Hayes, *The Last Invasion of Ireland*, pp.40–41.
21 Hayes, *The Last Invasion of Ireland*, p.41.
22 Hayes, *The Last Invasion of Ireland*, p.41.

lines of infantry, ready to attack the enemy formations once they had been forced to retreat from sustained musketry and artillery fire. About half a mile to the rear, two field guns were positioned on Staball Hill near the entrance to Castlebar, while a number of small mobile artillery pieces were also placed in the town marketplace as a last line of defence.[23] In total, the Government force had an estimated 18 field artillery pieces of various sizes.

Initially the engagement did not go well for Humbert's force of 800 French soldiers and 1,500 Irish insurgents. When the French columns first approached at 8:00 a.m. on 27 August they were facing a formidable and well-equipped enemy who had superior numbers and was defending high ground. Humbert was fully aware of the critical position he was in and had consulted with his French and Irish officers to achieve some consensus as to the best approach to take. Although exhausted from the 16 hours of marching through the night, there was enthusiasm to launch an attack as this was believed as the only chance of victory.[24] After having first sought shelter behind hilly ground near Slievenagark from the Government artillery, Humbert ordered 500 Irish insurgents, armed mostly with pikes, under the command of Colonel Dufour and General Blake to advance in a mass column towards the centre of the Government line. This attack was supported by the advance of two French columns on the flanks. This attack was subjected to artillery fire directed by Lieutenant General Lake, who was confident he could break the enemy advance before it could reach the British line with canister. This certainly effected the Irish levies who broke and ran. However, Sarrazin, whom Humbert had promoted to *Général de brigade* on 23 August, was leading a column of 150 French grenadiers on the left of the line and charged forward along a ditch, which gave some protection from the artillery fire. Another French column under the command of *Chef de brigade* P. Ardouin also advanced under cover on the right. After a period of ineffectual firing at the British artillery, both columns renewed the attack by advancing up the slope of Sion Hill, but the sustained artillery fire proved deadly, and both withdrew with heavy losses.[25]

The situation was now desperate for Humbert who decided on a change of tactics to achieve victory. He had sustained heavy losses by attacking in close columns and the enemy line appeared unbreakable at this point, so he directed a general advance in open order that made the British artillery less effective. With the Irish levies renewing the advance in the centre and the two French detachments charging with the bayonet on the flanks, the front line of the Crown force appeared to be waiving under the French attack, resulting in confusion and panic among the Government troops. Some officers endeavoured to restore discipline, but a sudden order for the withdrawal of troops from the front line caused panic among the second and third lines of defence, leading to a rout.[26]

---

23   Pakenham, *The Year of Liberty*, pp.355–356.
24   Hayes, *The Last Invasion of Ireland*, p.43.
25   Hayes, *The Last Invasion of Ireland*, pp.44–47.
26   Hayes, *The Last Invasion of Ireland*, pp.44–47.

However, there is evidence that some of the Government troops showed great courage in attempting to mount a defence during this time of confusion. Captain Shortall did good service with his exposed battery on the right until the guns were overrun, while the disciplined musketry of Fraser's Fencibles checked Ardouin's troops for a time while the main Government line disintegrated. A few officers managed to rally together small knots of resistance, particularly at Staball Hill where a stubborn defence was marked by the casualties from both sides resulting from hand-to-hand fighting that continued along the road to the bridge in the centre of Castlebar.[27] And despite Hutchinson and Lake later blaming the defeat on the ill-discipline and disaffection of the Irish Militia, it was the Longford Militia under the command of Lords Granard and Ormond that held the bridge in Castlebar until forced to surrender, losing 28 killed and 138 wounded or taken prisoner. It was recorded that 50 men from the regiment were to have supposedly then joined the French, but eye-witness statements concurred that militiamen obeyed their orders and did their duty.[28]

Castlebar was a spectacular victory for the Franco-Irish force, marked by the capture of 11 artillery pieces, five regimental colours, and much needed weapons and military stores.[29] But it came at a cost. It was estimated that about 150 French soldiers and Irish insurgents were either killed or wounded during the battle, most due to the very effective artillery fire during the initial advance. The British losses were even heavier, with over 350 casualties, of which an estimated 80 being killed, with the others being wounded or captured. It was thought that over 150 militiamen became 'turn-coats' and joined Humbert's force. Success at Castlebar was the high point of the French invasion and it allowed Humbert the opportunity to proclaim the 'Republic of Connacht' on 31 August, resulting in thousands of disaffected Irish joining his force. However, the republic was short-lived, lasting only three days and collapsed once he marched towards Dublin and the town was recaptured.[30]

The Longford and Kilkenny militias were made the scapegoats for the ignominious rout that quickly became known as the 'Castlebar Races,' which proved a major embarrassment for the British Army. The traditional historiography surrounding the battle places the blame for the sudden government retreat on the Longford Militia who were placed at the rear of the government defence line. Criticism of the militia came from both Major General Hutchinson and Lieutenant General Lake, who were the senior officers present and although disagreeing over who was in command, concurred that the whole force broke due to the militiamen suddenly falling back from their position.[31]

However, both Hutchinson and Lake were attempting to deflect blame from their own part in the debacle. In a letter to Cornwallis after the battle, Lake attempted to avoid any responsibility by blaming the militia:

---

27 Hayes, *The Last Invasion of Ireland*, pp.46–47.
28 Nelson, *The Irish Militia*, p.222.
29 Hayes, *The Last Invasion of Ireland*, p.51.
30 Hayes, *The Last Invasion of Ireland*, p.70.
31 Ross, *Correspondence of Charles, First Marquis Cornwallis*, pp.388–389.

REBELLION, INVASION AND OCCUPATION

Lieutenant General Gerard Lake. (New York Public Library Free Image Collection)

I think that it is absolutely necessary to state for your Lordship's information that it is impossible to manage the militia; their whole conduct has been this day most shameful, and I am sorry to say that there is a strong appearance of disaffection … I have thought it necessary to march to this place in hope that the soldiers will get the better of their panic, which is beyond description.[32]

In a letter of resignation sent by Hutchinson to Cornwallis at the end of September he claimed that the two militia regiments under his command had been 'previously tampered with' by the United Irish and that their known disaffection had induced the French to attack.[33] He further laid blame on the militia stating that they had run off after having fired volleys on the French without orders and before the French were in musket range.[34] Such comments were conveniently used by the military establishment to cover up mistakes made by the senior commanders and cemented the lasting poor reputation of the Irish militia.

It seems quite clear that the decisions made by Hutchinson were directly responsible for the disastrous defeat at Castlebar. His first mistake was that he failed to seize the opportunity to have his cavalry charge the inferior enemy force when it was in disorder and retreating from the two failed attacks. It could be argued that the ground was unsuitable for horses; but such a move would have most likely caused panic among the untrained and ill-disciplined Irish insurgents providing an opportunity for his infantry to advance down-hill against the greatly outnumbered French infantry. This would have provided an opportunity to destroy the small invasion force and quell further insurgency among the Irish in the west of Ireland as a result.

Hutchinson's second mistake was to order his forward line to withdraw at a time when the enemy were advancing and when the fire of his troops was proving effective in holding the enemy advance. Evidence of this came from officers within the militia who were confused when they, suddenly and without reason, received an order to withdraw, as their troops were doing good work in holding the French and were gaining confidence as the engagement progressed:

> The Kilkenny Regiment formed a portion of the first line of the British force under the command of Lord Ormonde. The French advanced in close column – a favourite of attack with the great Napoleon, and which those soldiers had often practiced with success against the Austrians. Lord Ormonde, who was as brave as

---

32 Ross, *Correspondence of Charles, First Marquis Cornwallis*, pp.388–389.
33 Ross, *Correspondence of Charles, First Marquis Cornwallis*, pp.408–411.
34 Ross, *Correspondence of Charles, First Marquis Cornwallis*, pp.408–411.

he was generous and popular with his men, flinched not but twice gave the very intelligible word of command, 'Kilkennies, make ready, present, fire!' and two volleys were fired at the French as they continued to advance. If the first discharge was too distant to allow of its having much effect, the result of the second was very different … Whilst the Kilkenny Regiment was … thus displaying "great steadfastness before the enemy" an Aide-de-Camp from the generals arrived with an order that they should retire. Lord Ormonde consulted Colonel Wemys and they coinciding in opinion as to the madness of any retrograde movement at such a moment, declined to act upon the order, stating that it must be a mistake of the messenger. Major William Cunningham, who commanded part of the Aberdeenshire, or Prince of Wales Regiment of Fencible Infantry, forming a portion of the line with the Kilkennies, received the same directions, but consulting with Lord Ormonde and Colonel Wemys, he decided to disobey them also. Thus the stout Kilkennies and equally brave Aberdeenshire Fencibles were prepared to meet the advancing Frenchmen with the bayonet … a second Aide-de-Camp from the General rode up to Lord Ormonde with a peremptory order he should retire, and a threat of punishment for disobedience of orders.[35]

It seems clear that Hutchinson's order to retire directly resulted in the outcome of the battle. It obviously caused confusion among the senior officers within the front line as it appeared to them incredulous to be ordered to withdraw and surrender a commanding position in the face of the enemy. This is clear from the description of what occurred from an anonymous officer who was present at the time of the withdrawal who stated, 'The enemy, instead of retreating, as they were preparing to do, instantly rushed forward and gained the advantageous ground which our troops by order quitted; the whole were in motion, confusion ensued, and as there was no plan of retreat, it became extremely disorganised.'[36] Upon seeing the infantry of the first line retreating, the cavalry units turned and galloped off towards Castlebar, causing havoc among the infantry of the second line which disintegrated. The retreat quickly turned into a rout where horses, waggons, baggage, and cannons were abandoned and blocked the roadway to the bridge in the town. However, one cavalry unit, Lord Roden's Fox Hunters, along with the Longford Militia, gallantly stood their ground near the bridge attempting to protect the bulk of the retreating infantry. Close quarter fighting with the pursuing Irish pikemen and French grenadiers resulted in heavy casualties on both sides. A small detachment of Highlanders manning two curricle guns also put a up a stout resistance in the public square until surrounded, but otherwise the majority of the survivors continued running towards Tuam and Athlone.[37] Ultimately, it was easier for Hutchinson to lay the blame for the disaster on the poorly-trained Irish militia, especially after a small number deserted to the French following the battle, than it was to admit his

---

35 'The Old Kilkenny Militia', *The Kilkenny Moderator*, 30 July 1859.
36 Sir Richard Musgrave, *Observations on a pamphlet published by an officer entitled 'Impartial relation of the military operations which took place in Ireland'* (Dublin, T. Stuart, 1799), in Nelson, *The Irish Militia*, p.221.
37 Hayes, *The Last Invasion of Ireland*, pp.48–49.

own error in judgement as a senior professional officer with limited fighting experience at that level of command. Politically it was also convenient to make the militia the scapegoats for the defeat and the perception of the unreliability and mistrust of the Irish troops was perpetuated throughout the nineteenth century.

However, it was plain to Cornwallis where the real blame should lie. In a reply to Major General Hutchinson's letter of resignation as commander in Connacht, the commander-in-chief stated that he believed the general had made a rash 'error in judgement' in moving forward too early without orders. He further stated that it was not prudent or advisable to place inexperienced troops in a situation of being attacked by seasoned regular forces or to have to make a 'precipitate' retreat.[38] However, Cornwallis did not accept the general's resignation and only added to the false reputation of the native troops through his official correspondence where he claimed he could not release any regular troops from Ireland for the campaign in Egypt due to him being burdened 'with a militia on which no dependence whatever can be placed.'[39] His opinion of the militia was obviously influenced by the reports of his subordinates and the views of the Ascendancy from what he stated in a letter to Major General Sir Charles Ross in September 1798: 'the Irish militia, from their repeated misbehaviour in the field, and their extreme licentiousness, are fallen into such universal contempt and abhorrence, that when applications are made for the protection of troops, it is often requested that Irish militia may not be sent.'[40]

In truth, Hutchinson was responsible for the defeat and not the militia. His order in the midst of the battle for the first line to retire proved disastrous in that not only did the French then seize the favourable ground, but the confusion and disorder in the government army led to a rout. The first unit to break was a regular cavalry regiment, the 6th Dragoon Guards, which rode through the Longford Militia who were being held in reserve. The disorderly retreat continued through Castlebar where the Longford Militia made a determined stand against experienced French grenadiers at the bridge in an effort to allow the government forces to escape.[41] The defenders eventually surrendered only when the French had cut off their line of retreat. The courageous actions of the militia were tainted by 53 members of the Longford regiment joining the French forces once captured, although this was obviously just an attempt to escape captivity for most of them as the majority had deserted before they reached Ballinamuck.[42] This was accepted by some military authorities who showed clemency to one of the alleged deserters when he stated that he had stood his ground at Castlebar and that it was the army that had deserted him.[43]

---

38   Ross, *Correspondence of Charles, First Marquis Cornwallis*, pp.411–412.
39   Ross, *Correspondence of Charles, First Marquis Cornwallis*, pp.411–412.
40   Ross, *Correspondence of Charles, First Marquis Cornwallis*, pp.414–415.
41   Richard Francis Hayes, 'An Officers Account of the French Campaign in Ireland in 1798', *The Irish Sword*, vol.2, issue 6-7 (1955), pp.161–171.
42   Richard Francis Hayes, 'The Battle of Castlebar', *The Irish Sword*, vol.3, issue 11 (1957), pp.107–114.
43   Nelson, *The Irish Militia*, p.230.

DEFEAT OF THE FRENCH INVASION

After his victory at Castlebar, Humbert immediately set up a provisional government in the town, which according to his second-in-command, *Général de brigade* Sarrazin, was mainly for the purpose of providing bread for the troops.[44] The French remained in the town for nine days awaiting news of a landing by Hardy and were disappointed with the small number of disaffected Irishmen that had joined them.

Without receiving any reinforcements from France and with news of four columns of government troops, amounting to 11,000 men, converging on his position, Humbert was now on the defensive. He was convinced by Sarrazin that their best option was to march into the interior to support the insurgents who had risen in counties Westmeath and Longford, before continuing their march onto Dublin with the intention of releasing imprisoned United Irish leaders.[45] On 4 September, the day before Cornwallis began his advance on Castlebar from Hollymount, less than 20 miles to the south, Humbert led a column of 840 Frenchmen, 600 Irish and four cannon, north toward Ulster.[46] Marching in this direction was meant as a *ruse de guerre* to convince Cornwallis to directly follow, ensuring that Humbert would not be outflanked before crossing the river Shannon.[47]

Near the village of Collooney, County Sligo, a skirmish took place on the morning of 5 September that was celebrated as a victory by the Ascendancy, even though it led to the defeat of the small government force that defended against Humbert's march on the town of Sligo. That morning, after receiving word of the French approach, the commander of the garrison at Sligo, Lieutenant Colonel Charles Vereker, marched out of the town with the 300–400 men of the Limerick Militia, 20 men of the Essex Fencibles, 30 Yeomanry infantrymen, 20 troopers of the 24th Light Dragoons, 30 Yeomanry cavalry, and two light cannons (curricle guns). Vereker took up a defensive position north of Collooney, with his left flank protected by the river Ballysadare and his right flank positioned on a steep, wooded hill. Although outnumbered, the Government force was able to hold Humbert's advance for a time, notably due to the effective gunnery of those manning the two light guns. However, with the French advancing on the right along the river and the Irish rebels to the left, Vereker's small force was eventually outflanked and forced to retreat, losing both guns, one officer and six men killed, with 27 wounded, along with three officers and 65 men captured.[48]

This proved to be a pyrrhic victory for the French who not only sustained 40 casualties, but who were now hotly pursued by the converging Crown troops.[49] Humbert could not afford such costly skirmishes and after receiving news of the United Irish rising in the Midlands, he decided to abandon his advance into Ulster and to try to link up with the Irish insurgents of counties Longford and Westmeath at Granard. However, three days later, after a forced

---

44 Hayes, 'An Officers Account of the French Campaign in Ireland in 1798', pp.161–171.
45 Hayes, 'An Officers Account of the French Campaign in Ireland in 1798', p.163.
46 Hayes, 'An Officers Account of the French Campaign in Ireland in 1798', p.163.
47 Hayes, 'An Officers Account of the French Campaign in Ireland in 1798', p.163.
48 Nelson, *The Irish Militia*, pp.225–226.
49 Hayes, 'An Officers Account of the French Campaign in Ireland in 1798', p.165.

march of 120 miles, the exhausted French and Irish rebel column was finally surrounded at Ballinamuck, County Longford.

Ballinamuck and Aftermath

The Battle of Ballinamuck on 8 September 1798 was more of a brief skirmish than a battle. The British army of 7,824 men led by Cornwallis heavily outnumbered the exhausted French and Irish force and comprised of four divisions commanded by Major Generals Campbell, Hutchinson, Hunter, and Moore. Campbell commanded the fencibles; Hutchinson commanded the Antrim, Armagh and Downshire militia regiments; Hunter led two of the three regular infantry battalions, along with the Louth Militia; while Moore commanded the third regular infantry battalion, two battalions of Irish Militia light infantry, and two companies of English militia.[50] The majority of this force was not used in the engagement, except the light company of the Armagh Militia who charged the French and captured the regimental colour of the 2nd battalion of the 70e Demi-Brigade. Indeed, the only Crown infantry who fought in this encounter were from the Irish Militia – with the 3rd battalion of Militia Light Infantry also engaged.[51] With only 850 French regulars and now around 1,000 Irish rebels in his small army, Humbert knew his position at Ballinamuck was hopeless. Cornwallis, with his superior force, was blocking his advance on Dublin, and Lieutenant General Lake was pursuing him from the west and preventing any retreat to the coast. He ordered his troops to put up some brief resistance for about half an hour, as honour demanded, before surrendering. This was followed by the massacre of hundreds of the Irish insurgents whose surrender was not accepted by Lake and who had ordered his dragoons to pursue and dispatch them in the field. This was followed by the hanging of numerous Irish officers of the Irish Legion who were considered traitors rather than legitimate prisoners of war.[52]

The surrender of Humbert effectively ended the French invasion, although the final military action did not occur until 15 days later at Killala on 23 September. It was here that Brigadier General Trench led a force of approximately 3,000 men, comprising Irish militia, English dragoons and Scottish fencibles, that surrounded the town and routed the smaller force comprising of a cadre of French officers and around 800 Irish Legion insurgents who had mounted a brief defence of the approaches to the town. This was followed by the indiscriminate killing of those attempting to escape the slaughter that occurred in the streets, as well as the hanging of some officers of the Irish Legion; a repeat of what occurred at Ballinamuck.[53]

Three main factors determined the failure of the French invasion. Firstly, the inability of the French to effectively coordinate the simultaneous

---

50   Nelson, *The Irish Militia*, pp.226–227.
51   Nelson, *The Irish Militia*, pp.226–227.
52   Pakenham, *The Year of Liberty*, p.373.
53   Hayes, *The Last Invasion of Ireland*, pp.170–177.

landing of all the troops allocated for the campaign hindered any chance of success. The force of 8,000 experienced men intended for the invasion would have posed a serious military threat to Dublin Castle, who could only rely on the few regular regiments that had remained in the kingdom after being sent from Britain during the rebellion.[54] An even larger expedition under the command of Irish-born, *Général de division* Charles Edward Saul Jennings of Kilmaine, County Mayo, was being gathered at Brest to reinforce Hardy, and had it actually sailed to Ireland, avoiding the naval blockade, the French would have been able to field an army of nearly 20,000 experienced troops.[55] However, the French plan was flawed through the near impossibility of having the separate forces embarking from Rochefort, Dunkirk and Brest converging on the west coast of Ireland at the same time. The weather determined when the fleets could sail and then they had to negotiate the blockade of the Royal Navy. Secondly, the location of the landing was unsuitable. The province of Connacht was the least likely region to rise in support of the invasion. Although there was widespread sympathy for the rebel cause, the United Irish were poorly organised in the western counties, with the Catholic Defenders very weak as a result of Carhampton's counter-insurgent measures in 1795.[56] The French were reliant on the population rising up against the government not only to provide an auxiliary force to augment their army, but also to ensure the dispersal of Crown troops to counter insurrection. The third factor that finally sealed the fate of the French invasion was the ability of the Royal Navy to intercept the subsequent French fleets carrying reinforcements. On 12 October a British naval squadron of frigates under Commodore John Borlase Warren engaged a French fleet commanded by *Vice amiral* Jean Baptiste François Bompard near Lough Swilly, Donegal. Bompard was carrying *Général de brigade* Jean Hardy and a force of 3,000 men, which was the largest of the expeditionary forces sent to Ireland. Six of the nine French ships were taken, along with Wolfe Tone, the United Irishman who had been instrumental in persuading the French to invade. Four days before the surrender at Ballinamuck, a small expedition of only 270 grenadiers had sailed from Dunkirk, which included another Irish republican, Napper Tandy. However, by the time the fleet had reached Rutland, County Donegal on 16 September, news of Humbert's surrender resulted in its immediate return to France and the abandonment of Kilmaine's reinforcing expedition. Depending on what could be captured through invasion, realistically, the dominance of the Royal Navy would have made the resupply of any sizable French force in Ireland near impossible, ensuring its isolation and eventual defeat.

The increase in the military establishment of Ireland during the rebellion ensured Cornwallis's defeat of the French invasion. Camden's repeated calls for reinforcements during the uprising had led to an influx of British regular, fencible and militia regiments into the kingdom. At the time of the French

---

54 Murtagh, 'General Humbert's Futile Campaign', p.176.
55 Murtagh, 'General Humbert's Futile Campaign,' p.176.
56 Murtagh, 'General Humbert's Futile Campaign', p.176.

REBELLION, INVASION AND OCCUPATION

The French frigate *La Bellone* engaged with the British 80-gun, HMS *Foudroyant*. (Public Domain)

landing Cornwallis had approximately 100,000 men under his command in Ireland, although only 10,000 were regulars. News of the invasion ensured that another 10,000 were sent from Britain in September, but the French had been defeated before most had arrived.[57] The inexperienced militia, fencibles and yeomanry remained the greater part of the government force available to meet the threat. The most professional element of Cornwallis's force was the Royal Irish Artillery which consisted of a battalion of 6-pounder cannon that had a round-shot range of 600–800 metres. These guns proved most effective in engaging and dispersing the enemy well before they could get into musket range.

It was the ability to coordinate and concentrate superior forces that ensured victory for Cornwallis. When Humbert landed at Killala, the government had less than 4,000 troops in Connacht, and those they had were mainly militia and yeomanry under the command of Major General Hutchinson.[58] In a rash move, and against the orders of Cornwallis, Hutchinson divided his forces and marched from Galway with a combined force of 1,700 men to take up a position at Castlebar in an effort to gain intelligence regarding the movements of the enemy.[59] The new lord lieutenant had dispatched Lieutenant General Lake to take command of the government troops west of the River Shannon, and he arrived at Castlebar on 26 August, the night before the French attack. By this time, Cornwallis himself was heading towards Connacht with a column of 7,000 men hoping to engage the French only once

---

57 Ferguson, 'The army in Ireland from the restoration to the act of Union', pp.179–183.
58 Murtagh, 'General Humbert's Futile Campaign', p.181.
59 Ross, *Correspondence of Charles, Marquis Cornwallis*, pp.411–412.

he had reinforced Lake.[60] However, as a result of Humbert's victory at Castlebar, the commander-in-chief had to formulate a new strategy that involved the convergence of three columns to surround the invaders. Cornwallis then ordered Major General Nugent to march to Enniskillen to prevent Humbert from moving into Ulster, while he directed Major General George Hewitt to assemble the available troops from the south and east at Portumna to create a blocking force to prevent any movement on Dublin. Cornwallis took control of the offensive in the west and followed the French, hoping to prevent them crossing the Shannon. A light force commanded by Lieutenant Colonel Robert Craufurd, constantly harried the French column from the rear, leading to exhausting forced marches by the French which eventually led to a breakdown of morale.[61] Although Cornwallis was criticised in some quarters, especially from prominent members of the Ascendancy with whom he had previously clashed, for initially being too timid in his handling of the campaign, his strategy proved effective. The French were defeated and captured at Ballinamuck on 8 September, only 18 days after they had landed, while the few Irish rebels that rose in support of the invasion had either been killed, captured, or dispersed. This second defeat, coupled with the oppressive mopping-up operations, proved devastating for the republican cause, with the enduring images and experiences of death and destruction remaining with an Irish population that never again challenged the might of the military establishment in open combat until the Easter Rising of 1916, more than a century later.

Charles, 1st Marquis of Cornwallis – Governor General of his Majesty's Kingdom of Ireland. (Anne S.K. Brown Military Collection)

The atrocities committed by the government forces in the rebellion were repeated during the French invasion campaign. Unlike the earlier uprising, the French received minimal popular support. The insurgents that did rise up were mainly restricted to around 600–700 rebels that joined Humbert when he landed at Killala, followed by around 3,000 after the victory at Castlebar, which included some militiamen and yeomen.[62] However, apart from the few middle-class Catholics, such as James MacDonnell, who were made officers, the majority of rebels were of poor peasant stock and prone to desertion. A

---

60 Murtagh, 'General Humbert's Futile Campaign', p.183.
61 Hayes, 'An Officers Account of the French Campaign in Ireland in 1798', p.165.
62 Hayes, 'An Officers Account of the French Campaign in Ireland in 1798', p.165.

small number of rebels also enlisted in the French force when the column marched into the interior, while several thousand had risen in Counties Longford and Westmeath hoping to link up with Humbert. Once defeated, the French were humanely treated as prisoners of war, especially the officers who were paroled and entertained in Dublin. However, the Irish officers, including those officially in the French army, such as Humbert's adjutant, Bartholomew Teeling, were treated as traitors and subsequently executed, mostly without trial. At Ballinamuck, Lieutenant General Lake promoted the slaughter of the Irish levies by encouraging the cavalry to run the rebels down instead of accepting their surrender.[63] Captain Thomas Pakenham, who had been appointed the honorary title lieutenant general of the government ordnance, told the rebels to run before they were cut down, but the warning came too late. Of the 1,000 rebels still with the French at the time of surrender over 200 were indiscriminately killed while either trying to surrender or attempting to escape.[64] However, about 90 insurgents were taken prisoner on the battlefield only to be executed a short time later, including nine deserters from the Longford Militia who had joined the French at Castlebar.[65] Prior to this the rebels in the Midlands suffered the same fate. On 5 September at Wilson's Hospital, near Longford, more than 200 rebels were hunted down and killed by a force of local yeomanry and Highland fencibles while the insurgents were negotiating a surrender, while at Granard an unsuccessful attack on the garrison led to a rout of the rebels and the massacre of more than 400 insurgents, many of them while attempting to surrender.[66] The bloodshed continued with the end of the campaign in County Mayo, where 400 rebels were sabred to death by fencible cavalry in the streets of Killala on 23 September after their attempts to surrender were refused.[67] Subsequently, the zeal of the military forces, especially the yeomanry, ensured that many innocent civilians, including women, children and priests, became victims of an unofficial counter-insurgent policy of extermination that remains a stain on the reputation of the Irish army of the period.

Ultimately, the defeat of the rebellion and the French invasion marked a turning point in the military establishment of Ireland. The violent times had ensured that attitudes had hardened with sectarianism coming to the fore. The Protestant Ascendancy would no longer tolerate the defence of the kingdom being left to the militia, which was seen by many as providing the Catholic peasantry with the means to rise again. The uprising and subsequent invasion had ensured that the British government were determined to maintain the security of Ireland as part of the defence of Britain, which necessitated political dominance from London through an act of union. Ireland was now to be not only a major recruiting ground for the expanding armed forces of Britain, but it was to be turned into a military bastion that would effectively lead to a lasting military occupation of the kingdom.

---

63 Hayes, *The Last Invasion of Ireland*, p.297.
64 Pakenham, *The Year of Liberty*, p.373.
65 Pakenham, *The Year of Liberty*, p.374.
66 Pakenham, *The Year of Liberty*, pp.371–372.
67 Murtagh, 'General Humbert's Futile Campaign', p.186.

7

The British Military Occupation of Ireland

The upheavals of 1798 were to have a lasting effect on the military establishment of Ireland. Post-rebellion politics heavily influenced the composition and use of the armed forces in the kingdom, with the Act of Union bringing Ireland under the direct control of the Westminster parliament in 1801. The importance of Ireland in the overall security of Britain was more appreciated during the continuing wars with France, where the country was perceived acutely as the soft underbelly in the defence of the realm. The potential for invasion and the constant fear of renewed insurrection prompted Pitt and Cornwallis to convince the various factions within the Irish society that their interests would now best be served by being governed from London. Surprisingly, it was the mistrusted Catholic population that gave the greatest support to the Union, with the Protestant Ascendancy hesitant to relinquish political control.[1] However, it was the Act of Union that eventually brought greater stability to the country, while strengthening the position of the Protestant minority. This came about by the rapid augmentation of the yeomanry through the mobilization of the Protestant male population, which in effect supplanted the role of the militia in the garrison. The political and sectarian-motivated attitudes which led to the poor reputation that the Irish militia had been labelled with from the events of 1798 ensured that this force could not be trusted by the Ascendancy and government in the defence of the kingdom. This ensured that the militia was now seen as an institution for providing semi-trained recruits to the regular army or relegated to provide garrisons where loyal forces could supervise them. Ireland became a major source of military manpower, especially when the threat of invasion lessened after 1805 and with the renewed determination of the Irish Catholics to prove their loyalty to the Crown in the hope of emancipation, ensuring little support for any future attempted uprising, such as Emmet's rebellion in 1803.[2] British regular, fencible (until 1802) and militia regiments were continually posted and rotated throughout Ireland post-1798 to counter the

---

1 Cronin, *A History of Ireland*, pp.114–116.
2 Bartlett, 'Defence, counter-insurgency and rebellion', p.288.

perceived unreliability of the militia, ensuring that, in effect, the Catholic population were placed under the military occupation of Protestant forces.

Pitt and his supporters were of the opinion that it was better to have the Ireland included in the British state and governed from a single parliament than to allow the continuation of a neighbouring semi-independent state, whose volatile domestic issues and poor state of defence seriously compromised the defence of the realm.[3] Pitt was hopeful that by drawing Ireland into the British union the power of the Irish Ascendancy could be broken, leading to a greater inclusion of Catholics and Presbyterian dissenters in the political process through emancipation, which he had indicated would occur through the union, thus, ultimately ensuring less internal tension.[4] The violence and destruction experienced in the rebellion and French invasion ensured that more factions within Irish society were now amenable to a union with Britain. Pitt had gained general Catholic support for the move by indicating full emancipation for Catholics under the union, an entitlement that they were unlikely to receive from the Ascendancy, especially in the wake of the uprising which had seen the destruction of the independence movement. Yet, the move also gained support from many Protestants who preferred a reduction in their political powers and the protection of Britain rather than face further domestic insurrection and invasion.[5] However, not all the Irish oligarchy favoured surrendering their power, especially those members of Orange orders who were against the franchising of the Catholic majority.

In January 1799, just four months after the last action of the campaign against the French invasion force, the Irish parliament rejected the proposed union. Determined to see the Act of Union come into force, Pitt, assisted by Cornwallis and his chief secretary, Lord Castlereagh, used patronage, bribery and bullying tactics to ensure they gained sufficient support in the Irish parliament for the bill to proceed.[6] This ensured that the act was passed when the government next debated the issue on 15 January 1800, where the vote resulted in 138 members supporting the move with 98 opposing it.[7] The parliament had voted itself out of existence with the Act of Union taking effect on 1 January 1801, ensuring Ireland was now completely controlled from London.

The continued insurgency from 1798 and 1803, which ended with the failure of Emmet's rebellion in Dublin in July 1803 and the subsequent surrender of Michael Dwyer and his followers, prompted a vital change in the composition of the military force that was to garrison and police the kingdom.[8] In the aftermath of the rebellion the yeomanry increasingly replaced the militia in the vanguard of the defence force, where internal security remained the main priority. This shift in military policy was not

---

3   Jacqueline Hill, 'Convergence and conflict in Eighteenth Century Ireland', *The Historical Journal*, vol.44, no. 4 (December 2001), pp.1039–1063.
4   Cronin, *A History of Ireland*, pp.114–116.
5   Bartlett, 'Defence, counter-insurgency and rebellion', p.292.
6   Dickson, *New Foundations: Ireland 1660-1800*, p.217.
7   Hill, 'Convergence and conflict in Eighteenth Century Ireland', pp.1039–1063.
8   Bartlett, 'Defence, counter-insurgency and rebellion', p.290.

through any official directive but more from necessity and a lack of faith in the loyalty and capabilities of the militia. As a professional soldier, Cornwallis was angered and reluctant to have to rely on a yeomanry force that he perceived as ill-disciplined and lacking in training: 'these men have saved this country, but now they take the lead in rapine and murder.'[9] Major General Sir Arthur Wellesley (later the Duke of Wellington), Chief Secretary of Ireland in 1807, had a similar view and was a proponent of increasing the number of regular troops to secure the defence of the country: 'Let those who think that the yeomanry and loyal inhabitants would keep down the rebels in the country in case of the occurrence [French invasion] of the event supposed, consider what would be the state of Ireland even at this moment, or at any other moment, if the regular troops were withdrawn.'[10]

However, the yeomanry was militarily essential in the defence of Ireland in a period when the demand for regular regiments in foreign campaigns ensured that very few were posted to the Irish establishment. Those units that were sent to Ireland were generally numerically weak, where it was intended that they recruit up to strength before embarking for other service.[11] A proposal for militia interchange with Britain was on the agenda soon after 1798 but was initially rejected due to the anti-Catholic attitude of the king.[12] Unwilling to rely on the Irish militia and without a substantial number of regular troops to count on, the lord lieutenant was forced to become reliant on the Protestant yeomanry at a time when problems of rising sectarianism in Ireland were secondary to the greater military needs of Britain.

Table 7.1 – Yeomanry Cavalry and Infantry Numbers, 1796-1815

Date	Cavalry	Infantry
Dec. 1796	10,000	10,000
Dec. 1797	18–20,000	15–17,000
May 1798	15,000	21,000
1799	13,000	53,000
Oct. 1801	10,000	40,000
Dec. 1803	9,000	57,000
Dec. 1804	7,000	52,000
Dec. 1805	8,000	58,000
Dec. 1806	6,000	53,000
Dec. 1807	7,000	50,000
Mar. 1810	9,000	71,000
Dec. 1815	100	43,000

Source: Blackstock, *An Ascendancy Army*, p. 116.

---

9 Ross, *Correspondence of Charles, First Marquis Cornwallis*, pp.370–371.
10 2nd Duke of Wellington (ed), *Civil Correspondence and Memoranda of Field Marshal Arthur Duke of Wellington, K.G.* (London: John Murray, 1860), pp.28–36, Letter to Lord Hawkesbury, 7 May 1807.
11 TNA: HO 100/55: Earl of Camden to the Duke of Portland, 28 November 1795.
12 BL: Add. MSS 37845: ff. 77, Duke of Portland to Lord Windham, quoted in J.R. Western, 'Roman Catholics Holding Military Commissions in 1798', *The English Historical Review*, vol.70, no. 276 (July,1955), pp.428–432.

The Dominance of the Yeomanry

The rapid augmentation of the yeomanry post-1798 made it the largest element of the Irish military establishment. When the rebellion erupted in May 1798 the official number of men enlisted in the yeomanry was 50,000, which included 15,000 cavalrymen.[13] However, the perceived threat of invasion, but more importantly the constant fear of rebellion, ensured that yeomanry numbers continued to increase after the crisis of 1798. There was some fluctuation in numbers, mainly due to the short-lived peace following the Treaty of Amiens, but by 1810 the yeomanry had reached its greatest strength, amounting to 85,000 effectives.[14] The greatest period of augmentation took place under Henry Addington's administration which restored only a numerically small Irish militia, but increased the yeomanry from 45,000 in 450 individual corps to 80,000 in 800 corps by 1804.[15] However, experience during 1798 led to a change in the structure of the corps (Table 7.1). Prior to the rebellion the yeomanry consisted of a high proportion of cavalry, but these proved unsuitable against the rebel pikemen who inflicted high casualties on the mounted yeomen. The cost of maintaining such large numbers of cavalrymen also proved prohibitive for the government and local gentry, ensuring that yeomanry corps was increasingly made up of infantrymen from as early as 1799. An examination of available returns provide evidence of this: in May 1798 the yeomanry corps consisted of 15,000 cavalry and 21,000 infantry; in 1799 there were 13,000 cavalrymen and 53,000 infantrymen, while by 1810 the yeomanry consisted of only 9,000 cavalry but included 71,000 infantry.[16] And although the force was truly a national institution with corps being established in every county, city and major town throughout Ireland, the largest concentration of yeomen remained in Ulster which had 36,782 enlisted yeomen in 1810.[17] By this time, and mainly in response to the rebellion, the yeomanry was almost exclusively Protestant, with Catholics being purged from many corps due to their perceived unreliability.[18] In effect, the yeomanry had now become the established military arm of the Ascendancy who were determined to maintain control over the Catholic population.

When Cornwallis took office as commander-in-chief in 1798, he formulated a new plan for the defence of Ireland. This involved dividing the army into five separate military districts where the available units were to be brigaded into stationary and movable forces. It was intended that these troops were to be engaged in normal garrison duties but could be rapidly concentrated to counter any invasion force.[19] The yeomanry became part of the stationary force where individual corps came together to form infantry battalions and cavalry squadrons. Cornwallis considered the yeomanry unfit

---

13 Blackstock, *An Ascendancy Army*, p.114.
14 Blackstock, *An Ascendancy Army*, p.114.
15 Cookson, *The British Armed Nation*, p.167.
16 Cookson, *The British Armed Nation*, p.116.
17 TNA: HO 100/155: Abstract of Yeomanry Inspection Report, 24 March 1810.
18 Hill, 'Convergence and Conflict in Eighteenth Century Ireland', p.1057.
19 Ross, *Correspondence of Charles, First Marquis Cornwallis*, p.298.

for field service with regular units and intended that these formations be used to occupy strategic strongpoints, bridges, passes and supply depots.[20] In the case of insurrection the yeomanry were primarily intended to defend their immediate locality in the first instance. This policy emphasized the main feature of the corps as a military force in that it had a vested interest in local defence where propertied Protestants were most likely to be the first victims of any rising.

Essentially, during the post-rebellion period, the yeomanry established itself as an important armed political force. With the militia being tainted with the unjustifiable reputation of being disloyal and unreliable, the government and the gentry became reliant on the yeomanry to maintain the rule of law through power and control. This was formalised through the Irish Yeomanry Act of 1802 that legalised the continuation of the yeomanry during times of peace, ensuring the Ascendancy had a permanent armed formation to protect their interests.[21] This strengthened the political position of the Protestant gentry who established a greater relationship with the government through ties of patronage, political expediency, and mutual inter-dependence. The British government became reliant on the yeomanry to maintain law and order, where the corps functioned as a deterrent and whose very existence meant a constant local armed presence. An example of this was the period from 1803 to 1805 when martial law was enforced resulting from Emmet's failed *coup*.[22] However, this relationship with the government had a negative impact for Irish Catholics whose support for the union in the hope of emancipation was in vain. The political strength of the Ascendancy was maintained through the government reliance on the yeomanry, with any move to alter this balance gaining minimal support. This ensured Irish Catholics remained disenfranchised for a further two decades.

The increase in size of the yeomanry directly corresponded with the rapid growth of the Orange orders. Although initially wary of the radicalism of the various loyalist lodges, Dublin Castle had agreed to the incorporation of the societies into newly raised yeomanry corps early in 1798 prior to the rebellion when insurgent activities where becoming increasingly violent.[23] During the uprising and the years following the yeomanry proved to have self-discipline and were effective when defending their own property, but were often 'licentious' when attacking property of others, especially Catholics and dissenters.[24] Such behaviour can be understood when examining the ethos that the Orangemen brought to the organisation. Irish society had been polarised by the violence of the 1790s leading to the rise in sectarianism. The incorporation of the Orange factions into the yeomanry further fostered the growth of loyalism and Orange traditions in the corps through memories of the Williamite wars of the 1690s.[25] This led to the rise in 'popular loyalism'

---

20   Ross, *Correspondence of Charles, First Marquis Cornwallis*, p.73.
21   Blackstock, *An Ascendancy Army*, pp.189–190.
22   Bartlett, 'Defence, counter-insurgency and rebellion', p.293.
23   TNA: HO 100/77: Camden to the Duke of Portland, 11 June 1798.
24   Bartlett, 'Indiscipline and disaffection in Ireland in the 1790s', pp.130–131.
25   Blackstock, *An Ascendancy Army*, p.273.

throughout the Protestant population, with the yeomanry providing an opportunity to revive the self-defence traditions that had been stifled through the abolition of the volunteer movement in 1793. It is estimated that when the yeomanry reached its zenith around 1810 the Protestant population of Ireland was approximately one million, which included 500,000 males of all ages.[26] Taking into consideration that the official strength of the corps was 80,000 at this time, this indicates that one in six of Protestant males were enlisted in the yeomanry. John Cookson's estimation that one-in-three of all Protestant males fit for military service joined the yeomanry seems reasonable when considering those who would have been excluded due to age, illness and deformities, and that age structure of the time indicated that about one-third of the population was aged between 18 and 45.[27] Strong social and religious links bound the yeomen through blood and kin, where the need to protect family and home determined excessive behaviour towards the perceived enemy. Attitudes had hardened from experience of the uprising, with many loyalists viewing the rebellion as a purely religious war, where victory over the Catholic peasantry was seen by some as divine intervention in securing the survival of the true faith.[28]

Ultimately, the yeomanry became the military expression of the Protestant state where it symbolized the physical embodiment and security of the Ascendancy. With the denial of Catholic emancipation in 1800, which was reaffirmed throughout the Napoleonic wars and after, Dublin Castle became exclusively committed to the dominance of the Protestant population. During this era the term 'loyal' became synonymous with Protestantism and the Ascendancy, while 'disaffected' meant Catholic and disloyal.[29] This could account for the significant number of ex-radical Presbyterians who enlisted in the yeomanry in the post-rebellion period to prove their allegiance to the Protestant cause.[30] Loyalism was seen as support for the status quo in the dominance of church and state, and led to the emergence of a new Protestant Irish nationalism that was promoted within the yeomanry. It was such beliefs that led to the exclusion of many Catholics from the corps following the rebellion, ensuring that from 1800 the yeomanry was a nearly exclusive Protestant force.

However, the British government never truly trusted the yeomanry and from 1798 it achieved greater control of the corps with the employment of brigade majors from each county who were appointed by the lord lieutenant. This ensured that individual corps commanders were more answerable to the direction of central government, ensuring Dublin Castle controlled the paramilitary force at a national level. This provided the commander-in-chief of the army with more flexibility in determining its use. After the rising the function of the yeomanry changed in that the corps were now not only to be used as a local police force, but also as a reserve of light troops, permanently

---

26   Blackstock, *An Ascendancy Army*, p.271.
27   Cookson, *The British Armed Nation*, p.167.
28   Hill, 'Convergence and Conflict in Eighteenth Century Ireland', pp.1041–1043.
29   Blackstock, *An Ascendancy Army*, p.298.
30   Blackstock, *An Ascendancy Army*, p.299.

on duty for the duration of the war and no longer limited to service in their immediate locality.[31] In effect, the yeomanry had become a permanent army which was readily available to counteract any perceived internal or external threat. The yeomanry had now evolved from a corps established for the protection of lives and property to one of defence of the Protestant state.

The Denigration of the Militia

The poor reputation of the Irish militia was fostered by the criticism of British generals and other senior regular officers. Critics such as Abercromby, Cornwallis and Moore believed that the militia was inefficient due to nepotism, where colonels nominated mainly inexperienced relatives and close associates for commissions based on their social connections rather than ability.[32] Moore recorded in a diary entry that the militia officers were 'profligate and idle, serving for the emolument, but neither from a sense of duty nor of military distinction.'[33] Such criticism had some justification, although this system of patronage was an accepted practise throughout eighteenth century British and Irish society, and was recognised within the British militias, fencibles and yeomanry corps, along with the Irish militia. Wellesley, also had little faith in the reliability of the militia, but realised that it was required in the defence of Ireland:

> In respect to the militia, the general opinion here is that they are disaffected, that as a military body they are not to be relied upon, and that they ought to be disbanded or removed from the country. I cannot say whether this opinion is well or ill founded; I know that they are liable to great temptations, that at this moment plans are in agitation to prevent them from volunteering into the line, and that the same persons (the priests) might equally endeavour to attain any other object by their influence over their minds. However, to disband them is out of the question, it is equally impossible to remove them from Ireland, and we must endeavour to find out the means of making them better troops be removing them from the temptations which affects their discipline and their loyalty, and by the establishment of a better system among them.[34]

The poor reputation of the Irish militia determined the role of the organisation in the Irish establishment in the post-rebellion years. Prior to the uprising the 38 militia regiments formed the nucleus of an Irish army that had very few regular troops on strength, and it remained the largest part of the army up until 1802, comprising an average of 53 percent of the Crown forces in Ireland between 1793 and 1802.[35] However, although

---

31 Bartlett, 'Indiscipline and disaffection in Ireland in the 1790s', p.131.
32 Brownrigg, *The Life and Letters of Sir John Moore*, p.76.
33 Brownrigg, *The Life and Letters of Sir John Moore*, p.76.
34 Wellington, *Civil Correspondence and Memoranda*, pp.28–36, Letter to Lord Hawkesbury, 7 May 1807.
35 Nelson, *The Irish Militia*, p.248.

the militia lacked the discipline of regular infantry units, the regiments proved loyal and performed well when led by competent officers. Official correspondence to the contrary, as well as popular anti-Irish Catholic caricatures by Gillray and Cruikshank, have been used by numerous historians to substantiate the negative view that was promoted by the Irish Ascendancy. The militia was made the 'scape-goat' of the few reverses that the Crown forces suffered in 1798 and it was eventually superseded by the yeomanry as the main internal defence force. However, it was the perception that the militia was a solely Catholic institution that was the main reason for its eventual relegation to a recruiting corps for the regular army. And although those militiamen who enlisted in regular regiments were volunteers, such religious bias led to post-rebellion policies that ensured thousands of young Catholic men were either shipped off for foreign military service or posted to locations in Britain where they were considered unlikely to desert or rebel.

Table 7.2: Irish establishment, 1793-1802

Date of Return		Militia	Fencibles	Regulars	Other	Total	Percentage Militia
1793	July	5,150		11,094		16,244	32
1794	Jan.	9,495		8,514		18,009	53
	July	11,967		4,134		16,101	74
1795	Jan.	13,336		6,708		20,074	67
	July	15,959		13,335		29,294	54
1796	Jan.	17,437	10,068	1,676		29,181	60
	July	18,093	8,612	1,936		28,641	63
1797	Jan.	18,132	9,141	1,906		29,179	62
	July	20,753	11,874	1,821		34,448	60
1798	Jan.	22,728	10,751	1,830		35,309	64
	July	22,930	13,247	2,380	2,516	41,073	56
1799	Jan.	22,383	12,490	2,335	14,339	51,547	43
	July	16,765	14,661	2,839	6,843	41,108	41
1800	Jan.	18,183	16,934	2,338	2,108	39,589	46
	July	16,765	15,965	8,258	2,787	43,775	38
1801	Jan.	16,473	16,368		8,259	41,100	40
	July	25,337	16,368	8,259		49,964	51
1802	Jan.	25,245	14,827	10,407		50,479	50

Sources: Kilmainham Papers- National Library of Ireland; Rebellion Papers- National Archives of Ireland; Ferguson, 'Army in Ireland,' quoted in Nelson, *The Irish Militia*, p.248.

Contrary to the propaganda of the Ascendancy, the militia proved to be an effective and loyal component of the Irish establishment. The constant rotation of regular regiments to and from Ireland ensured that the government was still reliant on the militia to provide the majority of its permanently mustered infantry force throughout the years of war with France. An example of this can be found in a report published in the *Dublin Evening Post* on 16 July 1808 after Wellesley had embarked from Cork to Portugal with his small expeditionary force made up of regular army regiments that had been recruiting while being part of the Irish garrison:

> In consequence of the reduction of the troops in this garrison by the late embarkation, the duty has fallen so heavily upon the Roscommon and Wexford Militia Regiments, which remain in barrack, that the Yeomanry Corps of this city have very handsomely volunteered their services to take guards occasionally to lighten it. This spirited and considerate offer has been received with proper acknowledgements; and on Sunday next the city duty will be committed to the Yeomanry, for that day only.[36]

At that time many of the new recruits into the regular units where volunteers from the Militia.

When Cornwallis formulated his new strategy of defence for Ireland in April 1800, he was forced to include the militia in the field force due to the lack of available troops. This policy involved the creation of a mobile force of 20,000 and a stationary force of 15,000.[37] It was intended that the mobile force would assemble at various locations before concentrating to challenge any invasion force. The stationary force, which was to comprise primarily of the militia, supported by fencibles and yeomanry, was intended to provide local defence and garrison strategic ports and cities. However, by May 1801 the Antrim, Roscommon, Fermanagh, and Londonderry regiments, predominantly Protestant in rank and file, were included with the four battalions of light infantry, formed from the light companies of various militia regiments, in the mobile force.[38] From this time the militia became more effective and professional through improved drills and training. In the same year drill books were issued to all sergeants and ranks above to counteract the inadequacies that had been exposed during the rebellion. And although the militia was never to be involved in any further action after Humbert's invasion, the subsequent training received by the militiamen after 1798 ensured that the militia became a more professional military organisation than the semi-trained establishment of the early 1790s. It had to be, as the militia veterans of 1798 constituted the bulk of those that volunteered for regular service in the British army from 1800, ensuring that for a time the militia comprised largely of raw and undisciplined recruits.[39]

The loyalty of the Irish militia towards the Crown was obvious from the large number who volunteered for long-term service in the regular army. In March 1799, less than a year after the rebellion, Cornwallis had been approached by Dundas with a proposal of procuring recruits for regular regiments from the militia due to the deficiency in the British offensive force; 'how far it is possible for you to prevail on the Irish Parliament to give us the power of recruiting into your regular regiments … volunteers from the Irish militia. I understand from everybody that the men are excellent, and the defect in these militia corps arises from their being badly

---

36 *Dublin Evening Post*, 16 July 1808.
37 Nelson, *The Irish Militia*, p.245.
38 Nelson, *The Irish Militia*, p.245.
39 McAnally, *The Irish Militia*, p.151.

officered.'[40] At this time Britain was desperate to replace the troops it had lost in the campaigns in the West Indies and on the continent. Dundas stated that if such a policy was followed the Irish establishment would be strengthened by having a complement of 10 full-strength regular regiments, which together with the battalions of fencibles, would be of a sufficient force to counter any possible invasion, negating any reliance on either English or Irish militia.[41] Cornwallis was mindful that such a move would upset the militia colonels, whose regiments would in effect be relegated to training cadres for the army. He was also wary that once line units had recruited to their full complement in Ireland that they would be immediately posted elsewhere, such as what happened in 1808, negating Dundas's argument of strengthening the military forces of the kingdom.[42] However, there was little opposition to the proposal, ensuring that volunteers were called for from January 1800. A ceiling of 10,000 men from the militia was stipulated, with each regiment being delegated a quota based on their established full complement.[43] The total number of volunteers received in this initial call was 8,138, with them being distributed amongst the nine regular regiments that were stationed in Ireland at the time. To encourage the militiamen, bounties of eight guineas were offered for general service at a time when many were due for release from service into a country that was suffering from a poor harvest and unemployment.[44] Although the economic crisis may have accounted for many who enlisted, some also volunteered through loyalty to their comrades from their militia regiments who had enlisted at the same time, as well as loyalty to the Crown. Thirteen militia regiments either reached or exceeded their quota of volunteers, with many militiamen joining particular regiments *en masse*; the 68th Foot was the most popular with 1,777 enlistments, the 54th received 800, the 64th gained 592, while the 13th enlisted 535.[45] Most of these volunteers were to see active service with Abercromby in Egypt the following year, where they were considered a superior class of recruit due to their previous military training.[46] This mirrored what was also occurring in England, Scotland and Wales at the time, where the augmentation and efficiency of the regular army relied heavily on the semi-trained volunteers from the militia, fencibles and yeomanry. By 1805 an average of 3,000 Irish militiamen annually were enlisting into regular regiments.[47] Their service and the constant demand for reinforcements for regular overseas campaigns ensured that the call for recruits from the Irish militia was eventually to become an annual event during the wars with France, as it was for the British militias.

The unsavoury reputation that the militia had gained from the events of 1798 ensured that many regiments wanted to prove their loyalty through

---

40 Ross, *Correspondence of Charles, First Marquis Cornwallis*, pp.78–79.
41 Ross, *Correspondence of Charles, First Marquis Cornwallis*, pp.78–79.
42 McAnally, *The Irish Militia*, p.150.
43 TNA: HO 100/90/41: Circular to general officers, 7 February 1800.
44 TNA: HO 100/90/37: Circular to general officers, 23 January 1800.
45 TNA: HO 100/90/37: Circular to general officers, 23 January 1800.
46 Nelson, *The Irish Militia*, p.241.
47 Bartlett, 'Counter-insurgency and rebellion', p.290.

service outside of Ireland. Although there was no legal authority to allow such service, some officers and enlisted men felt they could prove their questioned loyalty as part of a greater defence force. As early as 1796 individual regiments, such as the Dublin City and Queen's County militias offered to serve in England but such offers were rejected.[48] Dublin Castle continued to receive offers from regiments volunteering to serve anywhere in the British Isles, with the Queen's County Militia even offering to serve on the continent.[49] Such proposals are understandable when coming from the predominantly Protestant officer corps, but some written offers had either been signed by the senior NCOs on behalf of their men or by the rank and file themselves, who were largely Catholic in composition. Dublin Castle had also favoured such moves in June 1798 where a system of interchange of militias between Britain and Ireland had been argued by Castlereagh. However, the infamy of the militia resulting from the debacle at Castlebar, together with the negative response of King George III, ensured such measures were shelved, as argued by Lord Cornwallis: 'I can by no means encourage the idea of any of the Irish militia coming to Great Britain; it would with reason offend the English militia; some going to Jersey, Guernsey, or North America might be countenanced.'[50] The compromise offered by the king led to the King's County Militia embarking in June 1799 for a one-year garrison duty in Jersey, with the Wexford Militia sailing to Guernsey for similar service in August of the same year.[51] Although the king relinquished his opposition to the proposed system in 1804, it was not until 1811 that there was sufficient political support for parliament to pass an act that provided for the interchange of the British and Irish militias.

Table 7.3: Irish Militia: Rank and File Strength

Revolutionary War		Napoleonic War	
July 1794	11,967	Jan 1804	18,639
July 1795	15,959	Jan 1805	19,423
July 1796	18,093	Jan 1806	18,750
July 1797	20,753	Jan 1807	21,473
July 1798	22,930		
July 1799	16,756 in Ireland	Jan 1811	24,733
Aug 1800	18,118	Feb 1812	14,149 in Ireland
Feb 1801	22,886	Dec 1812	12,550 in Ireland
July 1801	25,337	Dec 1813	12,901 in Ireland
Jan 1802	25,245		

Source: Return of Effectives –State Papers office, Ireland, 620/50; Official Returns of Irish establishment. TNA: Home Office Papers: HO 100/35-102.

---

48   McAnally, *The Irish Militia*, p.146.
49   McAnally, *The Irish Militia*, p.146.
50   Ross, *Correspondence of Charles, First Marquis Cornwallis*, pp.79–80.
51   McAnally, *The Irish Militia*, pp.147–148.

The Militia Interchange Policy

The interchange system was not without controversy. Claims that the introduction of the interchange system formalized the 'Britannicisation' of the Irish garrison and the military occupation of Ireland have merit.[52] As a result of the rebellion two distinctive strains of nationalism developed in Ireland. The loyalist Protestant minority displayed their British nationalistic fervour through service in the yeomanry, while Catholic military service was firmly identified through enlistment in the militia and regular regiments, encouraged more by the opportunities for regular better-than-average pay, improved living conditions and adventure than any strong sense of British nationalism.[53] The polarisation of the population intensified with the Ascendancy fearful of the military potential of the militia, whose association with the discontented peasantry was perceived as a continued threat. However, the Catholic population essentially remained loyal, with Catholics now concentrating on seeking representation and other rights from the British state rather than seeking any alliance with France. There was some concern from Catholic quarters that service in Britain would lead to Catholic militiamen being forced to attend Protestant church services, but such fears were soon abated when steps were taken for them to attend mass instead.

Eventually, there were only two periods of interchange; 1811 and 1813 where a total of 29 regiments out of 38 served in Britain as part of the new system.[54] Initially 14 units were exchanged with British militia regiments in 1811, with all these Irish corps remaining stationed in Britain until 1813. That year a second exchange was carried out where 14 Irish units transferred to Britain where they remained until late 1814 after the cessation of hostilities with France.[55] The Meath Militia was the only regiment to be exchanged in 1812, while nine units were never exchanged. The Irish Catholic emancipationist, Daniel O'Connell, vigorously protested against the bill in parliament, claiming (amongst other points) that the act was a conspiracy to take away Ireland's native army and that it would lead to an annihilation of the Irish militia.[56] What gives credence to the theory of 'Britannicisation' is that in 1811 when the first exchange took place, 27 English militia and Scottish fencible regiments were transferred to Ireland compared to the 14 Irish posted to Britain.[57] It could be argued that the large number of regiments transferred from Britain to Ireland were simply to boost the strength of the garrison at a time when there were only a few weak regular battalions in the kingdom. However, whether by design or not, such moves ensured a significant increase in the number of perceived loyal Protestant troops in Ireland at the time that there was a dramatic decrease of Catholic soldiers in the country through the combination of interchange and enlistment in regular regiments.

---

52   Cookson, *The British Armed Nation*, p.12.
53   Nelson, *The Irish Militia*, pp.142–143.
54   *Journal of the House of Commons*, vol.59, pp.645–647.
55   *Journal of the House of Commons*, vol.59, pp.645–647.
56   McAnally, *The Irish Militia*, p.245.
57   *Journal of the House of Commons*, vol.59, pp.645–647.

Prominent members of the Ascendancy, such as Castlereagh, may well have seen the interchange of militias as an opportunity for the de-Catholicisation of the armed forces in Ireland, though there is no surviving correspondence that openly confirms this. Ironically, the militia was primarily seen by loyalists as a Catholic institution even though most of its officer corps, and at least a quarter of the rank and file, were Protestant. This fact has influenced the historiography surrounding the interchange system where it has been argued that it was predominantly 'Catholic' regiments that were posted out of Ireland. The problem with this theory lies in determining what constituted a Catholic corps. There are insufficient surviving records of the Irish militia to confirm the religious composition of every regiment, with any estimation being based on the documentation regarding the composition of the light battalions and the comparison of the population of each corresponding county. However, this too may be misleading as there was a tendency in some counties for a higher proportion of Protestants to enlist than the religious ratio of the population.[58] What is clear is that a greater number of regiments from the Protestant stronghold of Ulster were never exchanged. These included the Armagh, Cavan, Donegal, and Tyrone militias, while only three regiments from provinces with high Catholic populations remained in Ireland.[59]

There is evidence to suggest that decisions regarding what Irish militia regiments were to be interchanged were determined by the regiments themselves. It appears that most of the militiamen favoured service in Britain. Subsequent to the bill being first introduced to parliament in May 1811, the lord lieutenant submitted a list of 23 regiments that had volunteered to serve in Britain, which included 929 sergeants, 415 drummers and 16,218 other ranks.[60] By the end of July, 34 out of the 38 units had volunteered, with the prospect of service in England acting for example as a stimulus in recruiting for the Clare Militia.[61] The act stipulated that service in Britain and Ireland was to be limited to two years, with no more than one quarter of the English militia to serve in Ireland at any one time, while no more than one third of the Irish regiments were to be posted to Britain at one time.[62] This ensured that no more than 14 Irish regiments could serve outside Ireland at any time. Overseas service for existing personnel was to be voluntary, where they had to swear a new oath to serve faithfully in any part of the United Kingdom. It was the recommendation of the lord lieutenant that the regiments should be exchanged according to the order in which their tender of service had been received.[63] This may be one reason that few Ulster regiments were exchanged, in that there were no units from that province in the first interchange. This indicates that perhaps the Ulstermen were more interested in protecting their interests in Ireland than experiencing the excitement of service abroad

---

58   Nelson, *The Irish Militia*, pp.124–125.
59   *Journal of the House of Commons*, vol.59, pp.645–647.
60   McAnally, *The Irish Militia*, p.245.
61   McAnally, *The Irish Militia*, p.245.
62   McAnally, *The Irish Militia*, p.244.
63   McAnally, *The Irish Militia*, p.245.

and that the aforementioned Ulster regiments may have been amongst the four units that declined to volunteer.

Irish Recruitment into the British Army

Ireland's greatest military role in the years 1799 to 1815 was as a source of recruits for the British army. The demands of war had ensured Catholics, as well as Protestants, had been recruited from the kingdom during the Seven Years war and the American War of Independence, even though at the time it was illegal for 'Papists' to serve in His Majesty's forces.[64] The repeal of the Penal laws and continued war with France ensured that Ireland was to provide Britain with a readily available supply of volunteers in the post-rebellion period. It was to this end that during this time the Ireland was to see a constant rotation of regular British regiments. Although there were numerous invasion scares in 1799, 1804, 1808 and 1811, the country was considered stable enough by the British government to allow the gradual reduction of regular troops from the Irish establishment. Britain's army was relatively small compared to those of the major continental states, with the defence of the realm traditionally falling upon the might of the Royal Navy. However, campaigns in Flanders, the West Indies, the Iberian Peninsula (Spain and Portugal) and North America necessitated the augmentation of the army and the constant need to provide replacements for casualties. And although the garrison of Ireland was increased to safeguard against any possible insurrection or invasion, Ireland proved to be an untapped source of manpower that would eventually see 159,000 Irishmen integrated into British regiments.[65]

An examination of official returns shows to what extent Ireland proved important to recruitment in the British army. The Irish establishment reached its greatest strength in January 1799, when there were 60,820 troops recorded in the kingdom.[66] Only 11,183 of these were regular soldiers, with the rest being either fencibles, yeomanry or militia.[67] However, there was a decline in the size of the establishment, especially in the number of regular troops from this time. By the following year the establishment had been reduced to 50,502, with a massive reduction of regulars which then only equated to 3,976 remaining in Ireland.[68] From 1800 the number of regular troops permanently stationed in Ireland remained static, while the number of line regiments sent to the country increased. The disembarking and embarkation returns showed a trend that continued up to the end of hostilities with France in 1815. Most regular units sent to Ireland were seriously under-strength on arrival but within a matter of months had recruited up to a full complement. These regiments were then posted elsewhere and replaced by other 'skeleton'

---

64   Reid, *King George's Army 1740-1793*, pp.19–20.
65   Karsten, 'Irish soldiers in the British Army, 1792-1922: Suborned or subordinate?', pp.31–63.
66   NLI: MS 8351: Statement of Troops in Ireland, 1 January 1799.
67   NLI: MS 8351: Statement of Troops in Ireland, 1 January 1799.
68   NLI: MS. 8351: Statement of Troops in Ireland, 1 January 1800.

units where the process was repeated. An example was the two battalions of the 20th Foot, as well as the 36th Foot, that arrived in Ireland in February 1800 and embarked the following month after reaching full strength.[69] The 63rd Foot arrived in February and took four months to reach its full complement before being posted elsewhere, while the 82nd Foot arrived and left in the same month.[70] Most of those Irishmen recruited into these regular units came from the militia, with numerically weak British battalions being sent to Ireland at a time when the period of service for many of the militiamen was due to expire.

The offer of lucrative bounties, coupled with the promise of regular income and the chance to experience action and adventure in foreign service enticed thousands of young Irishmen to 'take the king's shilling'. Militiamen were the most preferred recruits for regular regiments as they were considered semi-trained and had already experienced the discipline of military life.[71] The success of recruiting in Ireland is obvious when comparing the strength of regiments on their arrival to when they embarked for other service; the 13th Foot had only 271 rank and file on its arrival but left with 806; the 64th disembarked with 318 and left with 910; while the most popular regiment appears to have been the 68th Foot that only had 199 men when posted to Ireland but recorded a strength of 1,976 when it was posted elsewhere.[72] It is true that some of the new recruits would have been posted to the 1st battalion of the regiment recruiting in Ireland from understrength 2nd battalions in Britain, but Ireland proved to be a lucrative manpower source for the British Army throughout the period. Another source of volunteers came from the Scottish fencibles. In July 1800 Cornwallis reported that 2,500 men from the 19 Scottish fencible units currently stationed in Ireland had volunteered for regular service in six Scottish line regiments.[73] The criticism from colonels of the militia who argued that the bounties offered by the regular regiments would prevent the militias from securing enough recruits to replace those who had volunteered or were discharged generally proved unfounded. Ironically, another notable source of recruits came from captured Irish rebels who chose to enlist rather than face execution or transportation to the prison colony at Botany Bay.[74] The significance of Irish recruitment into the rank and file of the British regular regiments, especially during the campaigning years of the Peninsular War, is evident by examining the composition of the battalions; in 1809 34 percent of the 57th Foot were Irish, while in 1811 Irishmen accounted for 37 percent of the 29th Foot.[75] Such ratios were typical of English infantry battalions throughout the period.

However, there were some regiments within Wellesley's Peninsular and Waterloo armies that had a significantly much higher percentage of Irish

---

69 TNA: HO 100/92: Disembarkation-embarkation Return, 20 September 1800.
70 TNA: HO 100/92: Disembarkation-embarkation Return, 20 September 1800.
71 Bartlett, 'Defence, counter-insurgency and rebellion', p.290.
72 TNA: HO 100/90: Official Return, 19 February 1800.
73 TNA: HO 100/91: Cornwallis to Portland, 31 July 1800.
74 TNA: HO 100/102: Earl of Hardwicke to Lord Pelham, 13 May 1802.
75 Philip J. Haythornthwaite, *Wellington's Military Machine* (Tunbridge Wells, Kent: Spellmount, 1988), p.24.

within their ranks, giving them a distinction of being known as 'Irish' regiments. These include: the 4th (Royal Irish) Regiment of Dragoon Guards; the 18th Regiment of Light Dragoons (Hussars) – sometimes called the 'King's Irish Hussars'; the three battalions of the 27th (Enniskillen) Regiment of Foot; the two battalions of the 87th (The Prince of Wales's Irish) Regiment of Foot; and the two battalions of the 88th (Connaught Rangers) Regiment of Foot. All these regiments forged histories of meritorious service throughout the Napoleonic wars, with the exploits of some individuals from these units becoming legendary. An example is the actions of Sergeant Patrick Masterson of the 87th Foot in capturing a French eagle at the Battle of Barossa in Spain in March 1811. It is estimated that 40 percent of the personnel within the British Army during the Napoleonic Wars were Irish, many of whom had volunteered directly from the militia.[76] This emphasizes the significant part Ireland played in the defence of Britain during the period.

Experience during 1798 also ensured a change in the components of the Irish army. Most notable was the reduction of cavalry and the increased reliance on British fencibles. In a letter addressed to the Duke of York in 1802 where Cornwallis outlined his recommendations for the force required to successfully garrison the kingdom, he argued for less cavalry; 'there is no part of the whole island where that species of troops can act in a body … I am of the opinion that 2,500 would be sufficient for any purposes which the services of that country could require.'[77] His argument that heavy cavalry was impracticable and that only light dragoons should be employed influenced the increased reliance on the mounted corps of the yeomanry. Light cavalry was required to provide reconnaissance and intelligence, which the yeomanry with their local knowledge could provide. A second consideration in the reduction of this arm of the establishment post-1798 was the poor performance of cavalry against the rebel pikemen who caused considerable casualties when making a determined stand. The discipline and the loyalty of the 'Irish Horse' regiments, namely the 4th, 5th, 6th and 7th Dragoon Guards who had been a permanent feature of the establishment throughout the eighteenth century, was also in question due to the perceived disaffection within the ranks, leading to these formations being transferred to England in 1799.[78] Of lesser importance was the disestablishment of the Royal Irish Artillery in 1801, when the ordnance and personnel were transferred to the Royal Artillery due to the Act of Union. With the demands for regular troops for overseas service constant, greater reliance was placed on British fencibles to provide a reliable infantry force in Ireland. This was emphasized in a letter from Pitt to Cornwallis in December 1799 when he was attempting to raise an army to attack Brest for which fencible regiments in Ireland had volunteered; 'This … force of fencibles I think amounts to about 15,000 or 16,000 men, and would make a most valuable and important addition, but I doubt whether any large part of it could be spared from Ireland … as we could hardly trust the internal safety of that country to a small body of regular

---

76   Mike Chappell, *Wellington's Peninsula Regiments: The Irish* (Oxford: Osprey, 2003), pp.5–7.
77   Ross, *Correspondence of Charles, First Marquis Cornwallis*, vol.3, pp.488–491.
78   Fortescue, *A History of the British Army*, vol.4, p.597.

cavalry, with Irish militia and volunteers.'[79] This ensured that contrary to the composition of the establishment of the 1790s, by the end of the Napoleonic war the Irish garrison was predominantly an infantry force.

A main feature of the British response to the threat of French invasion in the post-rebellion era was the proliferation of barracks and military posts established throughout the kingdom. This came about due to the greater reliance on British fencible and militia regiments in the kingdom, ensuring a substantial increase in the number of military barracks needed to house these troops. The construction of new permanent barracks, and improvements made to existing military posts, had been occurring prior to 1798 but without urgency and not in great numbers.[80] The experiences of that year heightened the fears of insurrection and invasion which resulted in a greater permanent military presence. An example was the use of fencibles and militia from 1800 to build a military road through the Wicklow Mountains, which from 1803 was to be supported by the erection of a series of fortified barracks. These strongholds were garrisoned by 100 men and were to serve a local or regional need, as opposed to being part of a national system of defence.[81] It was posts of this size and smaller that became a permanent feature of the Irish establishment. According to an Army Medical Board report, by 1804 there were 94 permanent military barracks established in the kingdom of various sizes and states of repair.[82] However, a return submitted in 1811 reveals the extent to which Ireland was under military occupation: there were 106 permanent barracks that were occupied by 46,351 men; as well as 163 temporary barracks or other buildings that were housing 24,073 men at the time.[83] Sir Arthur Wellesley, serving as Chief Secretary of Ireland in 1807, wrote that it was necessary to build and increase the number of new barracks to replace the old temporary barracks that were unfit for service and had been 'injurious to the soldiers' health and discipline.'[84] The greatest example of the military domination of Ireland can be seen by comparing this garrison of 70,424 to the Irish establishment of 1793, which had a paper strength of around 15,000 but an effective strength of much less.[85] And although the Irish population were generally no longer burdened with the system of 'free quartering' from 1800 onwards, it was the spread of barrack building throughout the country that became the catalyst for the military occupation of Ireland.

It is evident that post-1798 the British establishment saw Ireland as a constant weakness to the defence of the realm, leading to the construction

---

79 Ross, *Correspondence of Charles, First Marquis Cornwallis*, vol.3, pp.154–155.
80 TNA: HO 100/108: Army Medical Board Report, January 1802.
81 Paul M. Kerrigan, 'The Defences of Ireland, 1793–1815', *An Consantoir*, vol.34 (1974), p.109.
82 TNA: HO 100/108: Army Medical Board Report, January 1802.
83 NLI: MS 10217: Clinton Papers, 'A return of the permanent and temporary barracks in Ireland', August 1811.
84 Wellington, *Civil Correspondence and Memoranda*, Letter to Lord Hawkesbury, 7 May 1807, pp.28–36.
85 NLI: MS 10217: Clinton Papers, 'A return of the permanent and temporary barracks in Ireland', August 1811.

of military instillations and the posting of regular troops in the areas they deemed vulnerable to French invasion. Wellesley was certain of this view:

> The first point to which I will draw your attention is the general military system adopted in Ireland, with a view to its defence. All those who have considered this subject appear to agree in the following propositions, although they may differ in opinion many questions of details: That Ireland is assailable by the enemy on all parts of its southern, its western, and its northern coasts; that in case it could be attacked by a body of the enemy sufficiently large to give employment to a large proportion of the regular troops, the people in all parts of the country would rise in rebellion; that Ireland must ultimately depend on its defence upon the resources of men and military equipment which it should receive from Great Britain.[86]

This approach led to the construction of artillery batteries at strategic points such as Bantry Bay, Lough Swilly, the Shannon estuary, as well as improvements to the forts guarding the harbours at Dublin, Cork and Waterford.[87] Much of this work was undertaken in response to the military memorandum of the defence of Ireland submitted to the British government in 1808 by Charles François Dumouriez, a French *émigré* army officer who was well informed of the details of the French invasion plans of 1796 and 1798.[88] At the same time a system of signal towers, known as 'telegraph' stations was introduced to provide rapid news of coastal shipping movements to the naval and military authorities, especially any which indicated a French invasion force.[89] The 'semaphore' system of signalling with pivotal arms fixed to a vertical staff was also used to provide better communications between local forces and the high command in Dublin. These stations were prominent along the south and west coasts and were intended to be manned by 'sea fencibles' recruited from members of the local population who had some nautical experience.[90] A series of Martello towers were also constructed at strategic coastal points from 1804 (following the same approach taken along the south east coast of England), such as Dublin, Bantry Bay and Rosslare in an effort to hinder any landing at those locations.[91] Each tower generally mounted one 18 or 24-pounder cannon and with an extreme range of a mile was intended to provide mutual support to other towers or batteries in the vicinity.[92] A small number of towers were also constructed in the interior along the River Shannon to protect strategic crossings. Although records indicate that 74 such towers were planned, less than 50 were built, with the greatest concentration protecting Dublin.[93]

---

86 Wellington, *Civil Correspondence and Memoranda*, Letter to Lord Hawkesbury, 7 May 1807, pp.28–36.
87 Kerrigan, *Castles and Fortifications in Ireland*, p.152.
88 Kerrigan, 'The Defences of Ireland', p.109.
89 Kerrigan, 'The Defences of Ireland', p.225.
90 Kerrigan, 'The Defences of Ireland', pp.226–227.
91 Kerrigan, *Castles and Fortifications in Ireland*, p.152.
92 Kerrigan, 'The Defences of Ireland', p.149.
93 Kerrigan, 'The Defences of Ireland', p.149.

The greater reliance on British fencible and militia regiments in Ireland led to a substantial increase in the number of military barracks being built to house these troops. The augmentation of the military forces coupled with the establishment of 269 permanent and temporary barracks in the country post-1798 provide convincing evidence of the military occupation by Britain of Ireland. Such moves would have ensured that the Irish population would be left in no doubt as to the control Britain had over the country, with the posting of troops into garrisons throughout the country, no matter how small, serving as a permanent reminder of that. This strategy was obviously aimed at discouraging any further armed dissent from the rebellious and disaffected elements within Irish society, and to this end it proved successful. However, such moves were also instigated to counter the growth of the yeomanry whose self-interested policing policies against the Catholic majority had the potential to inflame further rebellion. Clearly, from 1798 the British government approach was that neither the external or internal defence of Ireland could be entrusted to the Irish, whether Protestant or Catholic, and that it could only be maintained through British domination.

8

Conclusion

The period 1793 to 1815 proved to be a defining period in Irish history. The relaxation of the Penal Laws towards the end of the eighteenth century saw Irish Catholic gentry reclaiming wealth and influence, which was then seen as a threat by the Protestant minority.[1] War with France amplified these fears with the arming of the Catholic peasantry through the creation of the Irish militia. The rise of the republican United Irish movement, coupled with the traditional agrarian protests of the Catholic peasantry, led to an increase in violent activity throughout the Midlands and the border counties of Ulster and Leinster from 1795.[2] This in turn prompted the formation of the yeomanry in an effort to provide local defence, especially in areas not garrisoned by the army.[3] The ruthless methods promoted by some senior army officers and the government in the disaffected areas subsequently fostered an increase in support amongst the peasantry for open rebellion. The turning point proved to be in 1798 when popular insurrection and the French invasion divided the nation. Sectarianism then halted the civil advances of the Catholic majority, while the Protestant Ascendancy was able to protect their interests in the kingdom, albeit, through political union with Britain. From this time British dominance of Ireland was asserted through military occupation, characterised by the augmentation of the garrison with loyal British fencible and militia regiments, coupled with the removal of a significant portion of the Irish militia through the interchange system from 1811.[4] Without doubt, the views of Major General Sir Arthur Wellesley, himself a member of the Irish Ascendancy, mirrored those of other senior military officers and senior government administrators in Ireland at this time, which led to increased military occupation during the Napoleonic era:

> I am positively convinced that no political measure which you could adopt would alter the temper of the people of this country. They are disaffected to the British Government; they don't feel the benefits of their situation; attempts to

---

1   Bartlett, 'Defence, Counter-insurgency and rebellion: Ireland, 1793–1803', pp.247–249.
2   Bartlett, 'Defence, Counter-insurgency and rebellion: Ireland, 1793–1803', pp.247–249.
3   Blackstock, 'The Irish Yeomanry and the 1798 Rebellion', p.334.
4   McAnally, *The Irish Militia*, p.62.

render it better either do not reach their minds, or they are represented to them as additional injuries; and in fact, we have no strength here but our army. Surely it is incumbent upon us to adopt every means which can secure the position and add to the strength of our army.[5]

The continual construction of barracks, coast defences and smaller army posts, especially after 1798, in line with the prolific building of the same throughout Britain at this time, became viewed by many Irish as a permanent expression of British military occupation. With the rebellion and the reverses suffered by government forces being blamed on the Catholic peasantry and militia, the Protestant oligarchy cemented the yeomanry as the defending military arm of the ruling minority, while welcoming the increased presence of British forces to minimise the perceived internal and external threats. The religious bias that was resurrected during this time was to become a permanent feature of Irish society and ultimately influenced events in Ireland up to the present time.

The fears held by the Ascendancy against Catholics in the 1790s were unfounded. Throughout the period the bishops of the Catholic Church in Ireland had actively discouraged any rebellious activity against the government as it was not under any threat from the Ascendancy.[6] The Catholic peerage and gentry were determined to maintain and improve their circumstances, while proving their loyalty to the Crown through military service either in the regular army, militia, or yeomanry. The predominantly Catholic militia had proven itself to be loyal to the Crown throughout the period and instrumental in dealing with the uprisings. In general, the Catholic population failed to give active support to the rebellion, essentially due to limited influence of the United Irish in many counties, and that the concept of a republic was foreign to the uneducated peasantry.[7] This ensured that the uprisings were nothing more than isolated revolts, stimulated by local circumstances rather than a religiously motivated insurrection. The rebellion in Wexford, which although being the only county in which any significant popular support was evident, and where several Catholic priests were amongst its leaders, was mainly motivated by local issues regarding the experiences of their flock rather than religious fervour.[8] Localised economic stress and United Irish propaganda had ensured that the rebellion in the county was initially led by aggrieved members of the Protestant gentry, such as Bagenal Harvey, with support from the Catholic peasantry mainly motivated by the recent counter-terror activities of the yeomanry and militia.[9] One aspect of the rising in Ulster was that the rebellion there erupted without the support of the Catholic 'Defenders' which the United Irish leadership had been counting on to provide the majority of their forces. It appears

---

5   Wellington, *Civil Correspondence and Memoranda*, Letter to Lord Hawkebury, 7 May 1807, pp.28–36.
6   Nelson, *The Irish Militia*, pp.55–56.
7   Foster, *Modern Ireland*, p.265.
8   Dickson, *New Foundations*, pp.215–217.
9   Gahan, 'The Rebellion in South Leinster', pp.109–111.

that those Catholics that did rise up throughout Ireland, did so either in protest to the government-instigated 'terror' or were forced to by pressure from United Irishmen within their community or neighbours.[10] The most obvious evidence of the allegiance of Irish Catholics remains the thousands who enlisted in the British army before the rebellion, and increasingly after it, with the Irish accounting for more than one third of Britain's Napoleonic and Victorian armies.[11]

Clearly, the poor reputation of the Irish militia, fostered by the Ascendancy and repeated by military historians such as Fortescue, was encouraged to cover the inadequacies of the high command and government policies. The dispersal of regiments in policing roles proved counter-productive in ensuring adequate training for the newly formed units, while the tolerated absence of regimental officers to pursue personal interests ensured a lack of leadership and further hindered any unit *élan*.[12] The training that the militiamen received was generally limited to musket drill and marching, with no provisions made for specific training for counter-insurgent duties.[13] The dispersal policies and insufficient training played a part in the few reverses that the militia suffered in the initial stages of the rebellion, such as Oulart Hill and Enniscorthy, where small company-sized garrisons were isolated and overwhelmed by the superior numbers of rebels. The ignominious defeat of the government forces at Castlebar by the French later in the year was squarely blamed on the lack of discipline of the 'Catholic' militia when facing the enemy, with such views being reinforced by official criticism from Cornwallis.[14] However, evidence indicates that such condemnation was unjustified and politically motivated. Contemporary statements from eyewitnesses, including French officers, indicate that the militia behaved admirably until the order to retreat was given by Major General Hutchinson which prompted a rout of the government troops at a time when the French were considering withdrawing from the field due to the stout defence of their foe.[15] Hutchinson had panicked, and he and Lieutenant General Lake officially criticised the militia to deflect the blame from themselves. In fact, part of the defeat at Castlebar was due to confusion of command caused by Hutchinson's superior, Lake, also being present.[16] It proved politically expedient for Cornwallis to divert the blame onto the militia rather than causing further embarrassment by having the competency of his experienced senior officers questioned. Thus, the reputation of the militia remained tarnished.

Prior to 1798 the Ascendancy had strengthened its position through political intrigue. This first came about through an outpouring of protest from influential Protestant peers and politicians regarding the liberal policies of Fitzwilliam, who as lord lieutenant, was keen to incorporate the Catholic

---

10 Hewitt, *Eye-Witnesses to Ireland in Revolt*, pp.104–108.
11 Chappell, *Wellington's Peninsula Regiments: The Irish*, p.5.
12 Nelson, *The Irish Militia*, p.108.
13 Nelson, *The Irish Militia*, p.78.
14 Ross, *Correspondence of Charles, First Marquis Cornwallis*, p.308.
15 Hayes, 'An Officers Account of the French Campaign in Ireland in 1798', pp.161–171.
16 Ross, *Correspondence of Charles, First Marquis Cornwallis*, pp.408–411.

peerage and gentry into the Irish political system.[17] Such protest led to his recall in 1795 and his replacement with the Earl of Camden. Camden proved to be weak, indecisive, and easily manipulated, ensuring internal government directives were heavily influenced by his council of Protestant Irish peers, led by Lords Clare and Carhampton.[18] Such men successfully argued for the formation of the yeomanry to protect their own interests, with their intention to maintain Protestant control throughout the country. Constant calls for protection from the gentry put further pressure on the beleaguered viceroy, with Ascendancy-minded and connected generals such as Carhampton, Lake and Knox eager to employ counter-terror operations against the disaffected population. Further pressure from the Ascendancy and within the army, ensured Camden failed to back the humane tactics encouraged by Abercromby, even though they proved more successful in recovering the arms of insurgents, while reducing civil unrest.[19] Ironically, the resumption of terror tactics directed by Lake, and widely supported within the Irish parliament when he replaced Abercromby in April 1798, proved the catalyst for insurrection. This convinced the Crown that the oppressive policies of the Ascendancy were only promoting instability at a time when the security of the country was essential to the defence of Britain.

Ireland was too important to the defence of Britain for it to be left in the hands of the Irish Ascendancy. The disorder within the kingdom proved an open invitation to the French who saw an opportunity to invade to destabilize Britain's defences. The French saw Ireland as the British did, as a weak link in Britain's chain of defence.[20] The rebellion and repeated invasion attempts provided Pitt, Dundas, Cornwallis and Castlereagh with sufficient evidence to promote British control of the kingdom through the Act of Union which had previously been universally rejected by all parties.[21] Once this had been achieved Britain could determine the defence strategies of Ireland that were considered insufficient while under control of the Irish parliament. It was necessary for Britain to secure control of the turbulent country to ensure that British troops were not unnecessarily drawn away from campaigns elsewhere to deal with insurgents, and that the French could not establish it as a base for expeditions to Britain. And although Pitt eventually gained sufficient support for the union from the Protestant oligarchy that was reliant on increasing British military presence to maintain its interests in Ireland, the move would ensure that Britain could weaken the political strength of the uncompromising and self-interested Ascendancy that was becoming problematic to Britain's defence strategies, which included taking advantage of the manpower resource provided by the Catholic population.

However, it was through the Act of Union that the Ascendancy maintained its dominance in Ireland. Although politically the country had been reduced to a collection of parliamentary constituencies within the

---

17   Smith, *Whig Principles and Party Politics*, pp.182–185.
18   Connelly, *The Oxford Companion to Irish History*, p.308.
19   Connelly, *The Oxford Companion to Irish History*, p.308.
20   Come, 'French Threat to British Shores, 1793–1798', p.180.
21   Cronin, *A History of Ireland*, pp.114–116.

Westminster parliament, the Protestant minority benefited from inclusion in the Union. The British government had chosen to appease the Ascendancy by taking into consideration its concerns regarding Catholics. The promised emancipation failed to happen through lack of support prior to the union and a later change to a conservative government that was more sympathetic to the Ascendancy.[22] In effect Britain had chosen to ally itself with the Ascendancy. This is understandable when considering the longstanding social, political, and religious ties that bound them. The Ascendancy was considered by many simply as Englishmen who lived and held lands in Ireland, and that their zealous loyalty would ensure Britain's best interests would be maintained there.[23] Furthermore, the strength of the yeomanry could not be ignored and was needed to provide internal security. Britain would most certainly have been in the impossible position of having to forcibly contain this sizable corps had the British government sided with the Catholic majority once union was complete. Such considerations ensured that, apart from the loss of legislative power, the Ascendancy maintained local control within Ireland. Any political support for the Catholics was limited due to the continued questions regarding their loyalty to the Protestant crown, especially after the rebellion.[24] However, the question of the Catholics remained an enigma in that Britain needed to encourage their loyalty to provide internal stability and utilize their military potential.

In contrast to the early 1790s, the Irish military establishment became 'Protestantised' in the post-1798 period. There is no doubt that the deployment of the Irish militia to Britain from 1811 led to an increase in the number of British regiments in Ireland until 1815. However, prior to 1798 there appears to be no pattern of deployment within Ireland that would indicate any official religious bias towards 'Catholic' regiments by the authorities at Dublin Castle.[25] Initially, regiments were not to garrison the county from which it recruited and were regularly transferred to various locations to prevent the troops from developing sympathies with the local populace.[26] The Ascendancy was certainly fearful of having formations of armed Catholics spread throughout the kingdom. However, the dispersal of the troops into small detachments in isolated locations, coupled with the massive reduction in the number of line battalions in Ireland, generally made it impossible for the militia to be placed under the supervision of regular troops. The rotation system continued after the event of 1798 but resulted in the militia being retained as garrison troops and formed reserves, increasingly relinquishing the policing role to the yeomanry. What is evident is that after 1798 any regiment involved in any unsavoury incident with the local population was usually transferred to prevent further confrontations.

There appears to have been little conflict between the 'Hibernianisation' of the armed forces of the British Crown and continued British rule in Ireland.

---

22   Cronin, *A History of Ireland*, p.116.
23   Blackstock, *An Ascendancy Army*, pp.55–56.
24   Cookson, *The British Armed Nation, 1793–1815*, p.156.
25   McAnally, *The Irish Militia*, p.42.
26   McAnally, *The Irish Militia*, p.62.

CONCLUSION

The thousands of Catholic soldiers who enlisted in the militia and regular regiments during 22 years of war with France provides proof of that. The British Army had been recruiting Irish Catholics, albeit illegally, since the 1750s and the removal of the Penal Laws in 1793 had only legalised a practice that was already in place. Although the reasons for enlisting were many and varied, some Irish militiamen chose to enlist in line battalions as they had become accustomed to military life. The army provided the peasantry with security through regular pay, pensions, education, and accommodation in an era of fluctuating economic uncertainty. Ireland proved a lucrative recruiting ground for British regiments who struggled to find sufficient replacements in Britain, with Irishmen equating to more than one third of the total of Wellington's army in the Peninsula, including 40 percent of the rank and file.[27] Religious bias may have hindered promotion of Catholics in the ranks, but this may have been due more to the lack of education than bigotry.[28] Military service was seen by the Catholic peerage and gentry as an opportunity to prove loyalty to the Crown once their traditional connection with Catholic Europe ended as a result of the French Revolution; a loyalty they hoped would be repaid through emancipation that would have been unlikely under the Ascendancy. Continued British rule in the kingdom during this period was considered essential for the political improvement of the Catholic population, and thus received their support.

Ultimately, the British successfully dealt with the situation in Ireland in 1798. Dublin Castle had made great use of the intelligence networks that had penetrated the United Irish movement. This resulted in the removal of the senior rebel leadership in Leinster, ensuring that the rebellion became a leaderless, disorganised, and spontaneous revolt which was quickly defeated.[29] The isolated rebel forces were easily contained by the government army, which was reinforced from Britain by the secure sea link of the Irish Sea. The rebel organisation had been seriously weakened prior to the rebellion due to the counter-terror operations, especially in Ulster, which limited the chance of success. The concentration of government forces, especially in and around Dublin, proved significant in preventing the capture of the capital which had been the main gaol of the insurgents. The United Irish attempt to engage the government forces in open battle proved a fatal flaw in their strategy, with any hope of success relying on a general popular uprising throughout the kingdom combined with a sizable French invasion. If this had been accomplished the British would have been forced to fight on two fronts, seriously stretching their military resources.

The operations of the British Army from 1795 up to 1798 left the Irish with historical memories of brutal repression. The ruthless counter-insurgent campaigns carried out by Carhampton and Lake prior to the rising resulted in a scale of death and destruction not seen in Ireland since Cromwell's invasion in 1649. This government-sponsored oppression only encouraged

---

27 Chappell, *Wellington's Peninsula Regiments: The Irish*, p.5.
28 BL: Add. MSS 37845: ff. 77, Duke of Portland to Lord Windham, quoted in J.R. Western, 'Roman Catholics Holding Military Commissions in 1798', pp.428–432.
29 Pakenham, *The Year of Liberty*, p.217.

further disorder and was the catalyst for the rebellion in 1798. The excesses of the army, prompted by the commander-in-chief and influenced by the Ascendancy, on the defeated rebels and unfortunate innocent population resulted in deaths far exceeding those sustained in open conflict and has remained a stain on the reputation of the British Army.[30] Although the post–rebellion years saw the demise of the Irish militia and the military occupation of the majority Catholic population by a Protestant para-military force that was determined to maintain the Ascendancy, the increased presence of the British Army in Ireland after 1798 ensured the excesses of the yeomanry were kept in check. However, the political and military circumstances dictated that the British government chose to align itself with the Protestant minority to secure its own interests. The British Army, including the Irish militia and yeomanry, was used to secure peace in Ireland during a time of war when national security remained the greatest priority. Unfortunately, the tactics used only led to further division and helped establish a sectarian tradition that has permeated Irish history ever since.

---

30 Ross, *Correspondence of Charles, First Marquis Cornwallis*, p.355.

Appendix I

Return of Permanent Barracks in Ireland, August 1811[1]

Permanent Barracks	Cavalry: Officers & Men	Infantry: Officers & Men	Permanent Barracks	Cavalry: Officers & Men	Infantry: Officers & Men
Ardglass		13	Carlisle Fort		238
Arklow		165	Camden Fort		211
Armagh		792	Haubolin battery		21
Athenry		109	Spoke Island		126
Athlone		1,486	Cove		128
Athy	64	86	Clogheen	76	
Aughavanagh		78	Dingle		84
Ballaghedenen		82	Donaghadee		21
Ballinrobe	119	157	Downpatrick		98
Ballyshannon		783	Drogheda		398
Banaghan		104	Drumgott		78
Bandon	116	1,035	Dungannon Fort		229
Belfast		1,186	Dundalk	249	739
Bellick battery		52	Dungarvan		102
Belturbet	161	324	Dunmore	74	
Boyle		289	Dunree Fort		32
Brey		67	Dunshaughlin		84
Cappoquin	38		Dublin City	827	4,031
Carlow	160	225	Enniskillen	111	549
Carrick-on-Shannon		284	Fethard	117	
Carrick-on-Suir	48	127	Fermoy	170	2,090
Cashel		333	Fork Hill		32
Castlebar	85	498	Foxford		83
Castlecomer		172	Galway		1,125

---

1   NLI: MS 10217: Clinton Papers.

REBELLION, INVASION AND OCCUPATION

Permanent Barracks	Cavalry: Officers & Men	Infantry: Officers & Men	Permanent Barracks	Cavalry: Officers & Men	Infantry: Officers & Men
Castle Island		84	New Geneva		1,790
Cavan		594	Glencree		78
Chapelizod		385	Gort	120	
Charles Fort		576	Granard		245
Clare Castle		154	Jonesborough		42
Clonakilty		69	Kelogue		53
Clonmel	147	1,223	Kilkenny	74	828
Cork City- old barracks		712	Killough		118
Cork City- new barracks	304	3,126	Kinsale		1,429
Total	1,242	15,370		1,818	15,082
Laragh		78	Portumna	93	
Leitrim		78	Roscommon	84	389
Limerick	300	2,614	Roscrea	22	353
Longford	209	210	New Ross	40	
Loughrea	84	798	Ross Castle		87
Mallow	92	1,046	Rostrevan		51
Man of War	43		Rutland		103
Meelick		33	Shannon Bridge		103
Middleton		865	Sligo	78	375
Mill Street		66	Swords		53
Monaghan	55		Tallagh	76	
Naas		169	Tralee		120
Navan	55		Tullamore	131	1,048
Naddeen		42	Waterford		596
Newry		1,168	Westport		188
Oughterrande		137	Wexford		616
Phoenix Park	45	302	Whiddy Island		267
Phillipstown	132		Youghall		445
Total	1,015	7,606		524	4,794

Barracks that could accommodate whole battalions (500 men) included:

Athlone
Belfast
Charles Fort
Cork
Dundalk
Dublin
Enniskillen
Fermoy
Galway
New Geneva
Kinsale
Limerick
Middleton
Newry
Waterford

Total: 106 Permanent barracks accommodating 46,351 officers and men.

Appendix II

Return of Temporary Barracks in Ireland, August 1811[1]

Temporary Barracks	Cavalry: Officers & Men	Infantry: Officers & Men	Temporary Barracks	Cavalry: Officers & Men	Infantry: Officers & Men
Abbeyfeale		72	Castlelacken		41
Adare		31	Celbridge		26
Aglish		31	Charleville		105
Antrim		252	Clerahan		23
Askeatow		159	Clononey		1,778
Aughnaclay		857	Coleraine		156
Ballyfernon		21	Croome		36
Balbriggan		62	Derry	98	830
Ballina		293	Drumcallaghan		31
Ballinamult		52	Dunboyne		62
Ballinasloe	350	830	Dundrum		31
Ballymena		60	Dungannon		52
Ballymore Eustace		51	Dublin-Old Custom House		622
Ballybunion		30	D- Mary St		350
Ballintobey		23	D- Abbey St		160
Ballypatrick		12	D- Henry & Sackville Sts		258
Ballinglass		100	D- Earl St		8
Bantry		426	D- St Stephen's Green	9	
Berehaven		75	D- Kenny House	327	
Bere Island		313	D- Leinster House	420	
Black Rock		32	D- Baggot St	219	
Bruff		120	D- Mespit St	83	
Bunoranna		62	D- Cork St		304
Bullivant		52	D- Portland St		6
Bunisoleigh		40	D- Recruiting Depot		232
Cahir	17	842	D- Marlborough St		451
Callan	12	24	D- Cope St		8

---

1   NLI: MS 10217: Clinton Papers.

REBELLION, INVASION AND OCCUPATION

Temporary Barracks	Cavalry: Officers & Men	Infantry: Officers & Men	Temporary Barracks	Cavalry: Officers & Men	Infantry: Officers & Men
Cappowhite		41	Eskey		44
Causeway		32	Ennnis		216
Carrickfergus		80	Enniscorthy		458
Ennistimond		52	Monkstown		309
Eyrecourt		538	Mt. Catherine	13	57
Elphin	58		Mullinahope		53
Fryarstown		27	Mocklesshill		52
Freshford		20	Michelstown		106
Garristown		31	Nenagh		638
Goldenbridge		69	New Castle, Co. Limerick		228
Gorey		94	New Castle, Co. Kildare		25
Green Castle		51	New Inn		21
Hospital, Co. Leitrim		50	Newtownbarry		190
Howth		38	New Birmingham		52
Hammondtown		21	Omagh		409
Keady		31	Palmerstown		43
Kells, Co. Tipperary		20	Parsonstown		1,040
Kenmere		–	Patrick's Well		41
Kilbiggan	154	412	Rathesole		25
Kilcock	41	77	Rathkeale		306
Kilcullen		222	Rathmullen		40
Kildare		99	Rathangan		31
Killarney		200	Skepsceene		–
Kilmanagh		14	Shanagolden	12	32
Kilmagany		12	Strabane		626
Kilrush		30	Templemore		60
Knockalla Fort		70	Tarbert		120
Killala		52	Templeodigan		25
Kilmacthomas		100	Three Mile Bridge		30
Kellinaule		80	Thurles		153
Kilmannan		14	Tipperary		258
Littlekenny		80	Trim		83
Lifford		489	Tuam		822
Lisburne	90		Tubbercorry		24
Listowel		196	Thomastown		16
Littleton		50	Tulsk		21
Magharafelt	30		Timolin		20
Maynooth	36	78	White Rock		328
Moate		371	Wicklow		89
Monasterwan		80	Urlingford		30
Mullingar		570			

Total: 163 Temporary barracks accommodating 24,073 officers and men
Grand total of permanent and temporary barracks: 241 throughout Ireland accommodating 70,424 officers and men.

Appendix III

Irish Militia Regiments by Seniority and Colour Facings, 1793[1]

Regiment	Facing Colour	Regiment	Facing Colour
Monaghan	white	Kilkenny	yellow
Royal Tyrone	blue	Limerick County	blue
North Mayo	yellow	Sligo	green
Kildare	black	Carlow	yellow
Louth	green	Drogheda	green
Westmeath	yellow	South Down	blue
Antrim	yellow	Clare	yellow
Armagh	white	Cork City	blue
North Down	blue	Tipperary	yellow
Leitrim	yellow	Fermanagh	yellow
Galway	yellow	South Mayo	white
Dublin City	blue	Roscommon	black
Limerick City	yellow	South Cork	white
Kerry	yellow	Waterford	yellow
Longford	blue	North Cork	yellow
Londonderry	yellow	Dublin County	white
Royal Meath	blue	Donegal	black
Cavan	black	Wicklow	yellow
King's County	blue	Wexford	yellow

Irish militia regiments were initially single-battalion units where the seniority was decided by ballot and the organisation followed the same 10-company system as regular units. The pattern of their uniforms and equipment also initially followed that of the regular foot regiments: large black cocked hats; red tailcoats faced in either yellow, blue, white, black, and green. White waistcoats and breeches were worn, along with black spatterdashes.

---

1 Reid, *Armies of the Irish Rebellion 1798*.

Appendix IV

English and Scottish Fencible Regiments that served in Ireland in 1798[1]

Infantry Battalions	Facing Colour and Dress
Princess of Wales's Aberdeen Fencibles	yellow, Highland dress
Angus Fencibles	yellow, bonnet and trews
Duke of York's Banffshire Fencibles	yellow, Highland dress
Caithness Legion	yellow, bonnet and trews
Devon & Cornwall Fencibles	unknown
Dunbarton Fencibles	black, bonnet and trews or kilt
Loyal Durham Fencibles	green
Lord Elgin's Fencibles	green, Highland dress
Loyal Essex Fencibles	buff
Fife Fencibles	yellow, not in Highland dress
Fraser Fencibles	black, Highland dress
Glengarry Fencibles	yellow, Highland dress
Inverness-shire Highlanders	buff, Highland dress
Royal Lancashire Volunteers (Fencibles)	blue
Leicester (Prince of Wales's) Fencibles	unknown
2nd Royal Manx Fencibles	blue, fur-crested round hats
North Lowland Fencibles	green, possibly wore trews
Northampton Fencibles	blue, red collar
Northumberland Fencibles	unknown
Loyal Nottingham Fencibles	green
Reay Fencibles	blue, Highland dress
Loyal Somerset Fencibles	yellow
Suffolk Fencibles	unknown
York Fencibles	unknown

---

1 Reid, *Armies of the Irish Rebellion 1798*.

APPENDIX IV

Cavalry Regiments
Irish Units (raised in 1794):
1st Fencible Cavalry (Lord Roden's Dragoons)   white, blue jackets
2nd Fencible Cavalry (Lord Glentworth's)   yellow, blue jackets

British Units:
Ancient British Fencible Cavalry	unknown, blue jackets
Dumfries Fencible Cavalry	unknown, blue jackets
Loyal Essex Fencible Cavalry	unknown, blue jackets
Midlothian Fencible Cavalry	unknown, blue jackets
Romney Fencible Cavalry	unknown, blue jackets
Duke of York's Fencible Cavalry	unknown, blue jackets

The two Irish units were recorded as having dark blue jackets and the usual white lace and cords, along with fur-crested Tarleton helmets and white breeches.

Roden's 'Foxhunters' had white facings, while Glentworth's had yellow facings displayed on their collars, cuffs and helmet turban. The British units originally had red jackets but were ordered to change to blue jackets when serving in Ireland in 1798 to distinguish them from the red-jacketed yeomanry.

A small number of regular units were also sent to Ireland after the outbreak of the rebellion which included the 100th Regiment of Foot, landed at Dublin, along with two battalions of the 3rd Regiment of (Scots) Foot Guards under the command of Lieutenant Colonel Lord Dalhousie, landed at Waterford, and four companies of the 5/60th and Hompesch's Mounted Rifles at Cork.

Appendix V

Camden's Proposed Changes to Irish Garrison – 21 March 1796[1]

Camden sought authority to establish permanent camps at Loughlinstown (to protect Dublin), Ardfinnan (near Clonmel, Co. Tipperary) and Blaris (near Lisburn, Co. Antrim) as part of his defensive strategy. He argued that a large body of troops were required to defend Dublin, while Clonmel was considered the best place for a reserve should the ports of Cork, Waterford or Limerick be attacked. He also pushed for a considerable force to be stationed in the north to protect from invasion and internal rebellion.

Dublin Garrison		**Loughlinstown Camp**	
Unit:	Strength:	Unit:	Strength:
Tyrone Militia	700	Kildare Militia	350
Kilkenny Militia	560	Clare Militia	420
North Mayo Militia	490	Donegal Militia	560
Elgin Fencibles	500	Inverness Fencibles	500
9th Dragoons	unknown		
Total (excl. cavalry)	2,250	**Total**	1,830

Ardfinnan Camp		**Northern Camp**	
Unit:	Strength:	Unit:	Strength:
Antrim Militia	560	Limerick City Militia	420
Armagh Militia	560	Cavan Militia	420
Louth Militia	420	Queen's County Militia	420
Wexford Militia	700	Fife Fencibles	500
Balfour's Fencibles	500	York Fencibles	500
Total	2,740	**Total**	2,260

---

1   TNA: HO 100/60: Home Office Correspondence: Ireland, 1792–1802.

APPENDIX V

Other Garrison Postings

Cavalry

Unit:	Location:
4th Dragoon Guards	Belturbet
7th Dragoon Guards	Longford
5th Dragoons	Tullamore
22nd Light Dragoons	Athlone
23rd Light Dragoons	Castlebar
24th Light Dragoons	Armagh
1st Fencible Light Dragoons	Mallow
2nd Fencible Light Dragoons	Clonmel

Regular Infantry

Unit:	Location:
6th Foot	Kilkenny
89th Foot	Wexford

Fencibles

Unit:	Location:
Strathspey (Grant's)	Inniskillen
Hall's	Ross Castle, Killarney
Leith's	Monaghan
Clavering's	Dungannon
Perthshire	Galway
Dunbar's	Cork
Prince of Wales	Westport
Northampton	Granard
Angushire	Athlone
Reay's	Belfast
Caithness	Armagh
Fraser's	Cavan
Breadalbane	Kells

Militia

Unit:	Location:
Carlow	Trim
North Cork	Sligo
South Cork	Clare Castle
Downshire	Drogheda
Derry	Limerick
Dublin County	Cove Forts
Dublin City	Dundalk
Drogheda	Ballyshannon
Fermanagh	Waterford
Galway	Macroon
Kerry	Newry
King's County	Roscommon
Leitrim	Charles Fort

REBELLION, INVASION AND OCCUPATION

Limerick County
Longford
South Mayo
Meath
Monaghan
Roscommon
Sligo
Tipperary
Waterford
Westmeath
Wicklow

Derry
Coleraine
Naas
Youghal
Maryborough
Cork
Kinsale
Carrick-on-Shannon
Mullingar
Carrickfergus
Portarlington

Invalid Companies at:
Dublin, Kinsale, Charlemont, Clonakilty, Carrickfergus, and Duncannon Forts

Appendix VI

Selected Orders of Battle – Ireland, 1798

Battle of New Ross, Co. Wexford – 5 June 1798

Crown Forces – Commanded by Major General Henry Johnson:
Donegal Militia
Dublin County Militia
Meath Militia
4th Battalion, Militia Light Infantry (including companies from North Mayo, Antrim, Kilkenny, Clare, and Queen's County militia regiments)
Royal Irish Artillery (including several 12-pounder and 9-pounder field guns, two howitzers and 12 light swivel guns)
4th Dragoons (approx. 50 troopers)
5th Dragoons (approx. 50 troopers)
Midlothian Fencible Cavalry (approx. 50 troopers)
Local Mounted Yeomanry (numbers unknown)
(Total force estimated at 1,500–2,000)

United Irish Forces – Led by Bagenel Harvey and Father Philip Roche
(Total force estimated at around 10,000 insurgents)

Battle of Arklow, Co. Wicklow – 9 June 1798

Crown Forces – Commanded by Major General Francis Needham:
Dublin City Militia
Antrim Militia
Armagh Militia
Londonderry Militia (Grenadier company only)
1st Battalion, Militia Light Infantry
Durham Fencibles
Dumbarton Fencibles
Royal Irish Artillery (detachments)
Local Mounted Yeomanry
(Total force estimated at 1,335 infantry and 500 cavalry)

REBELLION, INVASION AND OCCUPATION

United Irish Forces – Led by Father John Murphy
(Total force estimated at around 19,000 insurgents)

Battle of Ballynahinch, Co. Down – 13 June 1798

Crown Forces – Commanded by Major General George Nugent:
Monaghan Militia
Argyll Fencibles
Yeomanry Infantry
22nd Light Dragoons
Royal Irish Artillery (detachments)
(Total force estimated at 1,500 troops)

United Irish Forces – Led by Henry Munro
(Total force estimated at around 7,000 insurgents)

Battle of Vinegar Hill, Co. Wexford – 21 July 1798

Crown Forces – Commanded by Lieutenant General Gerard Lake:
Armagh Militia
Antrim Militia
Cavan Militia
Donegal Militia
Dublin County Militia
Londonderry Militia
Meath Militia
Roscommon Militia
Sligo Militia
Tyrone Militia
1st Battalion, Militia Light Infantry
4th Battalion, Militia Light Infantry
Local Yeomanry Cavalry (numbers unknown)
Royal Irish Artillery (detachments)
(Total force estimated at 13,000)

United Irish Forces – Led by Father John Murphy, Anthony Perry, and Myles Byrne)
(Total force estimated at around 16–20,000 insurgents)

Battle of Castlebar (the 'Castlebar Races'), Co. Mayo – 27 August 1798

Crown Forces – Commanded by Lieutenant General Gerard Lake
6th Foot (small detachment)
Kilkenny Militia (6 companies)
Longford Militia (4 companies)
Prince of Wales Fencibles
Fraser Fencibles

Galway Yeomanry Infantry
6th Dragoon Guards (small detachment)
23rd Light Dragoons
Roden's 1st Fencible Cavalry
Royal Irish Artillery (detachment – approx. 10 field guns of various calibres)
(Total force estimated at 1,100 infantry and 500 cavalry)

French Forces – Commanded by *Général de brigade* Jean Joseph Humbert:
2e Bataillon, 70e Demi Brigade (843 men)
Company of Grenadiers (51 men)
3e Régiment de Chasseurs à Cheval (43 troopers)
11e Compagnie des Canonniers (42 men)
Staff officers (39 officers)
Medical officers (4 officers)
Irish Legion/United Irish Volunteers (estimated at 500–1,000)
(Total force estimated at 1,500– 2,000 troops – although probably only half of this force would have taken part in the engagement)

Battle of Collooney, Co. Sligo – 5 September 1798

Crown Forces – Commanded by Colonel Charles Vereker:
Limerick City Militia (200–300 men)
Essex Fencibles (20 men)
Local Yeomanry Infantry (30 men)
24th Light Dragoons (20 troopers)
Local Yeomanry Cavalry (30 troopers)
2 x light curricle guns
(Total force estimated at 300–400 troops)

French Forces – Commanded by *Général de brigade* Jean Joseph Humbert:
2e Bataillon, 70e Demi Brigade (843 men)
Company of Grenadiers (51 men)
3e Régiment de Chasseurs à Cheval (43 troopers)
11e Compagnie des Canonniers (42 men)
Staff officers (39 officers)
Medical officers (4 officers)
Irish Legion/ United Irish Volunteers (estimated at 500–1,000)
(Total force estimated at 1,500–2,000 troops – although probably only half would have taken part in this engagement)

Bibliography

Primary Sources

Manuscript
Public Records Office of Northern Ireland, Belfast (PRONI):
    D 607/D/142, Downshire Papers
    U840/0174/15, K.A.O. Pratt Papers
National Library of Ireland, Dublin (NLI):
    MS 464, Paymaster General's Officer Register
    MS 809, Pelham Papers
    MS 8351, Statement of Troops in Ireland, 1 January 1799
    MS 10217, Clinton Papers
    MS 1081 Kilmainham Papers
The National Archives, Kew (TNA):
    WO 68/221, War Office correspondence: Donegal Militia, letter book and general orders
    HO 100/35-102, Home Office correspondence: Ireland, 1792-1802
British Library, (BL):
    Dublin Journal, (17 October 1782–12 December 1799)

Printed: Books
Anon., *Journal of the House of Commons*, vol.59 (London: House of Commons, 1803)
Brownrigg, Beatrice, *The Life and Letters of Sir John Moore* (Oxford: Blackwell, 1923)
Byrne, Miles, *Memoirs of Miles Byrne* (Dublin: Maunsel, 1907)
Dobbs, J., *Recollections of an Old 52nd Man* (Waterford: Harvey, 1859)
Hewitt, James (ed.), *Eye-Witnesses to Ireland in Revolt* (Reading, Berkshire: Osprey, 1974)
Londonderry, Charles, Marquis of (ed.), *Memoirs and Correspondence of Viscount Castlereagh* (London: Henry Colburn, 1848)
Maurice, Major General Sir J.F (ed.), *The Diary of Sir John Moore* (London: Arnold, 1904)
Myers, Steven W. & Delores E. McKnight (eds), *Sir Richard Musgrave's Memoirs of the Irish Rebellion of 1798* (Fort Wayne, Indiana: Round Tower Books, 1995)
Ross, Charles (ed.), *Correspondence of Charles, First Marquis Cornwallis* (London: John Murray, 1859)
Vattel, E., *The Law of Nations or Principles of the Law of Nature Applied to the Conduct and Affairs of Nations and Sovereigns* (London: S. Sweet, 1834)
Wakefield, Edward, *An Account of Ireland, Statistical and Political* (London: Longman, Hurst, Rees, Orme & Brown, 1812)
Wellington, 2nd Duke of, (ed.), *Civil Correspondence and Memoranda of Field Marshall Arthur, Duke of Wellington, K.G.* (London: John Murray, 1860)

Printed: Articles
Hayes, Richard Francis, 'An Officers Account of the French Campaign in Ireland in 1798', *The Irish Sword,* vol.2, issue 6-7 (1955), pp.161–171

BIBLIOGRAPHY

Printed: Newspapers
Dublin Evening Post
Freeman's Journal
The Kilkenny Moderator

Secondary Sources

Books
Abercromby, James, *Lieutenant General Sir Ralph Abercromby: a memoir by his son* (Edinburgh: Edmonston & Douglas, 1861)
Bartlett, Thomas (ed.), et.al, *1798: A Bicentenary Perspective* (Dublin: Four Courts Press, 2003)
Bartlett, Thomas & Jeffrey, Keith, (eds), *A Military History of Ireland* (Cambridge: Cambridge University Press, 1996)
Blackstock, Allan, *An Ascendancy Army: The Irish Yeomanry, 1796-1834* (Dublin: Four Courts Press, 1998)
Chappell, Mike, *Wellington's Peninsula Regiments: The Irish* (Oxford: Osprey, 2003)
Cookson, J.E., *The British Armed Nation, 1793-1815* (Oxford: Clarendon Press, 1997)
Connelly, S.J. (ed.), *The Oxford Companion of Irish History* (Oxford: Oxford University Press, 2004)
Cronin, Mike, *A History of Ireland* (Basingstoke: Macmillan, 2001).
Corish, Patrick J. (ed.), *Radicals, Rebels & Establishments* (Belfast: Appletree Press, 1985)
Curtain, Nancy J., *The United Irishmen: Popular Politics in Ulster and Dublin, 1791-1798* (Oxford: Clarendon Press, 1994)
Dann, Otto & Dinwiddy, J.R., (eds), *Nationalism in the Age of the French Revolution* (London: Hambleton Press, 1988)
Dickson, David, *New Foundations: Ireland 1660-1800* (Dublin: Irish Academic Press, 2000)
Dickson, David, Keogh, Daire & Whelan, Kevin, (eds), *The United Irishmen: Republicanism, Radicalism and Rebellion* (Dublin: The Lilliput Press, 1993)
Duffy, Michael, *Soldiers, Sugar and Seapower: The British Expeditions to the West Indies and the War Against Revolutionary France* (Oxford: Clarendon Press, 1987)
Elliott, Marianne, *Partners in Revolution: The United Irishmen and France* (New Haven, Connecticut & London: Yale University Press, 1982)
Fortescue, J.W., *A History of the British Army* (London: MacMillan, 1915)
Foster, R.F., *Modern Ireland, 1660-1972* (London & New York: Penguin Press, 1988)
Gough, Hugh & Dickinson, David, (eds), *Ireland and the French Revolution* (Dublin: Irish Academic Press, 1990)
Hall, Christopher D., *British Strategy in the Napoleonic War, 1803-1815* (Manchester: Manchester University Press, 1992)
Hayes, Richard, *The Last Invasion of Ireland: When Connacht Rose* (Dublin: Gill & MacMillan, 1979)
Haythornthwaite, Philip J., *Wellington's Military Machine* (Tunbridge Wells, Kent: Spellmount, 1989)
Houlding, J.A., *Fit For Service: The Training of the British Army, 1717-1795* (Oxford: Clarendon Press, 1981)
Keogh, Daire & Furlong, Nicholas, (eds), *The Mighty Wave: The 1798 Rebellion in Wexford* (Dublin: Four Courts Press, 1996)
Kerrigan, Paul M., *Castles and Fortifications in Ireland, 1485-1945* (Cork: Collins Press, 1995)
McAnally, Sir Henry, *The Irish Militia, 1793-1816: A Social and Military Study* (Dublin: Clonmore & Reynolds, 1949)
Moody, T.W. & Vaughan, W.E., *A New History of Ireland: Volume 4 – Eighteenth Century Ireland, 1691-1800* (Oxford: Clarendon Press, 1986)
Myers, Steven W. & McKnight, Delores E., (eds), *Sir Richard Musgrave's Memoirs of the Irish Rebellion of 1798* (Fort Wayne, Indiana: Round Tower Books, 1995)
Nelson, Ivan F., *The Irish Militia, 1793-1802: Ireland's Forgotten Army* (Dublin: Four Courts Press, 2007)
Newman, Peter R., *Companion to Irish History: From the submission of Tyrone to Partition, 1603-1921* (London & New York: Facts on File, 1991)
Pakenham, Thomas, *The Year of Liberty: The bloody story of the great Irish Rebellion of 1798* (London: Panther Books, 1972)

Pakenham, Thomas, *The Year of Liberty: The Great Irish Rebellion of 1798,* revised edition, abridged by Toby Buchan (London: Weidenfield & Nicholson, 1997)
Reid, Stuart, *Armies of the Irish Rebellion, 1798* (Oxford: Osprey, 2011)
Reid, Stuart, *British Redcoat, 1740-93* (London: Osprey, 1996)
Reid, Stuart, *King George's Army, 1740-93: Infantry* (London: Osprey, 1995)
Reid, Stuart, *Redcoat Officer, 1740-1815* (Oxford: Osprey, 2002)
Reid, Stuart, *Wellington's Highlanders* (Oxford: Osprey, 1992)
Shepperd, Alan, *The Connaught Rangers* (Oxford: Osprey, 1972)
Smith, Ernest, *Whig Principles and Party Politics: Earl Fitzwilliam and the Whig Party, 1748-1833* (Manchester: Manchester University Press, 1975)
Stewart, A.T.Q., *The Summer Soldiers: The 1798 Rebellion in Antrim and Down* (Belfast: The Blackstaff Press, 1995)

Articles

Bartlett, Thomas, 'An End to Moral Economy: The Irish Militia Disturbances of 1793', *Past and Present,* no.99 (May 1983), pp.41–64
Carswell, Allan L., 'The Scottish Fencible Regiments in Ireland', *The Irish Sword,* vol.21 (1998), pp.155–159
Chart, D.A., 'The Irish Levies during the Great French War', *English Historical Review,* vol.32 (1917), pp.497–516
Come, Donald R., 'French Threat to British Shores, 1793-1798', *Military Affairs,* vol.16, no.4 (Winter, 1952), pp.174–188
Ferguson, K.P., 'The Volunteer Movement and the Government, 1778–1793', *The Irish Sword,* vol.13 (1979), pp.208–216
Forde, Frank, 'The Royal Irish Artillery, 1755–1801', *The Irish Sword,* vol.11 (1973–74), pp.32–38
Hayes, Richard Francis, 'An Officers Account of the French Campaign in Ireland in 1798', *The Irish Sword,* vol.2, issue 6-7 (1955), pp.161–171
Hayes, Richard Francis, The Battle of Castlebar', *The Irish Sword,* vol.3, issue 11 (1957), pp.107–114
Hayes-McCoy, G.A., 'The Government Forces Which Opposed the Irish Insurgents of 1798', *The Irish Sword,* vol.4 (1959), pp.16–28
Hill, Jacqueline, 'Convergence and Conflict in Eighteenth Century Ireland', *The Historical Journal,* vol.44, no.4 (December 2001), pp.1039–1063
Karsten, Peter, 'Irish soldiers in the British Army, 1792–1922: Suborned or subordinate?', *Journal of Social History,* vol.17 (1983–84), pp.31–63
Kerrigan, Paul, 'A Military Map of Ireland of the Late 1790s', *The Irish Sword,* vol.12 (1975–1976), pp.247–251
Kerrigan, Paul, 'The Defence of Ireland, 1793–1815', *An Consantoir,* vol.34 (1974), pp.107–109, 148–149, 225–27, 285–290
McPeake, B.Y., 'Letters of General Lake, 1798', *The Irish Sword,* vol.1 (1953), pp.284–287.
Morris, William O'Connor, 'Ireland, 1793–1800', *The English Historical Review,* vol.6, no.4 (October 1891), pp.713–735
Morton, 'Plans for Ulster Defence,' *The Irish Sword,* vol.2 (1956), pp.270–274
Morton, R.G., 'The Rise of the Yeomanry', *The Irish Sword,* vol.8 (1967), pp.58–64
Murphy, Kathleen S., 'Judge, Jury, Magistrate and Soldier: Rethinking Law and Authority in Late Eighteenth-Century Ireland,' *The American Journal of Legal History,* vol.44, no.3 (July 2000), pp.231–256
Van Brock, F.W., 'Dilemma at Killala', *The Irish Sword,* vol.8 (1967–1968), pp.261–271
Western, J.R., 'Roman Catholics Holding Military Commissions in 1798', *The English Historical Review,* vol.70, no.276 (July 1955), pp.428–432

Unpublished Secondary Sources

Cookson, J.E., 'Arming Catholics: The Irish Militia, 1793–1815', unpublished paper –presented at AMBHA conference, February 1995
Ferguson, K.P., 'The army in Ireland from the restoration to the act of Union', Ph.D. thesis, Trinity College, Dublin, 1980
Martin, Andrew P.R., 'Reform and Change within the Irish Army and Military System, 1763–1818', M.A. thesis, University of Canterbury, 1990